PEARSON

my World

Social Studies™

Regions of Our Country

PEARSON

Boston, Massachusetts
Chandler, Arizona
Glenview, Illinois
New York, New York

ISBN-13: 978-0-328-63918-2
ISBN-10: 0-328-63918-4
17   17

Program Consulting Authors

The Colonial Williamsburg Foundation
Williamsburg, Virginia

Dr. Linda Bennett
Associate Professor, Department of Learning, Teaching, & Curriculum
College of Education
University of Missouri
Columbia, Missouri

Dr. Jim Cummins
Professor of Curriculum, Teaching, and Learning
Ontario Institute for Studies in Education
University of Toronto
Toronto, Ontario

Dr. James B. Kracht
Byrne Chair for Student Success
Executive Associate Dean
College of Education and Human Development
Texas A&M University
College Station, Texas

Dr. Alfred Tatum
Associate Professor, Director of the UIC Reading Clinic
Literacy, Language, and Culture Program
University of Illinois at Chicago
Chicago, Illinois

Dr. William E. White
Vice President for Productions, Publications, and Learning Ventures
The Colonial Williamsburg Foundation
Williamsburg, Virginia

Consultants and Reviewers

PROGRAM CONSULTANT

Dr. Grant Wiggins
Coauthor, *Understanding by Design*

ACADEMIC REVIEWERS

Bob Sandman
Adjunct Assistant Professor of Business and Economics
Wilmington College–Cincinnati Branches
Blue Ash, OH

Jeanette Menendez
Reading Coach
Doral Academy Elementary
Miami, FL

Kathy T. Glass
Author, *Lesson Design for Differentiated Instruction*
President, Glass Educational Consulting
Woodside, CA

Roberta Logan
African Studies Specialist
Retired, Boston Public Schools/ Mission Hill School
Boston, MA

PROGRAM TEACHER REVIEWERS

Glenda Alford-Atkins
Eglin Elementary School
Eglin AFB, FL

Andrea Baerwald
Boise, ID

Ernest Andrew Brewer
Assistant Professor
Florida Atlantic University
Jupiter, FL

Riley D. Browning
Gilbert Middle School
Gilbert, WV

Charity L. Carr
Stroudsburg Area School District
Stroudsburg, PA

Jane M. Davis
Marion County Public Schools
Ocala, FL

Stacy Ann Figueroa, M.B.A.
Wyndham Lakes Elementary
Orlando, FL

LaBrenica Harris
John Herbert Phillips Academy
Birmingham, AL

Marianne Mack
Union Ridge Elementary
Ridgefield, WA

Emily L. Manigault
Richland School District #2
Columbia, SC

Marybeth A. McGuire
Warwick School Department
Warwick, RI

Laura Pahr
Holmes Elementary
Chicago, IL

Jennifer Palmer
Shady Hills Elementary
Spring Hill, FL

Diana E. Rizo
Miami-Dade County Public Schools/Miami Dade College
Miami, FL

Kyle Roach
Amherst Elementary, Knox County Schools
Knoxville, TN

Eretta Rose
MacMillan Elementary School
Montgomery, AL

Nancy Thornblad
Millard Public Schools
Omaha, NE

Jennifer Transue
Siegfried Elementary
Northampton, PA

Megan Zavernik
Howard-Suamico School District
Green Bay, WI

Dennise G. Zobel
Pittsford Schools–Allen Creek
Rochester, NY

Social Studies Handbook

Reading and Writing

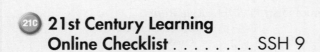
Map and Globe

Geography of the United States

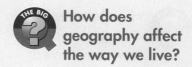

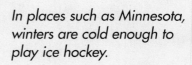
THE BIG ? How does geography affect the way we live?

In places such as Minnesota, winters are cold enough to play ice hockey.

Americans and Their History

 How have we changed and how have we stayed the same during our history?

These spear points are thousands of years old.

Government in the United States

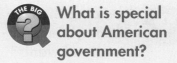
THE BIG
?
What is special
about American
government?

*The Declaration of
Independence*

The Nation's Economy

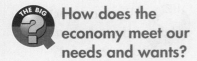 How does the economy meet our needs and wants?

Choosing what to buy is an economic decision.

Chapter 5

Regions: The Northeast

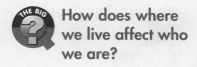

How does where we live affect who we are?

Blue crabs are a resource in the Northeast.

Regions: The Southeast

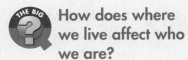 How does where we live affect who we are?

Quilting is part of the culture of the Southeast.

Regions: The Midwest

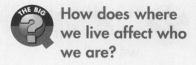

How does where we live affect who we are?

The first steam-powered tractors helped change the Midwest.

Regions: The Southwest

 How does where we live affect who we are?

Spanish and Mexican traditions are celebrated in the Southwest.

Regions: The West

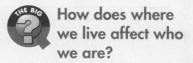

How does where we live affect who we are?

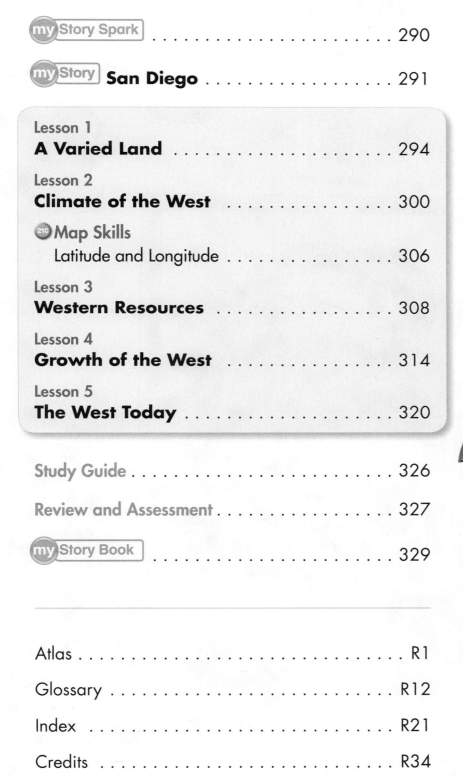
Totem poles are made by some Native Americans in the West.

Reading Skills

Main Idea and Details

The main idea is the most important idea about a topic. Details support the main idea.

Categorize

When we categorize, we look at how people or things are related based on their characteristics.

Compare and Contrast

To compare and contrast is to look for similarities and differences in things.

Reading Skills

Sequence

Sequence refers to the order of events in text. We also use sequence when we list the steps in a process.

Summarize

We summarize, or retell, to check our understanding of what we have read. A summary is usually short. We can sum up what we have read in just a few sentences.

Many people travel around the United States each year. They visit the beaches, theme parks, and cities.

Draw Conclusions

When we draw conclusions, we think about facts and details and then decide something about them.

Keys to Good Writing

The Writing Process

Good writers follow five steps when they write.

Prewrite	Choose a topic, gather details about it, and plan how to use them.
Draft	Write down all your ideas, and don't worry about making it perfect.
Revise	Review your writing, looking for the traits of good writing. Change parts that are confusing or incomplete.
Edit	Check your spelling, capitalization, punctuation, and grammar. Make a final copy.
Share	Share your writing with others.

The Writing Traits

Good writers look at six qualities of their writing to make it the best writing possible.

Ideas	Share a clear message with specific ideas and details.
Organization	Have a beginning, middle, and end that are easy to follow.
Voice	Use a natural tone in your writing.
Word Choice	Choose strong nouns and verbs and colorful adjectives.
Sentence Flow	Vary your sentence structures and beginnings to create writing that is easy to read.
Conventions	Follow the rules of spelling, capitalization, punctuation, and grammar.

21st Century Learning Online Checklist

You can go online to myworldsocialstudies.com to practice the skills listed below.
These are skills that will be important to you throughout your life.
After you complete each skill tutorial online, check it off here in your book.

Target Reading Skills

- [ ] Main Idea and Details
- [ ] Cause and Effect
- [ ] Categorize
- [ ] Fact and Opinion
- [ ] Draw Conclusions
- [ ] Generalize
- [ ] Compare and Contrast
- [ ] Sequence
- [ ] Summarize

Collaboration and Creativity Skills

- [ ] Solve Problems
- [ ] Work in Cooperative Teams
- [ ] Resolve Conflict
- [ ] Generate New Ideas

Graph Skills

- [ ] Interpret Graphs
- [ ] Create Charts
- [ ] Interpret Timelines

Map Skills

- [ ] Use Longitude and Latitude
- [ ] Interpret Physical Maps
- [ ] Interpret Economic Data on Maps
- [ ] Interpret Cultural Data on Maps

Critical Thinking Skills

- [ ] Compare Viewpoints
- [ ] Use Primary and Secondary Sources
- [ ] Identify Bias
- [ ] Make Decisions
- [ ] Predict Consequences

Media and Technology Skills

- [ ] Conduct Research
- [ ] Use the Internet Safely
- [ ] Analyze Images
- [ ] Evaluate Media Content
- [ ] Deliver an Effective Presentation

Five Themes of Geography

Geography is the study of Earth. This study can be divided into five themes: Location, Place, Human/Environmental Interaction, Movement, and Region. You can use the themes to better understand how each place on Earth is different from any other place, as the example of the Great Lakes shows.

Location: Where can the Great Lakes be found?

The Great Lakes are located in the United States and Canada. The five lakes include Lake Erie, Lake Huron, Lake Michigan, Lake Ontario, and Lake Superior.

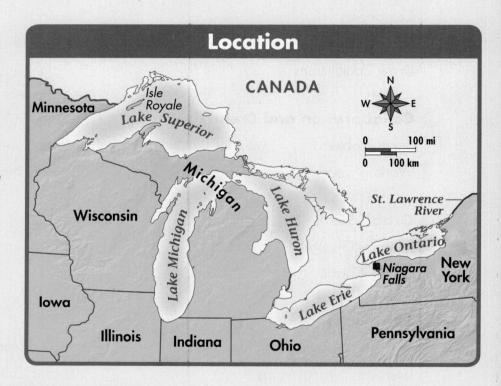

Place: How is this place different from others?

The Great Lakes have 35,000 islands. The islands in Lake Superior, which is the largest of the five lakes, include Isle Royale and the Apostle Islands.

Human/Environmental Interaction

Human Interaction: How have people changed a place?

Canals are man-made waterways that are dug across land. Canals around the Great Lakes connect these lakes to other lakes and to rivers in the area. In Illinois, for example, a canal connects Lake Michigan to the Illinois River.

Movement

Movement: How has movement changed a place?

Since the Great Lakes connect to the Atlantic Ocean by the St. Lawrence Seaway, shipping is a major industry here.

Region

Region: What is special about the region that includes the Great Lakes?

There are many natural areas where birds can nest or take shelter.

Reading Globes

This is an image of Earth. It shows some of Earth's large landforms, called continents. It also shows Earth's large bodies of water, called oceans.

Atlantic Ocean

North America

Pacific Ocean

South America

1. **Name** the two continents shown in this photo of Earth.

....

2. **Name** the two oceans shown.

....

To the right is a **globe**, a round model of Earth. Some globes are small enough to hold in your hands. It shows the true shapes and locations of Earth's continents and oceans.

A globe often shows two lines that divide Earth into halves. These two lines are called the prime meridian and the equator. You can see the equator on this globe.

Earth's Hemispheres

The equator and the prime meridian divide Earth into halves called **hemispheres**. The **prime meridian** is a line drawn from the North Pole to the South Pole that passes through Europe and Africa. That line divides Earth into the Western Hemisphere and the Eastern Hemisphere as shown below.

Vocabulary

globe
hemisphere
prime meridian
equator

The **equator** is a line drawn around Earth halfway between the North Pole and the South Pole. It divides Earth into the Northern and Southern Hemispheres.

Because Earth is divided two ways, it has four hemispheres.

Western Hemisphere	Eastern Hemisphere	Northern Hemisphere	Southern Hemisphere

3. Name the two hemispheres that North America is located in.

....

....

4. Identify whether Asia is north or south of the equator.

....

Maps Show Direction

Maps show real directions. A **compass rose** is a symbol that shows directions on a map. There are four **cardinal directions**—north, south, east, and west. North points toward the North Pole and is marked with an *N*. South points to the South Pole and is marked with an *S*.

Look at the compass rose on the map below. In addition to showing the cardinal directions, it shows directions that are midway between them. These are the **intermediate directions.** They are northeast, southeast, southwest, and northwest.

This map shows land use in the Southwest. It is called a special purpose map and has a compass rose to show direction.

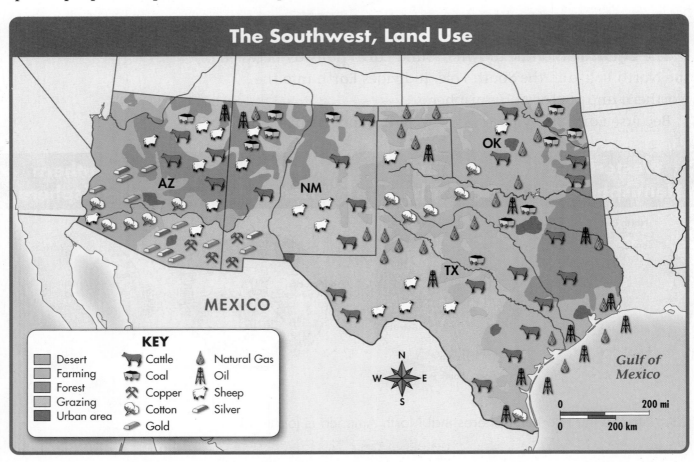

The Southwest, Land Use

KEY

- Desert
- Farming
- Forest
- Grazing
- Urban area

- Cattle
- Coal
- Copper
- Cotton
- Gold

- Natural Gas
- Oil
- Sheep
- Silver

Gulf of Mexico

0   200 mi
0   200 km

5. Name the resource in the northeast corner of Oklahoma.

....

6. Name the body of water that is southeast of Texas.

....

Maps Show Distance

A map is a very small drawing of a large place. However, you can find real distances in miles or kilometers from one point to another on Earth by using a map scale. A **map scale** shows the relationship between distance on the map and distance on Earth. One way to use the scale is to hold the edge of a piece of paper under the scale and copy it. Then place your copy of the scale on the map to measure the distance between two points.

The map below shows the path of Hurricane Katrina. You can use the scale to track the miles the storm traveled.

Vocabulary

compass rose

cardinal direction

intermediate direction

map scale

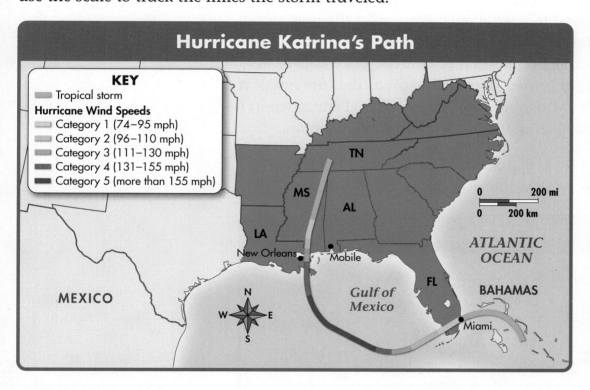

Hurricane Katrina's Path

KEY
Tropical storm
Hurricane Wind Speeds
Category 1 (74–95 mph)
Category 2 (96–110 mph)
Category 3 (111–130 mph)
Category 4 (131–155 mph)
Category 5 (more than 155 mph)

TN

MS

AL

LA

New Orleans
Mobile

ATLANTIC OCEAN

MEXICO

FL

BAHAMAS

Gulf of Mexico

Miami

N W E S

0   200 mi
0   200 km

7. **Identify** the body of water where Hurricane Katrina became a Category 5 hurricane.

....

8. **Identify** about how many miles Hurricane Katrina traveled north from New Orleans before it became a tropical storm.

....

....

Political Maps

A map is a flat drawing of all or part of Earth. It shows a place from above.

Different kinds of maps show different information. A map that shows boundaries for counties, states, or nations, as well as capital cities, is called a **political map.** This kind of map often shows major landforms and bodies of water to help locate places.

Each map has a title. The title tells you what the map is about. Maps use symbols to show information. A **symbol** is a small drawing, line, or color that stands for something else. The **map key** or legend tells what each symbol on the map stands for. On this political map, a star stands for the state capital. Lines show the state boundaries, or borders. Color is used to show the area that is the Midwest. The areas that are not part of the Midwest are a different color. For example, Pennsylvania is a lighter color to show that it is not the subject of the map.

9. **Circle** the symbol that stands for state capital in the key. Then **circle** the state capital of Nebraska on the map.

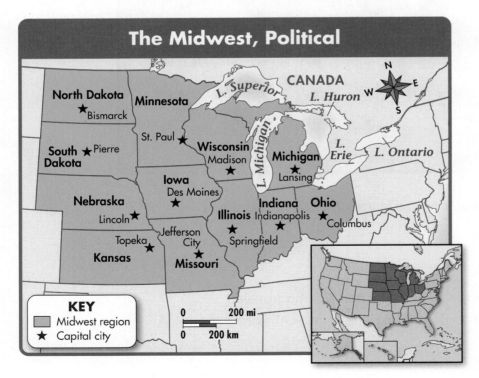

The Midwest, Political

North Dakota
★Bismarck

Minnesota

L. Superior

CANADA

L. Huron

N

W E

S

St. Paul ★

Wisconsin

L. Michigan

Michigan
★
Lansing

L. Erie

L. Ontario

South Dakota ★Pierre

Madison
★

Iowa
Des Moines
★

Nebraska

Indiana Ohio
Indianapolis ★
Columbus

Lincoln★

Illinois
★
Springfield

★

Topeka★

Jefferson City
★

Kansas

Missouri
★

KEY
▢ Midwest region
★ Capital city

0   200 mi
0   200 km

Physical Maps

A **physical map** shows landforms, such as mountains, plains, and deserts. It also shows bodies of water, such as oceans, lakes, and rivers. Physical maps often show borders between states and countries to help locate these landforms. A good place to look for political and physical maps is an atlas. An **atlas** is a collection or book of maps.

The physical map of the Northeast shown below includes labels for islands, or land that is completely surrounded by water. It also has labels for bays and capes. A bay is a body of water that is partly surrounded by land. A cape is an area of land that sticks out from the coastline into an ocean, sea, or lake. This physical map not only identifies mountains of the Northeast, it also tells you how high these mountains are.

Vocabulary

political map
symbol
map key
physical map
atlas

10. **Circle** the tallest mountain in the Northeast. **Draw an X** through the bay that is southeast of Washington, D.C.

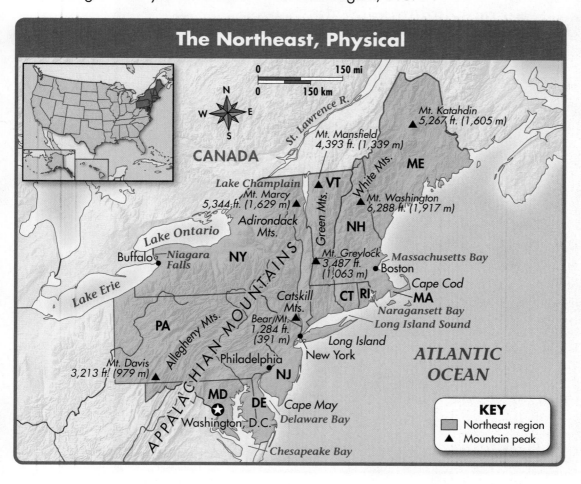

The Northeast, Physical

Elevation Maps

An **elevation** map shows you how high the land is. Elevation is height above sea level. A place that is at sea level is at the same height as the surface of ocean's water.

Elevation maps use color to show elevation. To read this kind of map, first look at the map key. Note that there are numbers next to each color on the map key. The numbers show the range of elevation that each color represents. On this Pennsylvania map, dark green represents the lowest elevation. The range for dark green is between 0 and 500 feet above sea level.

11. Identify the elevation range of the Allegheny Plateau.

....

....

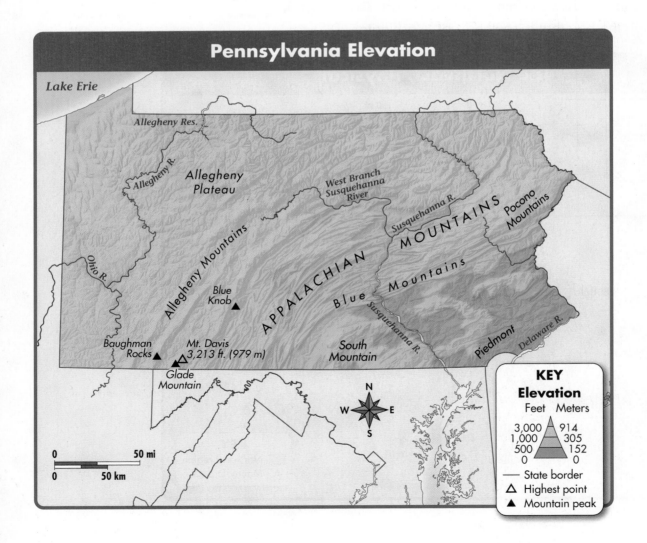

Pennsylvania Elevation

KEY
Elevation
Feet Meters
3,000 914
1,000 305
500 152
0 0
— State border
△ Highest point
▲ Mountain peak

Use a Grid

A city map shows the streets of a city. It might also show points of interest and natural features. To help locate places more easily, this city map has a **grid**. A grid is a system of lines that cross each other forming a pattern of squares. The lines are labeled with letters and numbers. These squares give every place on the map a location.

To find a specific location, the map has an index. An index is an alphabetical listing of places. The index gives the letter and number of the square where the place is located.

12. **Add** the number and letter set for Forest Park to the index.

Vocabulary

elevation

grid

Index	
Forest Park	
Lilburn	A4
Stone Mountain Park	B4

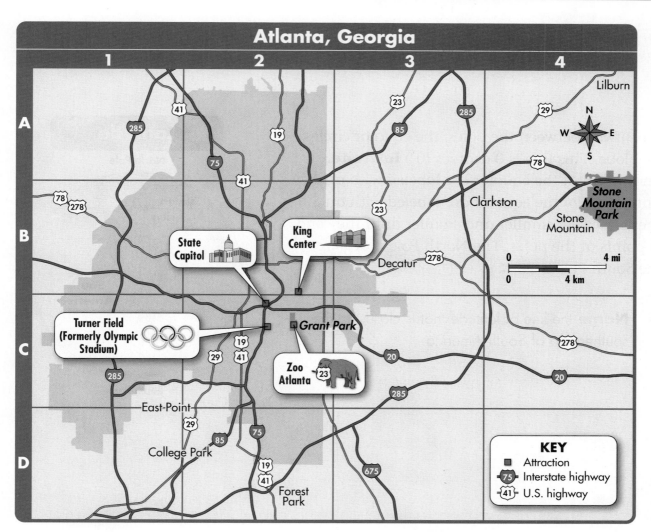

Use Latitude and Longitude for Exact Location

Long ago, mapmakers made a system for locating exact places on Earth. The system uses two sets of lines that form a grid around the globe. These lines are numbered in units called **degrees.**

One set of lines runs from the North Pole to the South Pole. These are lines of **longitude.** The prime meridian is labeled 0 degrees (0°) longitude. Lines of longitude are labeled from 0° to 180°. Lines east of the prime meridian are labeled with an *E*. Lines west of it are labeled with a *W*.

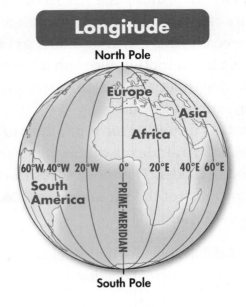

Longitude

13. **Identify** about how many degrees east the center of Africa is from the prime meridian.

....

Halfway between the poles, the equator circles the globe. This line is 0 degrees (0°) **latitude.** Lines north of the equator are labeled with an *N*. Lines south of the equator are labeled with an *S*. These lines get smaller and smaller until they end as points at the poles. The North Pole is 90°N. The South Pole is 90°S.

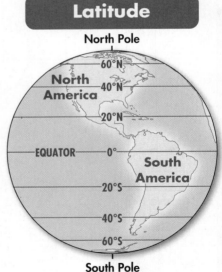

Latitude

14. **Name** the line of latitude that is closest to the southern tip of South America.

....

....

....

Maps Show Events

Maps can also show events. These might be current events, such as a map of battles that are being fought between different countries, or a weather map that shows the path of a severe storm. Another example of an events map is a map of special activities at a fairground or festival.

Maps can also show events from the past, or historic events. You can use the lines of longitude and latitude on the map of explorers in the Americas shown below to locate and compare events that happened long ago.

Vocabulary

degree
longitude
latitude

15. Circle the island that was explored at 80°W.

16. Identify the explorer who traveled above 50°N.

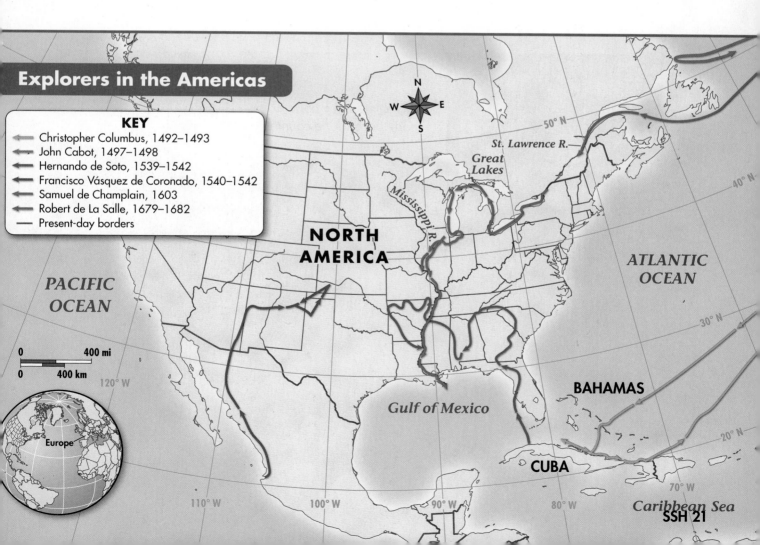

Explorers in the Americas

KEY
- Christopher Columbus, 1492–1493
- John Cabot, 1497–1498
- Hernando de Soto, 1539–1542
- Francisco Vásquez de Coronado, 1540–1542
- Samuel de Champlain, 1603
- Robert de La Salle, 1679–1682
- Present-day borders

NORTH AMERICA

PACIFIC OCEAN

ATLANTIC OCEAN

St. Lawrence R.

Great Lakes

Mississippi R.

Gulf of Mexico

BAHAMAS

CUBA

Caribbean Sea

Europe

0   400 mi
0   400 km

120° W
110° W
100° W
90° W
80° W
70° W

50° N
40° N
30° N
20° N

Geography of the United States

How does geography affect the way we live?

Describe how the land or outdoor weather where you live affects your daily activities.

....

....

....

....

Rock climbing is popular in many parts of the country.

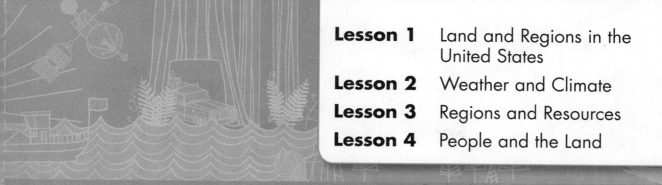

Marjory Stoneman Douglas
Rescuer of the Everglades

my Story Video

Some people really do change the world! Marjory Stoneman Douglas proved that. Douglas was a writer. In 1915, she moved from Massachusetts to Miami, Florida, to work for a newspaper.

Soon after Douglas arrived in Florida, she discovered how much her new state had to offer. She wrote about the people and different places in the state. Some of those stories were about the Everglades, a marshy area in South Florida.

Douglas found that the Everglades have a truly remarkable environment. Alligators, turtles, and panthers roam this watery world. Deer, gray foxes, and even marsh rabbits call the Everglades home. Countless birds and butterflies also live in this special environment.

In one description, Douglas wrote:

"There are no other Everglades in the world. They are, they always have been, one of the unique regions of earth; remote, never wholly known."

—*Marjory Stoneman Douglas*

Marjory Stoneman Douglas visited the Everglades in the 1920s.

1

In the late 1800s, workers dug canals to drain water from the Everglades.

People burned areas of the Everglades to clear land for farms.

Douglas also discovered that many people across the nation did not know of the Everglades. Few scientists studied the region, and few visitors went there. Many considered it a useless swamp. For years, people drained the slow-moving water and built on the land. Farmers burned large parts of the Everglades. Once the fires were out, some farmers grew crops such as sugar cane there. Others raised cattle on the open land.

These actions harmed the Everglades. In fact, by the 1940s, about half the marsh in the Everglades had been lost! This destruction worried Douglas. But what could she do?

In the early 1940s, Douglas made a plan. She would write a book. Her book would include the history of the Everglades and a description of the physical environment. She would also say why it was important to restore water to the marsh, and much more. Douglas hoped her book might stop the destruction.

In time, Stoneman met and learned from Miccosukee Native Americans who lived in the Everglades.

Douglas wrote a book that changed how people viewed the Everglades.

At the age of 103, Douglas received the Presidential Medal of Freedom for her work in protecting the Everglades.

For years, Douglas studied the Everglades. She walked the land and paddled the waters. She talked to historians, scientists, and ordinary people. Then she began to write.

Douglas finished her book in 1947. She called it *The Everglades: River of Grass*. The book not only told the story of an amazing environment, but it also explained why the Everglades are important to surrounding areas. The Everglades help keep the nearby drinking water fresh and protect parts of South Florida from floods.

The book was a sensation throughout the nation. Many people realized the need to protect the Everglades. The United States government heard Douglas's message, too. The Everglades was soon made a national park. Lands that are part of a national park are protected for the future.

Even so, the Everglades weren't exactly safe. Some people wanted to build an airport next to the national park. Others wanted to build a place to treat oil nearby. These projects could harm the Everglades. Douglas spoke out against the plans. In 1969, she started a group called the Friends of the Everglades. This group continues to work to preserve and look after the Everglades.

Douglas worked for the rest of her life to protect the Everglades. Florida had changed a great deal during her long life. Many people believe that Douglas helped to make the state a better place.

Think About It Based on the story, why is protecting the Everglades important? As you read the chapter, think about how people affect the environments in which they live.

Land and Regions in the United States

Envision It!

The Rocky Mountains are a physical feature found in the western United States.

No matter where you live in the world, you are near landforms. A **landform** is a natural feature of Earth's surface, such as a hill, a cliff, or even an island. The United States is a large country. A country this large has many different landforms.

Landforms and Bodies of Water

One of the many landforms in the United States is a mountain. Mountains rise high above the land around them. They can have steep sides, rocky cliffs, and towering peaks. Some mountains form in large chains or groups called mountain ranges.

Hills are also raised landforms. However, they are mostly rounded at the top and not as high as mountains. A **mesa** is similar to a hill, except that its top is flat and not rounded.

Landforms and Bodies of Water

Mountain Peak

Mountain Range

Plateau

Mesa

River

Flood Plain

Lake

UNLOCK
THE BIG
?

I will know that the United States is divided into five regions, each with unique landforms.

Vocabulary

landform	region
mesa	desert
plateau	boundary
canyon	
flood plain	

Label the landforms on the left. On the right, draw a picture of a landform you see in your community.

Other landforms include plains, plateaus, and canyons. A plain is an area of flat or gently rolling land. Plains may be large or small and are often covered with grasses. **Plateaus** are large, flat, raised areas of land. Some plateaus are cut through by rivers, which over time have worn away the soil to form a canyon. A **canyon** is a deep narrow valley with steep, rocky sides.

The United States also has many different bodies of water. Lakes, rivers, bays, and oceans are all unique shapes and sizes. Most lakes are made up of water that is fresh, not salty as the ocean is. Rivers carry fresh water to seas or oceans. The land along many rivers is called a flood plain. A **flood plain** is a plain that is formed from the dirt and silt that settle after a river has overflowed. The land along an ocean or bay is called the coast. Landforms along the coast include beaches, dunes, and cliffs.

1. **Label** the landforms in the pictures.

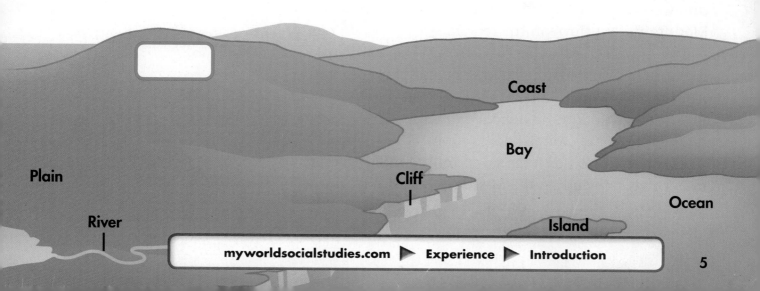

Plain

River

Cliff

Coast

Bay

Island

Ocean

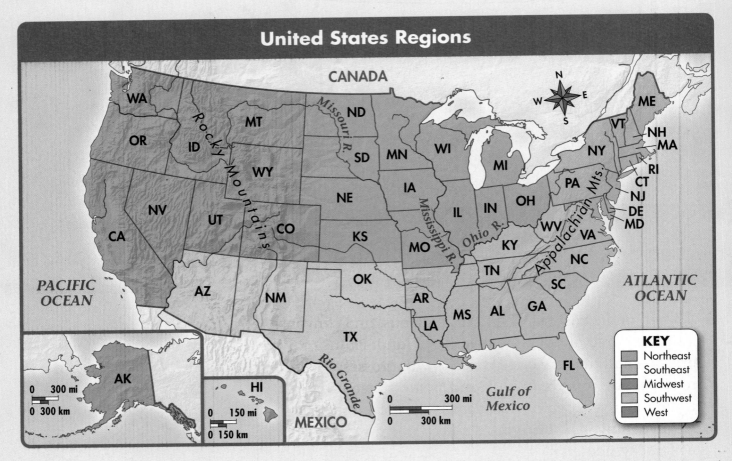

United States Regions

KEY
- Northeast
- Southeast
- Midwest
- Southwest
- West

Regions of the United States

To study the United States, geographers and others divide it into smaller areas called regions. A **region** is an area in which places share similar characteristics. This map shows the five regions of the United States: the Northeast, the Southeast, the Midwest, the Southwest, and the West. These regions are organized based on the location of the states.

In the Northeast region, along the northern coast, there are forests and hills. The soil is rocky. Farther south and west, the soil is good for farming. The Appalachian Mountains run through the region.

The Appalachians also run through the Southeast region. The Southeast has a low coastal plain along the Atlantic Coast and Gulf of Mexico Coast. The Mississippi River flows through the region.

The Midwest region is known for its broad grassy plains, but it also has forests and rolling hills. Several major rivers, including the Missouri, Mississippi, and Ohio, flow through the Midwest.

2. **Find** your state on the map. **Mark** it with an X. In which region do you live?

....

....

....

The land of the Southwest is very different from the land of the Midwest. Here there are low coastal areas, dry plains, canyons, and deserts. A **desert** is a dry area that gets little rain. One of the region's best-known landforms is the Grand Canyon. Formed by the Colorado River over millions of years, it cuts through the Colorado Plateau.

The West is the nation's largest, most varied region. There are forests, rich soil for farming, and a long coast. Its landforms also include plains and mountains. Both the nation's highest and lowest points are found in this region. Alaska's Mount McKinley is the highest point, and Death Valley, in California, is the lowest point.

Where People Live

In each region there are large cities where many people live and work. Our country's three largest cities are New York, New York; Los Angeles, California; and Chicago, Illinois. These cities have large populations, and people often live close to each other.

Each region also has areas where people live farther apart than in cities. On the plains of Texas, some people raise animals, such as cows and sheep. They live far from their neighbors because they use a large area of land to grow grasses for their animals to eat.

3. ⊙ **Cause and Effect**
Write the name of the river that formed the Grand Canyon.

....

....

4. Circle the name of the region with the smallest population.

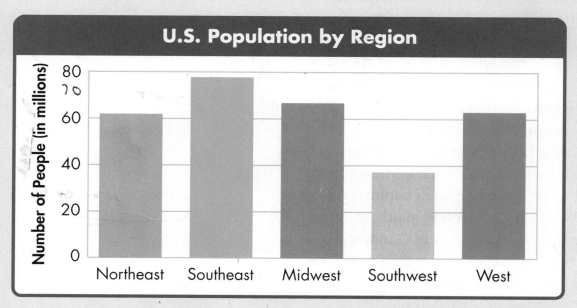

U.S. Census Bureau, 2009

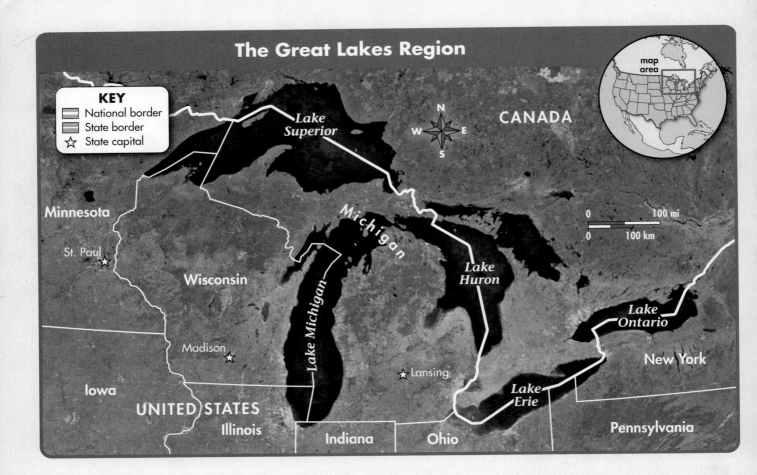

The Great Lakes Region

KEY
- National border
- State border
- ☆ State capital

Lake Superior

CANADA

Minnesota

St. Paul ☆

Wisconsin

Michigan

Lake Huron

Lake Michigan

Lake Ontario

Madison ☆

☆ Lansing

New York

Iowa

UNITED STATES

Lake Erie

Illinois

Indiana

Ohio

Pennsylvania

map area

0 ___ 100 mi
0 ___ 100 km

Boundaries and Borders

When you look at a political map of the United States, one of the first things you can see are lines that show boundaries. A **boundary** is a line that divides one area or state from another. Boundaries often follow natural features, such as rivers or lakes. On the map of the Great Lakes region, you can see that each state has a boundary drawn around it. Some boundaries appear as a straight line while others are curved or irregular. The irregular lines often follow a natural feature, such as a river.

The United States is organized into 50 states. The nation also includes the District of Columbia, or D.C. This land is set aside for the nation's capital city, Washington, D.C. To the north and south, the United States is bordered by the countries of Canada and Mexico. These borders are set and agreed to by the governments of each nation involved.

5. Circle the natural features that Michigan and Wisconsin share. **Draw** an X on a state border that is not a natural feature.

Regional boundaries are different from city, state, or national borders, since they are not set by laws. In fact, regions can be based on many other characteristics. Regions can be based on major landforms found in a given area. Regions can also be based on what the people there do for a living or on what language is spoken there. Unlike cities, states, and nations, most regions are not marked with signs.

The Four Corners is where New Mexico, Arizona, Utah, and Colorado meet. Since this is a unique area, people have marked the borders on the ground.

Got it?

6. ◉ **Cause and Effect** What can cause people to live far from each other?

....

....

....

7. ? **Describe** how the landforms in your region affect activities you do?   my Story Ideas

....

....

....

▢ **Stop!** I need help with ....

❚❚ **Wait!** I have a question about ....

▶ **Go!** Now I know ....

Lesson 2

Weather and Climate

Envision It!

Frederick

Baltimore

Washington, DC

The pictures of the suns and clouds show that on this day in Washington, D.C., no rain was expected.

In most parts of the country, the weather changes with the seasons. Seasonal changes are part of the climate of a place.

No matter where you live, weather affects you. **Weather** is the condition of the air at a certain time and place. The weather can affect what you wear and the activities you do. When it is warm outside, you may want to go swim. If it is raining, you may stay inside.

Weather and Climate

The weather can be hot, cold, rainy, or windy. It changes from day to day. **Climate** is the pattern of weather in a place over a period of time. For example, changes in weather that come with the seasons year after year are part of the climate of a place.

Two major factors of weather and climate are temperature and precipitation. **Temperature** is how hot or cold a place is. The **precipitation** of a place is the amount of rain or snow that falls there.

Draw a symbol to show if it is hot, cold, rainy, or snowing outside today.

UNLOCK THE BIG ?

I will know that weather and climate vary across the regions of the United States.

Vocabulary

weather   precipitation

climate   humidity

temperature   elevation

The United States includes places with a wide variety of weather and climates. In can be warm in one area and very cold in another. On a winter day, it might be far below freezing in Minnesota. On the same day, it might be over 50 degrees in southern Louisiana. A light jacket will keep you warm at this temperature. The map below shows that the temperature varies as you look at the different regions.

1. **Mark** where you live on the map with an X. **Circle** the average temperature in the map key.

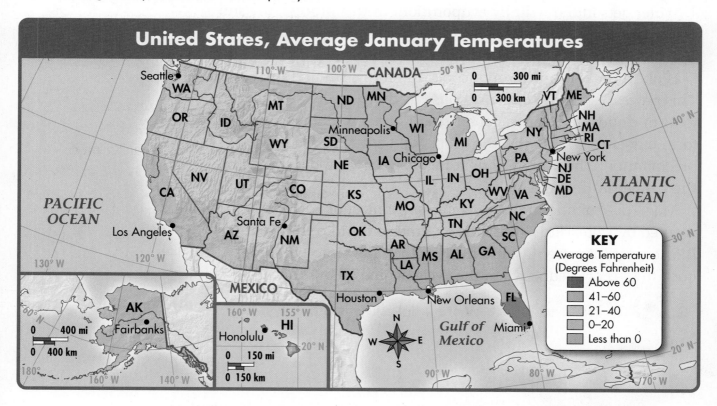

United States, Average January Temperatures

KEY
Average Temperature
(Degrees Fahrenheit)

- Above 60
- 41–60
- 21–40
- 0–20
- Less than 0

The Water Cycle

Condensation
Water vapor cools
and forms drops

Cloud

Precipitation
Rain or snow falls

Evaporation
Water changes
to water vapor

Lake

Water and Climate

Another important feature of weather and climate is humidity. **Humidity** is the amount of water in the air. You cannot see this water, but sometimes you can feel it. When humidity is high, the air feels damp.

Water gets into the air by evaporation. In this process, the sun heats the oceans, lakes, and rivers. Heat changes some of the water into a gas called water vapor. This vapor rises into the air.

High in the air, water vapor cools and forms small drops. This process is called condensation. The drops gather together to form clouds. Inside the clouds, small drops combine to form bigger drops. Finally, the drops fall to the ground as precipitation. The drops fall as rain, snow, or sleet, depending on the temperature of the air.

Much precipitation falls on water, since most of Earth is covered by water. Rain that falls on land soaks into the ground. It also runs into streams and rivers, which flow into lakes or back to seas or oceans. Then the cycle begins all over again.

2. ⊙ **Cause and Effect Write** what causes evaporation.

....

....

Other Climate Factors

What other factors affect the climate of a place? One factor is location. Places near the equator receive the most direct sunlight. The equator is an imaginary line that circles Earth halfway between the North Pole and South Pole. As you move away from the equator, the climate gets cooler.

Lakes and oceans also shape the climate of a place. They affect the amount of precipitation that falls. They also can affect the temperature, since lakes and oceans warm and cool more slowly than land does. In the winter, water is often warmer than the land. Winds from the water will warm the air nearby. In summer, breezes blow from the water and cool the nearby air.

Elevation also affects climate. The **elevation** of a place is how high the land is above sea level. Places at high elevations are generally colder than lower areas. In fact, high mountain peaks can be covered in snow all year!

Wind also contributes to climate and weather. Winds bring air of varying temperature and humidity from one place to another. In this way, winds help create the weather patterns that form different climates.

3. Plant life on the San Francisco Peaks in Arizona changes with elevation. What grows at 9,000 feet above sea level?

....

....

Plant Life and Elevation

Elevation (in feet)

12,000
10,000
8,000
6,000
4,000
2,000
sea level

Alpine

Conifer Forest

Aspen

Ponderosa Pine

Sage Brush

Mesquite

Climate Regions

The map below shows the different climate regions in the United States. Arctic or polar climates are the coldest. Places near the North Pole have arctic climates. The only place in the United States with this climate is northern Alaska. Here the summers are short and the winters are very cold.

Tropical climates are warm or hot all year. Places with tropical climates are located near the equator. South Florida has a tropical climate. In the winter, the temperature is often warmer than in other parts of the country. The summers can be hot with high humidity.

Most of the United States has a temperate climate. Places with temperate climates are not as cold as the arctic regions nor as hot as the tropical ones. For example, the Northeast has cold winters, but not nearly as cold as northern Alaska. Precipitation in the Northeast is moderate, which means it is neither extremely wet nor extremely dry.

To the west, however, less rain falls. Parts of Arizona and New Mexico are very dry. Summer days there are hot, but winters are cold in the Southwestern mountains.

4. Circle the climates in Wisconsin and Arizona. How are the climates of the two states different?

....

....

....

....

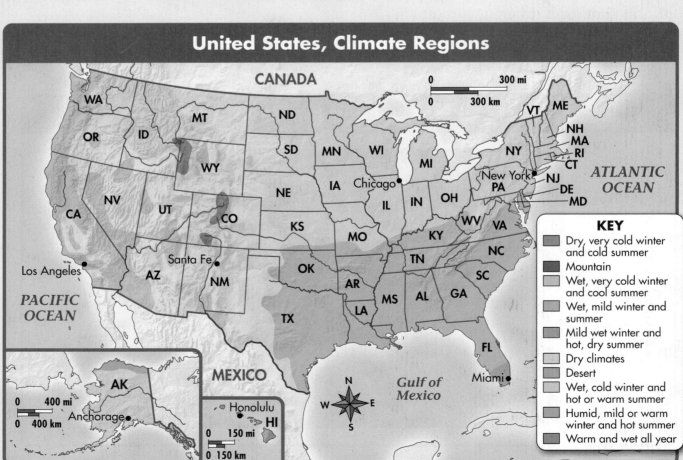

United States, Climate Regions

KEY
- Dry, very cold winter and cold summer
- Mountain
- Wet, very cold winter and cool summer
- Wet, mild winter and summer
- Mild wet winter and hot, dry summer
- Dry climates
- Desert
- Wet, cold winter and hot or warm summer
- Humid, mild or warm winter and hot summer
- Warm and wet all year

14

5. ◎ **Compare and Contrast** **Fill in** the chart to show how the climate of your region and one other region are alike or different.

Compare Climate

Other region	My region

Another beautiful winter day—70 degrees! I live in a tropical climate.

Got it?

6. ◎ **Cause and Effect** What effect does elevation have on climate?

....

....

....

7. ⓠ **Describe** how the changing seasons affect what you do outdoors.

....

....

....

⬛ **Stop!** I need help with ....

⏸ **Wait!** I have a question about ....

▶ **Go!** Now I know ....

Read Inset Maps

Below there is one large, main map and two smaller, separate maps. Each small map has its own map scale. Small maps that are related to a main map are called inset maps.

Inset maps give details that can't be shown on a main map. The places shown on the inset map may be too large, too small, or too far away to be included on the main map. Suppose you want to show a map of the United States. In order to include Alaska and Hawaii you would need to include Canada and a large area of the Pacific Ocean. The United States would be shown smaller with less room for details. If you use inset maps to show both Alaska and Hawaii, you can show more details of all of the states and less of the surrounding areas.

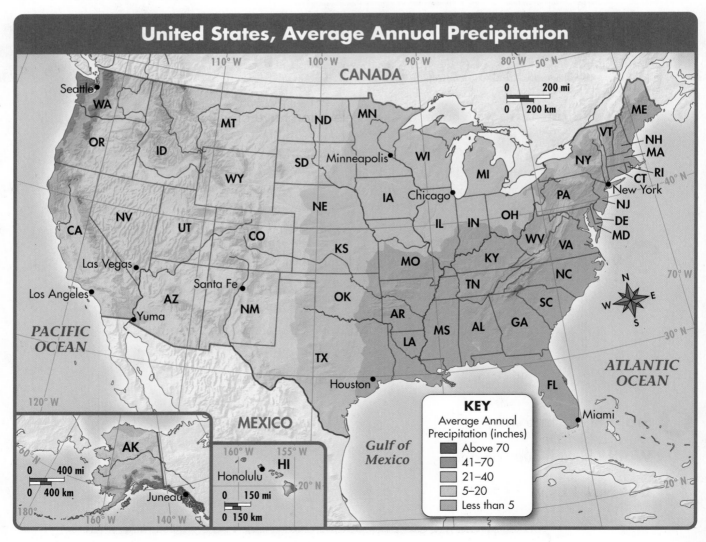

United States, Average Annual Precipitation

KEY
Average Annual Precipitation (inches)
Above 70
41–70
21–40
5–20
Less than 5

To read an inset map, first study the main map. Look at the title and scale. Then examine the inset maps. Ask yourself how they relate to the main map. What do the inset maps show that the main map does not?

1. What does the main map show?

    ....

    ....

2. What do the inset maps show?

    ....

    ....

3. How do the inset maps relate to the main map?

    ....

    ....

4. Why do you think the mapmaker used inset maps rather than one map to show the precipitation of United States?

    ....

    ....

    ....

    ....

    ....

Regions and Resources

Trees are used to make items such as furniture.

The United States is a nation that is rich in natural resources. A **natural resource** is something in the environment that people can use. Soil, water, and trees are all examples of natural resources.

Natural Resources in the United States

Each region of the country has many different natural resources. The Northeast has forests and fertile soil. It also has rivers and a long coast that make fishing possible. Coal, found in Pennsylvania, is another natural resource in the Northeast.

Fish and shellfish are brought to shore in the Northeast.

Draw an item that is made from corn.

UNLOCK THE BIG ?

I will know that each region has natural resources that are used to make products.

Vocabulary

natural resource	human resource
economy	nonrenewable
product	conserve
capital resource	renewable

In the Southeast, fertile soil is an important resource. The soil and the warm climate make farming a leading activity. Farmers grow cotton, rice, citrus fruits, peanuts, and other crops. The Southeast also produces oil, coal, and lumber.

Farming is a large part of the economy of the Midwest. An **economy** is the use of the wealth and resources in a place. The region's fertile soil is ideal for growing soybeans and corn. Farmers also raise hogs and cows. Cows' milk is used to make dairy products such as butter and cheese. **Products** are items people make or grow to sell. Coal, oil, and iron ore are also natural resources in the region. Iron ore is used to make iron and steel.

The plains of the Southwest are a major center for raising cattle and sheep. Cotton is the region's leading crop. Oil is a valuable resource found in Oklahoma and Texas. Copper is mined in Arizona and New Mexico.

The West is known for cattle ranching and copper, silver, and gold mining. In the warm valleys near the Pacific Coast, farmers raise fruits, nuts, and vegetables. Oil, lumber, and fish are also found in the West.

1. **Look** at the picture. **Label** the natural resource.

Farmers plow the soil before planting.

Using Resources

Natural resources are used to make the things we use every day. Your clothes, your books, your desk in school, what you eat for lunch, all come from natural resources. For example, trees are a natural resource. After trees are cut down, the wood is made into lumber. The lumber can be used to build houses or for other products. Wood, when it is shredded and softened, is also made into paper.

People also use **capital resources** to make products. Capital resources are the human-made things that we use to grow or make other things. Tools, machines, and buildings are examples of capital resources. A lumber company's capital resources might include the mills where trees are cut into lumber.

A third type of resource is also needed to make products. Can you guess what it is? It's people! **Human resources** include people and their skills, ideas, and hard work. Without human resources, nothing could be produced.

Some businesses in the Southeast and the Southwest drill for oil. The oil that is pumped from underground is not ready to be used. The oil is processed and made into gasoline or other products for people to use.

2. These pictures show the resources that are used to make oil into gasoline. **Label** the pictures to show what type of resource is being used.

Regional Industries

The natural resources in a region shape the economy and the businesses that are found there. A region with large deposits of iron ore will likely have steel factories. It may also have a port so that iron ore and steel can be easily shipped. For farms to thrive, a region must have rich soil and the right climate.

Similar businesses can vary from region to region. People across the country farm. However, what they grow differs from one place to another. In one part of the Southeast, the soil and warm climate are good for growing citrus trees. Here the trees grow through much of the year, and the winters are not too cold. In the Midwest region, however, the soil and climate are better for growing crops such as corn and soybeans.

3. ◉ **Compare and Contrast** Why might farmers in different regions grow different crops?

....

....

....

Once oil is made into gasoline, people use it to fill their cars.

21

Protecting Resources

The United States is so large that it might seem that we could never run out of natural resources. But that's not true. Some of the resources that people depend on most are **nonrenewable.** This means the resources cannot be replaced or would take a long time to form again. These resources exist in large but limited amounts. When they are used up, they are gone for a long time.

Coal, oil, and natural gas are nonrenewable resources. People use these fuels to heat their homes, cook food, and run their cars. People also use them to make electricity to power lights and machines.

Since these resources cannot be replaced easily, it is important to conserve them. To **conserve** means to save or protect them. There are many ways to do this. People conserve electricity when they turn off lights that are not being used. People can walk or ride their bikes instead of driving a car. In winter, some people limit how warm they keep their homes.

Some natural resources are **renewable.** This means they can be replaced. For example, when trees are cut down for lumber to make furniture, new trees are planted. Companies plant more so they will not run out of trees. However, trees take years to grow. Therefore, it is still important to conserve them.

4. ◉ **Draw Conclusions**
Why is it important to conserve resources?

....

....

....

....

....

Replanting trees and recycling paper are good ways to care for our forests.

Soil and water are also renewable resources. Soil can be used year after year if it is nourished and taken care of. Water is renewed through the water cycle. However, pollution is a particular danger to these natural resources. Pollution can dirty the water and damage the soil. It can also harm plants and animals. Many people work to limit the amount of pollution released into the environment.

Another way people care for natural resources is by recycling. To recycle means to reuse the things we often throw away. People recycle many items, including glass, metal, plastic, and paper. These materials are processed and used again.

5. Write each resource in the correct column: water, fish, coal, soil, trees, natural gas, wheat, oil.

Classify Resources

Renewable	Nonrenewable

Got it?

6. ● **Summarize Write** a summary of the ways people conserve natural resources.

....

....

....

....

7. ❓ **Think** of a business near you. **Write** about the types of resources   **my Story Ideas** that it uses to provide its product or service.

....

....

....

....

⬛ **Stop!** I need help with ....

⏸ **Wait!** I have a question about ....

▶ **Go!** Now I know ....

myworldsocialstudies.com ▶ **Experience** ▶ (Got it?)   23

People and the Land

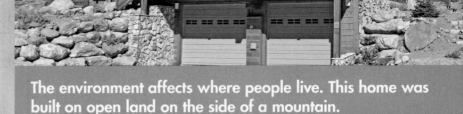

The environment affects where people live. This home was built on open land on the side of a mountain.

Steep roofs allow rain and snow to slide off.

What physical features are in your community? Are there plains, mountains, or a beach? Each of these features can affect the way people live. Some people live near the ocean because they enjoy the climate of areas along the coast. Others live near natural resources. These people might work in businesses that use the resources or have jobs that depend on those businesses. For example, since the late 1800s, miners have lived near the coal mines of Illinois.

People Adapt to the Environment

Wherever people live, they adapt to their environment. To **adapt** means to change to fit a new set of conditions. Suppose you moved from Florida to Wisconsin. The climates and landforms of these two states are different. How would you adapt to the land and climate of Wisconsin?

To begin with, you would wear different clothes. Instead of wearing lightweight clothes in winter, you would bundle up against the cold. You would also use more heat to warm your house. You may use less air conditioning in summer than you did in Florida.

Your activities would change, too. In Florida, you might have gone to the beach often to swim and surf in the ocean. Wisconsin has no ocean beaches. Instead, in summer you could swim in a freshwater lake. In winter, you could ski down snow-covered mountains. That is not possible in Florida.

Vocabulary
....

adapt
technology
irrigation
aquifer

Think about open land in your community. Draw what you would like to build on it.

People don't just adapt themselves to the environment. They also adapt how and what they build. In regions with lots of rain or snow, some people build houses with steep, sloped roofs. A slope keeps rain and snow from collecting on top. People may also build tunnels. In Minneapolis, Minnesota, people have built a system of glass tunnels that connect buildings. These tunnels link about 80 city blocks! The tunnels allow people to get around in the city without going outside during the cold, snowy winter.

In towns along the coast in North Carolina, beach houses might be raised to keep them from flooding when water levels rise. Along the coast, people also build their homes to withstand strong winds and heavy rainfall, since large and dangerous storms sometimes strike the area.

1. **Underline** how people in Minnesota have adapted to the environment.

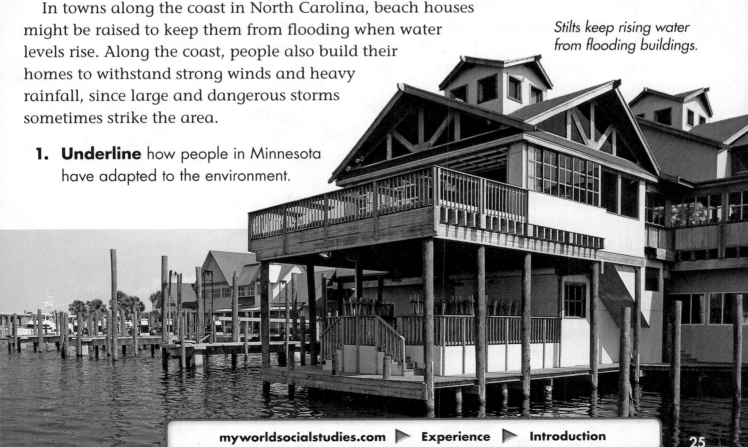

Stilts keep rising water from flooding buildings.

Workers today can easily clear land with heavy machines.

People Change the Environment

Since ancient times people have changed the environment to meet their needs. Long before the first explorers arrived, Native Americans burned prairies and forests. They did this to clear land, to make rich soil, and to create better grazing areas for animals. Early settlers in the Northeast also changed the land. They cut down forests to clear fields for planting. Today, people continue to change the environment. Land is cleared to build homes, shopping centers, and farms.

Over time, people have been able to make greater changes to the land. This is possible due to technology. **Technology** is the use of tools and scientific knowledge to do work. In the late 1800s, people cut trees down by hand with saws and axes. It could take many people a long time to clear a forest. Today, however, large machines are used to cut trees. People can clear a larger area much more quickly.

People today can more easily build large structures, too. People make roads on mountains, complex highway systems, and bridges that connect places that were once separated by wide rivers or streams. People also use new technologies to build dams to hold back rivers. The Oroville Dam in California is the tallest dam in the United States. It is about 770 feet high. That is more than twice as high as the Statue of Liberty in New York!

People use new technologies for irrigation, too. **Irrigation** is the use of technology to bring water to crops. In some states, farms are not located near a water source. People irrigate their crops with water brought in through pipes from lakes, streams, and rivers. In other states, people irrigate their crops with water from an aquifer. An **aquifer** is an underground layer of porous rock that holds water.

The Ogallala Aquifer (oh ga LAH la AH kwuh fur) is a large aquifer near the center of the United States. In fact, it lies beneath parts of eight different states in the Midwest, the West, and the Southwest. The aquifer is used to irrigate millions of acres, or large land areas, of wheat, corn, and other crops. People use many different machines to use and monitor the aquifer. Large pumps and tunnel systems bring the water up from underground and pump it to farms. Computers measure the amount of water that is drawn from the aquifer. They also track where the water is sent and how much water is left in the aquifer.

The Ogallala Aquifer

WY
SD
IA
NE
KS
CO
OK
NM
TX

0   100 mi
0   100 km

KEY
Area of aquifer

2. ◉ **Cause and Effect** **Write** an effect for this cause: People pump water from the Ogallala Aquifer.

....

....

Nearly all the water drawn from the Ogallala Aquifer is used for irrigation.

Saving Resources with Technology

Just as people use new technologies to change the land, people also use new technologies to conserve resources. When people first used the Ogallala Aquifer, they dug large ditches to carry the water to farms. Soon people realized that they were taking out water faster than it was replaced by rainfall. Some water was lost through evaporation from the open ditches. To conserve the aquifer, people used large machines to dig and connect underground tunnels to carry the water so it would not be lost through evaporation. They also created improved irrigation systems that wasted less water.

New technology allows factories to better conserve and protect resources as well. Today, factories can reduce the amount of pollution they release by sending the polluted air they produce through a scrubber. In the scrubber, water or chemicals are used to reduce the amount of harmful particles in the air. New technologies protect water resources, too. Some water treatment plants provide homes and businesses with clean, drinkable water. Other treatment plants filter waste water and treat it with chemicals before it flows into rivers and other bodies of water. This water is safer for fish or other wildlife.

New technologies allow people to use wind to make electricity cleanly.

New technologies also allow people to use other renewable sources of energy. These sources include wind, sunlight, and ocean waves. Solar panels, for example, change energy from the sun into electricity. Sunlight, wind, and waves are all resources that can be used over and over. Many of the resources people use for fuel, such as oil, are nonrenewable and limited. Other sources of energy allow people to conserve oil and other fuels.

3. ◉ **Main Idea and Details** **Fill in** the boxes with details.

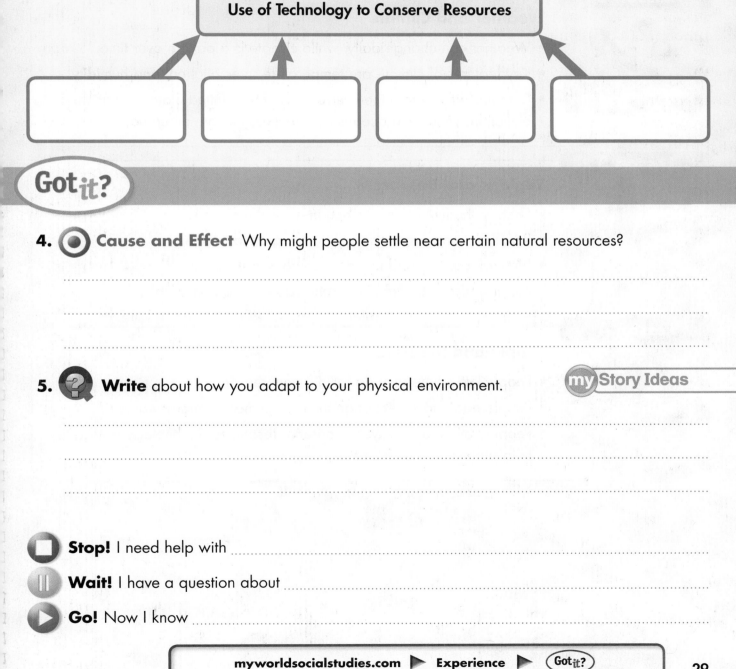

Technology at Work

Use of Technology to Conserve Resources

Got it?

4. ◉ **Cause and Effect** Why might people settle near certain natural resources?

....

....

....

5. ❓ **Write** about how you adapt to your physical environment.　my Story Ideas

....

....

....

⬛ **Stop!** I need help with ....

⏸ **Wait!** I have a question about ....

▶ **Go!** Now I know ....

Lesson 1

Land and Regions in the United States

- The United States is divided into five regions: the Northeast, the Southeast, the Midwest, the Southwest, and the West.
- Each region has landforms and bodies of water that make it special.
- Every region has cities as well as areas where fewer people live.

Lesson 2

Weather and Climate

- Weather can change daily, while climate is a pattern over time.
- Key features of climate are temperature, precipitation, and humidity.
- Climates vary across the five regions of the United States. Location, elevation, wind, and oceans contribute to climate differences.

Lesson 3

Regions and Resources

- Each of the five regions is rich in natural resources.
- Resources and products vary from region to region.
- Natural, capital, and human resources make products.
- Natural resources are either renewable or nonrenewable.

Lesson 4

People and the Land

- People live where they do for different reasons.
- People adapt to and change the environment in many ways.
- People have found ways to conserve resources. Technology is used to help protect the environment.

Review and Assessment

Lesson 1

Land and Regions in the United States

1. Match each word with its meaning.

_____ mesa   a. flat, raised land

_____ plateau   b. hill with a flat top

_____ flood plain   c. deep, rocky valley

_____ canyon   d. a plain along a river that floods

2. Write a sentence using the words *region* and *landform*.

....

....

....

3. Write the region for each state below.

Florida ....

Montana ....

Delaware ....

Wisconsin ....

Oklahoma ....

Lesson 2

Weather and Climate

4. How are weather and climate different?

....

....

....

5. Label part of the water cycle.

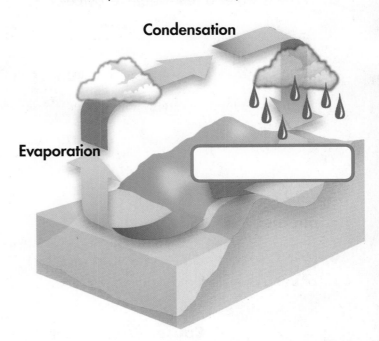

Condensation

Evaporation

6. Why does the Northeast have a colder climate than the Southeast?

A. It is not as windy as the Southeast.

B. It has more mountains than the Southeast.

C. It is farther from the ocean than the Southeast.

D. It is farther from the equator than the Southeast.

Lesson 3

Regions and Resources

7. **Fill in** the blanks. Trees are a .... resource used to make wooden furniture. The workers who make the furniture are .... resources. The tools and machines they use are .... resources.

8. Why is water a renewable resource?

   ....
   ....
   ....

Lesson 4

People and the Land

9. **Cause and Effect Fill in** an effect of using the Ogallala Aquifer.

Cause

Water from the Ogallala Aquifer was being lost through evaporation.

Effect

10. **List** three ways technology can be used to help the environment.

    a. ....

    b. ....

    c. ....

11. **How does geography affect the way we live?**

    Look at the picture and **answer** the question.

    How has this building been adapted to fit the environment?

    ....
    ....
    ....
    ....
    ....
    ....

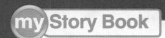

Go online to write and illustrate your own **myStory Book** using the **myStory Ideas** from this chapter.

 How does geography affect the way we live?

The United States has a variety of landforms, bodies of water, natural resources, and climate regions. This varied geography affects people in different ways, depending on where they live. Geography influences where we choose to live, what we wear, what we do for fun or work, and what our communities are like. How does it affect you?

Think about where you live and the activities you do. **Write** about how geography affects part of your life.

....

....

....

....

Now **draw** a picture to illustrate your writing.

While you're online, check out the **myStory Current Events** area where you can create your own book on a topic that's in the news.

Americans and Their History

my Story Spark

How have we changed and how have we stayed the same during our history?

Write something about yourself or your family that has changed in your lifetime. Then **write** about something that has stayed the same.

....

....

....

....

The Liberty Bell in Philadelphia, Pennsylvania, stands for American freedom.

Abraham Lincoln
Civil War President

my Story Video

President Abraham Lincoln stood in front of a large crowd. About 15,000 people were at the opening of the National Cemetery in Gettysburg, Pennsylvania. It was November 1863. Four and a half months earlier, nearly 8,000 soldiers died there. The Civil War was in its third year.

The ceremony at Gettysburg was held to honor soldiers who had died. Abraham Lincoln also wanted to honor something else. He wanted to honor what the United States stood for. The war, he said, was being fought so that

> *"government of the people, by the people, for the people, shall not perish from the earth."*

It was a time of great change in the nation. The North and the South had disagreed for years. Finally, the Southern states broke away from the United States. They created a separate nation and called it the Confederate States of America.

President Abraham Lincoln gave the Gettysburg Address on November 19, 1863.

35

Abraham Lincoln was born in Kentucky. He grew up on the frontier. He later moved to Illinois, where he worked as a lawyer.

President Lincoln led the nation through the Civil War. He visited Union generals and soldiers on the battlefield.

Abraham Lincoln believed in the Union. A union is a group that joins together. The union of states was created by the United States Constitution. Lincoln believed states could not leave that union.

At Gettysburg, President Lincoln spoke about the beginning of the nation. He said that the United States was "born in liberty." It was dedicated to the idea that all people "are created equal." This terrible war was testing these ideas. It was testing whether or not a nation based on liberty and equality could survive.

Abraham Lincoln looked tired and worried that day at Gettysburg. As president, he was the commander in chief of the United States Army and Navy. He was responsible for the lives of all Americans. Every day, more and more lives were lost in the fighting.

The war began in April 1861. Lincoln had just become president. He moved to Washington from Illinois. He brought his wife and three young sons to the White House.

The White House was a huge change from the Kentucky log cabin where Lincoln was born. When he was still a boy, his family moved to Indiana. Lincoln helped his family farm their land there. The young Lincoln was known for being honest and truthful. He also read every book he could find. By the time he was a tall, grown man, Abraham Lincoln had taught himself a lot. He became a lawyer and served in Congress. Then, in 1860, he was elected President of the United States.

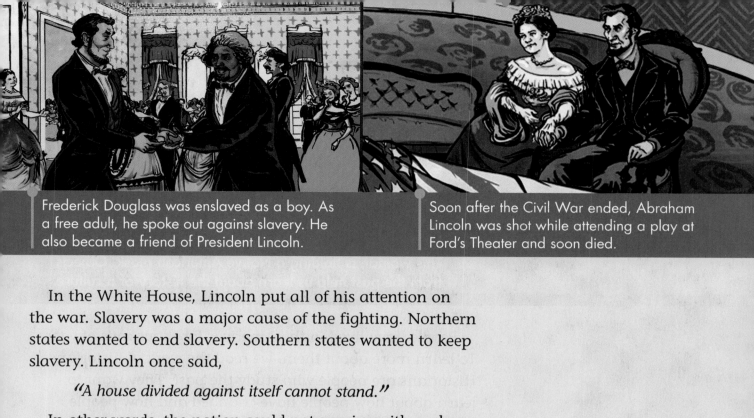

Frederick Douglass was enslaved as a boy. As a free adult, he spoke out against slavery. He also became a friend of President Lincoln.

Soon after the Civil War ended, Abraham Lincoln was shot while attending a play at Ford's Theater and soon died.

In the White House, Lincoln put all of his attention on the war. Slavery was a major cause of the fighting. Northern states wanted to end slavery. Southern states wanted to keep slavery. Lincoln once said,

"A house divided against itself cannot stand."

In other words, the nation could not survive with such a disagreement. Lincoln knew that something had to change.

After that day in Gettysburg, the war continued for another year and a half. Soon the states were reunited. The Union survived.

Just a few days after the war ended, Abraham Lincoln was shot and killed. He led the nation through the Civil War. Now others had to rebuild it.

Think About It Based on this story, how did the nation change in the Civil War? As you read this chapter, think about how the nation changed and how it stayed the same.

In 1865, Abraham Lincoln took the presidential oath for the second time.

America and Europe

Envision It!

This woman is holding a Native American mask. Objects from the past help us learn about the history of a culture.

People have lived in the Americas for thousands of years. To learn more about them, we read the work of historians. Historians are people who study the past. They want to learn about how people have changed and how people have stayed the same.

The First Americans

Historians work with archeologists to learn about the distant past. An **archeologist** (ar kee AHL uh jihst) studies artifacts and sites to learn about ancient people. An **artifact** is an object made by humans. Artifacts can tell a lot about the history of a place and its people.

Archeological sites like Blackwater Draw in New Mexico are important. About 80 years ago, a young man found a strange-looking stone tool there. Soon archeologists came and uncovered many other artifacts. The artifacts tell a story about the first humans in the Americas.

Most historians and archeologists believe the first Americans came from Asia. Thousands of years ago, land connected Asia and the Americas. Small groups of hunters crossed over from Asia. Others may have come by water. They were **hunter-gatherers.** They hunted animals and gathered plants for food. Over a very long time, these early people spread across North and South America.

The descendants of these early people are called Native Americans. A descendant is a person's child, grandchild, great-grandchild, and all the children that follow.

Native Americans hunted animals for food. These stone points would have been attached to a spear or a dart and used for hunting.

I will know that when Europeans and Native Americans met, their cultures changed forever.

What can you learn from studying masks, clay pots, or stone tools?

Vocabulary

archeologist	culture
artifact	colony
hunter-gatherer	enslaved
agriculture	tradition

From the far north to the tip of South America, from the Pacific to the Atlantic, many different Native American groups lived on the land. Then agriculture changed the way many of these people lived. **Agriculture** is the planting and growing of crops for food. Once people learned how to farm, they could stay in one place.

The environment affected the cultures they developed. A **culture** is the way of life of a group of people. In some places, Native Americans farmed and lived in small villages or large communities. In others, groups moved from place to place. They followed the animals they hunted. Across the Americas, Native Americans created a wide range of cultures. Today, their descendents value those ancient traditions.

1. Pueblo Bonito was a Native American village built in New Mexico about 1,000 years ago. Look at the baskets. **Circle** evidence of agriculture at Pueblo Bonito.

Europeans Explore

On a warm Friday morning in October 1492, three Spanish ships approached a small island off the coast of North America. Their leader was an explorer named Christopher Columbus. Like others in Europe, Columbus wanted to find a direct route to Asia. Europeans traded in Asia for spices and other goods but only knew long, dangerous routes to get there.

Columbus had no idea that North America even existed. Seeing land, he believed that he had reached the Indies. The Indies were islands near Asia. When he saw the people who lived on the island, he called them "Indians."

On that morning, Columbus claimed the land he found for Spain. He also claimed the people. For about 200 years, explorers would come to North and South America from Spain, France, Portugal, the Netherlands, and England.

Most explorers who came to North America were like Columbus. They were looking for a shorter route to the riches of Asia. Like Columbus, they would also claim the land of North America. The encounters, or meetings, between the two groups would change the lives of Europeans and Native Americans forever.

2. ◉ **Sequence** On the map key, **circle** the name of the earliest explorer in the Americas. Then **circle** the name of the explorer who explored 110 years later.

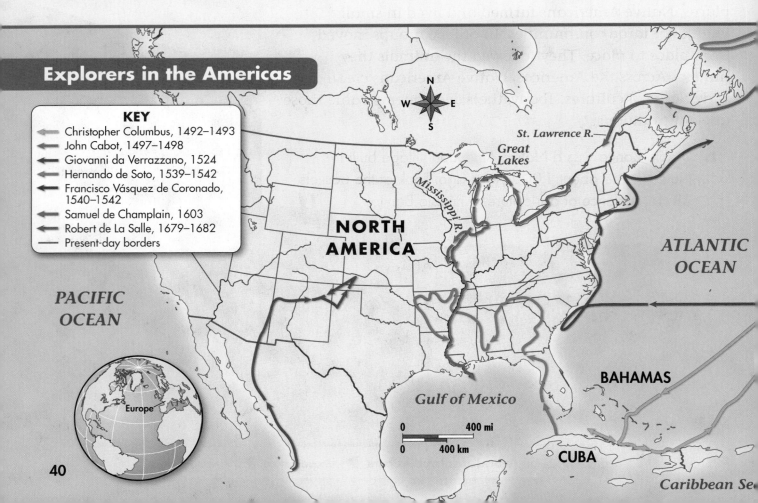

Explorers in the Americas

KEY
- Christopher Columbus, 1492–1493
- John Cabot, 1497–1498
- Giovanni da Verrazzano, 1524
- Hernando de Soto, 1539–1542
- Francisco Vásquez de Coronado, 1540–1542
- Samuel de Champlain, 1603
- Robert de La Salle, 1679–1682
- Present-day borders

NORTH AMERICA

PACIFIC OCEAN

ATLANTIC OCEAN

Great Lakes

St. Lawrence R.

Mississippi R.

Gulf of Mexico

BAHAMAS

CUBA

Caribbean Sea

Europe

0   400 mi
0   400 km

European Colonies

In the 1500s, Europeans began to settle the Americas. Countries like Spain, England, Portugal, the Netherlands, and France founded colonies. A **colony** is a settlement ruled by another country.

Europeans often built forts. A fort is a military settlement surrounded by walls. In 1565, Spaniards settled St. Augustine in what is now Florida. Later, English colonists came. Colonists are the people who settle a colony. Their first lasting colony was at Jamestown. It was formed in 1607. They named the surrounding land Virginia. In 1620, another group of English colonists called Pilgrims settled north of Virginia. They were looking for religious freedom. They named their community Plymouth.

For more than 200 years, Europeans colonized America. The French settled Canada and called it New France. Spanish explorers claimed much of the Southwest region. And by the early 1700s, thirteen English colonies stretched along the Atlantic coast.

Starting in 1619, another group of people arrived in America. European traders brought men and women from Africa to work. Gradually, farmers depended on the labor of enslaved Africans. A person who is **enslaved** is not free.

In 1492, America belonged to the Native Americans. Three hundred years later, Americans were a diverse people. Some had European backgrounds. Others were from Africa. Some were Native Americans. By 1790, almost 4 million colonists and enslaved Africans lived in North America along with the Native Americans.

This painting from the 1800s shows an early encounter between European colonists and Native Americans. Some encounters between Europeans and Native Americans were peaceful. Others, however, were not. The two groups fought over who owned land.

Native Americans shared plants and animals that were new to Europeans.

Europeans brought many plants and animals that were new to the Americas.

The Columbian Exchange

What did you have for breakfast this morning? Perhaps you had a glass of milk, a piece of toast, and maybe some applesauce. You probably did not thank Christopher Columbus, but you should have. Before 1492, there were no cows, no wheat, and no apples in the Americas!

For hundreds of years, the Americas, which are in the Western Hemisphere, were isolated from the Eastern Hemisphere. That all changed in 1492. Columbus and other explorers brought plants, animals, and more to the Americas. From Native Americans Europe got corn, potatoes, vast amounts of gold, and other resources. When Columbus returned to Europe from his travels, he brought plants that grew pineapples. He may also have brought tobacco. This was just the beginning of a giant exchange called the Columbian Exchange.

The Columbian Exchange was helpful in many ways. Corn and potatoes helped feed people in Europe. They helped the population grow. Wheat and rice did the same thing in the Americas. Horses improved work and transportation for everyone in the Americas.

Not all of the exchanges were good, however. Europeans brought germs that were deadly to the Native Americans. The results were terrible. Native Americans had no protection against the germs. Many thousands of Native Americans died of smallpox. Native Americans would continue to die from deadly germs.

3. ◎ **Categorize Look** at the pictures. Then **think** about the food you ate recently. **Write** some ingredients that came from Europe to the Americas. Then **write** some that went to Europe from the Americas.

....

....

....

....

Government in the English Colonies

The English colonists who lived on the Atlantic coast brought an important tradition with them. A **tradition** is a belief or custom handed down through generations. For many years, English people had played a role in their government. The new colonists expected to do the same. They wanted to make their own laws.

In 1619 the colonists of Virginia were allowed to create the House of Burgesses. Communities elected representatives to make laws for the colony. Representatives act on behalf of a group of people. The House of Burgesses started our tradition of self-government.

4. How might the idea of self-government lead the English colonists to want freedom from the King of England?

....

....

The Virginia House of Burgesses was an early institution of self-government in the colonies.

Got it?

5. ⊙ **Sequence Write** the numbers 1, 2, and 3 to arrange the following events in the order that they happened.

_____ House of Burgesses meets in Virginia.

_____ Christopher Columbus reaches the Americas.

_____ English people set up first colonies on the Atlantic coast.

6. ❓ **Describe** one building or place that tells something about the history of your community. How has it changed over time?

my Story Ideas

....

....

⬛ **Stop!** I need help with ....

⏸ **Wait!** I have a question about ....

▶ **Go!** Now I know ....

Graph Skills

Use a Timeline

Knowing the order of events is important when you study history. A timeline can help you understand sequence. Sequence means the order of events. A timeline is a kind of chart. It shows events and the dates they occurred. The events are placed in the order in which they happened. This can help you understand connections between events.

This timeline shows important events in colonial American history. The events are about Spanish exploration and settlement. Look at the timeline. You read it from left to right, like a line in a book. The earliest date on the timeline is on the left. The most recent date is on the right. A timeline is divided into equal units of time. On this timeline, each unit equals 20 years.

Timelines can also help you understand different periods of time. A timeline may be divided into years, decades, or even centuries. A decade is a period of ten years. A century is one hundred years.

Look at the timeline below. Then answer questions 1 through 5 on the next page.

By 1673, Spaniards in St. Augustine had built a strong fort called Castillo de San Marcos. The fort protected the settlement.

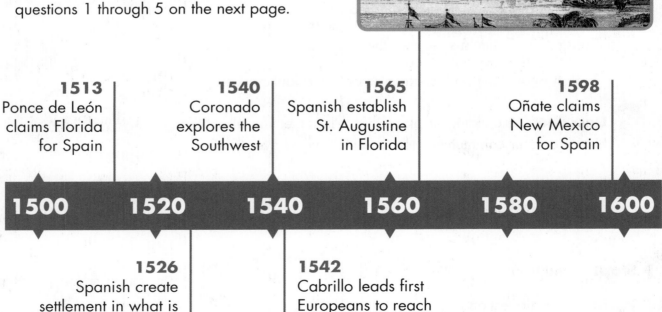

| 1513 Ponce de León claims Florida for Spain | 1540 Coronado explores the Southwest | 1565 Spanish establish St. Augustine in Florida | 1598 Oñate claims New Mexico for Spain |

1500 **1520** **1540** **1560** **1580** **1600**

| 1526 Spanish create settlement in what is now South Carolina. | 1542 Cabrillo leads first Europeans to reach California coast. |

Use the timeline to answer the following questions.

1. Does the timeline cover a period of one decade or one century?

   ....

2. How is the timeline divided?

   ....

3. Did Spain claim New Mexico or Florida first?

   ....

4. When was St. Augustine established?

   ....

5. **Apply** Now complete a timeline of your own life. **Write** three important events in your life that have already happened. Then **draw** lines that connect the events to their correct place on the timeline. Then **write** one event that you're looking forward to.

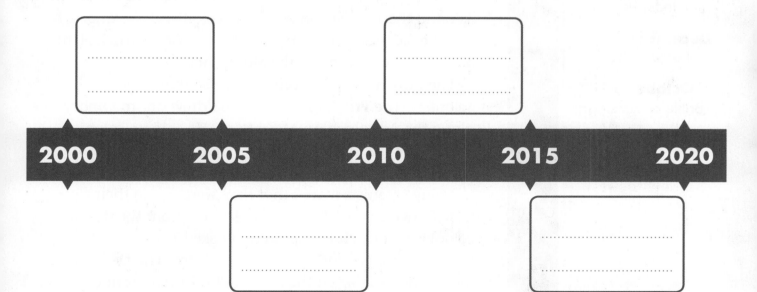

A New Nation

Envision It!

Your teacher probably has rules about what is allowed in class. George Washington helped make rules for America.

War for Independence

April 1775
Fighting at Lexington and Concord

1774

1775

June 1775
Battle of Bunker Hill

1776

July 1776
Declaration of Independence

1777

December 1776
Battle of Trenton

1778

October 1777
Battle of Saratoga

1779

1780

1781

October 1781
Battle of Yorktown

1782

It was July 1776. In Philadelphia, Pennsylvania, more than 50 men came together and said, "We . . . declare that these united colonies are . . . free and independent states." Each of the 13 colonies was governed by Britain. This made the colonists British subjects. Why were they declaring independence? **Independence** is freedom from rule by others.

Independence

In 1763, the British won an expensive war against France in North America. The British wanted to tax the colonists to help pay for it. They passed tax laws such as the Stamp Act and the Townshend Acts. The colonists were angry. A member of the Virginia House of Burgesses, Patrick Henry, gave a speech opposing the Stamp Act.

The British king did something else that angered colonists. The Proclamation of 1763 drew an imaginary line along the Appalachian Mountains. He said no colonists could live west of the line. Since colonies were expanding, colonists wanted to be able to move west to find new land.

Many colonists feared that they were losing their right to self-government. So, in 1776, leaders from the different colonies met in Philadelphia and asked Thomas Jefferson to write the Declaration of Independence. The Declaration marks the time when the colonies broke free from British rule and became independent. However, some Americans and most British disagreed and wanted the colonies to remain under Britain's government.

Why do you think both schools and countries need rules?
Write some reasons.

UNLOCK THE BIG ?

I will know that the United States grew out of the English colonies and became an independent nation.

Vocabulary

independence	delegate
confederation	ratify
congress	amendment
constitution	territory

The American Revolution

The colonists began organizing and planning to fight for independence. They formed the Continental Army. Its leader was General George Washington of Virginia. King George III, the British ruler, was furious. He sent soldiers to the colonies. Their job was to stop the independence movement.

The colonists were successful in small, early battles. But they faced a strong British army and navy. Soon it looked as if the colonists might lose. After a defeat in New York, Washington won a battle at Trenton, New Jersey.

In 1777, the Continental Army won an important battle. They defeated the British at Saratoga, New York. Seeing that the Americans could win, France agreed to help the colonists.

The following winter was a terrible time for the Americans. Washington and his army camped at Valley Forge in Pennsylvania. It was extremely cold. The soldiers also did not have enough to eat.

The revolution continued for six long years. Across the colonies, more people became involved. About 5,000 black colonists joined the Continental Army. Women worked at home to help. Some even fought on the battlefield. Finally, in 1781, George Washington led his soldiers to victory at Yorktown, Virginia. The long war was over.

1. **Sequence** On the timeline, **circle** the earliest fighting of the war. Then **circle** the last battle fought.

George Washington was a strong leader. He led the Americans to victory.

Many of the farmers in Shays' Rebellion had fought in the Revolution. They were disappointed in the government formed under the Articles of Confederation.

A Hard Job

After winning independence, the Americans had to build a nation. The 13 new states called themselves the United States of America, but the country was not united in the way it is today. Each state felt independent. They were not used to working together. In 1781 the states signed the Articles of Confederation to govern the country. A **confederation** is a union of states that agree to cooperate.

Leaders from the states met in a congress. A **congress** is a group of people who are responsible for making a country's laws. But soon they were arguing. They disagreed about money, so soon each state was printing its own money. They also disagreed about who owned land in the west.

The new Congress of the Confederation did make some important decisions. It set up a way for new states to join the United States, for example. However, money problems continued. Taxes went up, and the economy slowed down. Many people felt desperate in the bad times. In 1786, a farmer organized a revolt. Daniel Shays and about 1,200 Massachusetts farmers attacked government buildings. It was time for change.

A New Constitution

Once again, leaders felt the need to meet and discuss the country's future. They planned to revise the Articles of Confederation. Instead, they created an entirely new government. The plan they created is still the plan of government for our nation today. The planners held a Constitutional Convention. A **constitution** is a plan of government. In May 1787, 55 delegates met in Philadelphia. A **delegate** is someone who represents a group of people. These delegates represented their states.

2. ◉ **Cause and Effect** How did the Articles of Confederation lead to the Constitution?

....

....

....

The road to a new government was not smooth. The first problem was size. Some states had large populations. Other states were smaller. But every state wanted the same amount of power. The delegates argued for weeks. Eventually, they made a compromise. There would be a Senate, where each state would have two members. There would also be a House of Representatives. There, each state would send representatives based on the state's population.

The second argument was over how much power the government should have. Many people wanted a central government that was strong enough to solve the country's problems. Others wanted states to have more power. They worried that the leader of a strong national government might act like another king. The new constitution had to balance these concerns.

Finally, in September, the delegates were ready to sign the new Constitution. Then they faced a new challenge. They had to convince the people that the new Constitution could help save the nation.

One by one, each state ratified the new Constitution. To **ratify** means to approve. Some people said the new Constitution did not protect the rights of the people. So amendments were written. An **amendment** is a change or addition. These first ten amendments are called the Bill of Rights. The Senate and the House of Representatives urged the states to ratify, or adopt, these amendments.

The new nation needed a president. On April 30, 1789, George Washington took an oath. He promised to "preserve, protect and defend the Constitution."

3. Read the summary of the First Amendment. Then **write** why you think it is important.

....

....

....

....

James Madison played an important role at the Constitutional Convention. Sometimes he is called the Father of the Constitution.

The First Amendment

The First Amendment protects freedom of religion, speech, and the press.

It guarantees that people can assemble, or gather, peacefully.

It guarantees that people can petition, or ask, the government to make changes.

The New Nation Grows

After independence, the new nation stretched from the Atlantic Ocean to the Mississippi River. Only some of that land was organized into the 13 states. Soon people living in other parts of the United States wanted to become states, too.

The government set up territories first. A **territory** is an area that is governed by a country but is not a state. The Northwest Territory was organized under the Articles of Confederation. Eventually its land became the states of Ohio, Indiana, Illinois, Michigan, and Wisconsin. Other states were formed, too. The area between New York and New Hampshire became Vermont, for example.

A big change came in 1803. Thomas Jefferson was president then. The leader of France was a man named Napoleon. He offered to sell the United States land that would double its size for less than three cents an acre. For $15 million, Jefferson purchased the Louisiana Territory. It was an area of 828,000 square miles. Eventually it would become all or part of 15 new states.

4. **Compare and Contrast** What was the difference in the size of the country before and after the Louisiana Purchase?

....

....

....

....

....

....

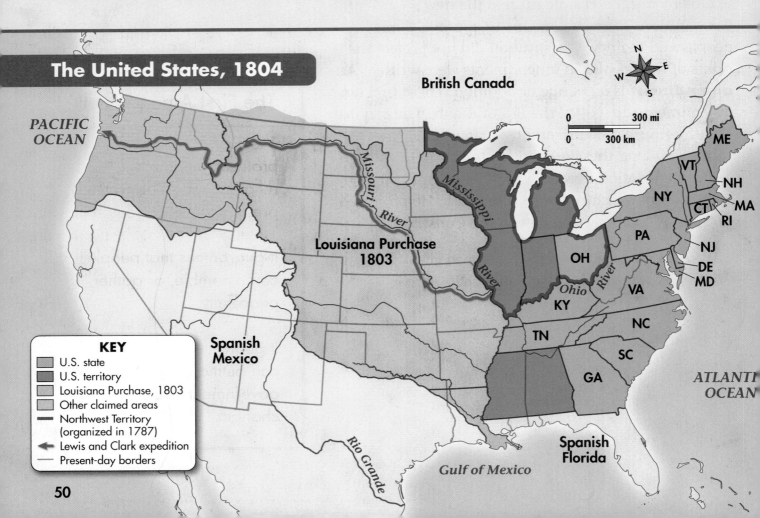

The United States, 1804

British Canada

PACIFIC OCEAN

Missouri River

Mississippi

Louisiana Purchase 1803

ME

VT

NH

NY

CT

MA

RI

PA

NJ

OH

DE

MD

Ohio River

VA

KY

NC

TN

SC

GA

ATLANTIC OCEAN

Spanish Mexico

Rio Grande

Spanish Florida

Gulf of Mexico

KEY
- U.S. state
- U.S. territory
- Louisiana Purchase, 1803
- Other claimed areas
- Northwest Territory (organized in 1787)
- Lewis and Clark expedition
- Present-day borders

Lewis and Clark Explore the West

Thomas Jefferson knew that the rivers of the United States were important. The Louisiana Purchase gave Americans control of the Mississippi River. Now Jefferson wanted to find a river route to the Pacific Ocean. He hoped the Missouri River could be part of that route. He also wanted to make contact with the Native Americans in the region. So he sent an expedition west. An expedition is a journey made for a special purpose.

Meriwether Lewis and William Clark led the expedition. They took about 50 men with them. They explored the rivers. The round trip was almost 8,000 miles long. It took more than two years. There was no river route to the Pacific, but they brought back important information about the land and people of the west.

Sacajawea, a Native American, helped Lewis and Clark. She was a valuable guide.

Got it?

5. ◉ **Summarize** **Write** a summary of Thomas Jefferson's contributions to the early history of the United States.

....

....

6. ❓ How has your state changed over time? In 1804, was it a state, a territory, or something else?

....

....

⬛ **Stop!** I need help with ....

⏸ **Wait!** I have a question about ....

▶ **Go!** Now I know ....

Lesson 3

Growth and Civil War

In the 1840s, many families moved west in covered wagons. Inside, the wagon was very small.

In 1847, San Francisco, California, was a tiny town. By 1849, after gold was found, about 25,000 people lived there. Other western towns were growing, too. Americans were on the move!

The Nation Grows West

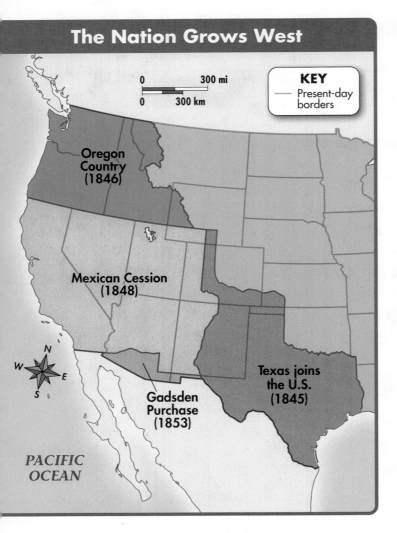

KEY
— Present-day borders

Oregon Country (1846)

Mexican Cession (1848)

Gadsden Purchase (1853)

Texas joins the U.S. (1845)

PACIFIC OCEAN

0   300 mi
0   300 km

Manifest Destiny

The Louisiana Purchase doubled the size of the nation. There was more territory to the west as well. Great Britain controlled much of Oregon. Spain, and later Mexico, controlled the Southwest.

Americans in the East began moving west to find land, gold, or furs. People spoke of Manifest Destiny. If something is manifest, it is obvious. Destiny is what must happen. In other words, some believed it was Americans' clear duty to expand the nation from coast to coast. However, Native Americans lived in these areas. The two groups were going to have to fight for control of the land.

The United States and Mexico also fought a war for control of land in the Southwest. The Treaty of Guadalupe-Hidalgo ended the war in 1848. The nation finally stretched from the Atlantic to the Pacific.

1. Sequence On the map, **circle** the last piece of land added to the United States.

Your family is moving west and you can take only one thing with you. Draw what would you take.

UNLOCK THE BIG ?

I will know that the growing nation had deep divisions that led to Civil War.

Vocabulary

immigrant	secede
industry	Reconstruction
states' rights	segregation
abolitionist	reservation

New Industries

The United States was growing in other ways, too. In the 1840s, many European immigrants arrived. An **immigrant** is a person who comes to live in a new land. These immigrants helped build the nation's growing industry. **Industry** is the part of the economy in which machines are used to do the work.

This period of change is called the Industrial Revolution. During this time, more and more goods were produced by machines in large factories. Later, farmers used machines to do work they once did by hand or with animal power. These changes made the economy very productive.

Inventions changed more than just farm and factory work. There were big changes in transportation, too. Railroads let people travel faster and easier. Better roads and the new Erie Canal helped Americans go west. The telegraph helped them communicate, or keep in touch. Inventions such as these played an important role in the nation's growth.

2. ◎ **Cause and Effect** This illustration shows how a cotton gin cleaned seeds from cotton. It was much faster than cleaning cotton by hand. Would this cause Southern planters to grow more or less cotton?

Raw cotton is fed into the hopper.

Cleaned cotton appears.

Seeds are removed and discarded.

Work in the North and the South was very different. Northern factories used free labor to weave cotton into cloth. Southern growers used enslaved workers to grow cotton.

Paid Factory Labor

Enslaved Agricultural Workers

The North and the South

The North and the South had different ways of life. The North had more people, cities, and factories. The South was largely a farming region. At the heart of all of the differences was slavery. The South depended on enslaved Africans to work in cotton fields. Northern factories needed cotton to make cloth. As a result, Southern growers needed more enslaved workers.

Southern states argued for **states' rights.** This was a belief that each state should solve its own problems. It also meant that new states could allow slavery if they wanted. Many Northerners, however, did not want slavery in new states. They believed in free labor. Many were abolitionists. An **abolitionist** is someone who wants to abolish, or end, slavery completely.

Free blacks were an important part of the abolitionist movement. Black and white Americans worked together to help men, women, and children escape from slavery. Abolitionists published newspapers. They spoke out at public meetings. They protected enslaved people who had run away. They told about the horrors of slavery.

By the mid-1800s, the nation was growing more divided and angry. In 1860, Abraham Lincoln was elected president. Southerners were furious after his election. Lincoln wanted to stop the spread of slavery. Southern states threatened to leave the Union. Many said Lincoln's election could lead to war. Sadly, it did.

The Civil War

Soon after the election, South Carolina seceded from the Union. To **secede** means to break away or officially withdraw. Soon ten more Southern states seceded. They called themselves the Confederate States of America. They elected a president: Jefferson Davis. The United States had become two nations. Southerners said they had a right to do this. President Lincoln said they did not.

The Civil War began in April 1861. It started with a battle over Fort Sumter. This fort belonged to the United States, but it was in Charleston, South Carolina. So now it was in the land of the Confederacy.

Soon the president called for 75,000 volunteers to fight for the Union. People believed the war would be over soon. They were wrong. It would go on for four years. More than 2.3 million soldiers fought in the war. More than 1 million of them died or were wounded.

The North and South fought on land and at sea. They fought along the Mississippi River and as far west as New Mexico. Each side had strong leaders. Robert E. Lee of Virginia was a Confederate general. Ulysses S. Grant of Ohio was a Union general.

Finally, the Union defeated the Confederacy. On April 9, 1865, General Lee surrendered. The terrible war was over. Now the job of healing the nation began.

President Lincoln was shot and killed just five days after General Lee surrendered to General Grant. The nation lost a strong leader.

3. **Summarize Write** short descriptions for the three Civil War figures in the bottom row.

Clara Barton
Nurse; founder of American Red Cross

Harriet Tubman
Abolitionist; guide for escaped slaves

Frederick Douglass
Abolitionist; newspaper publisher

Ulysses S. Grant

Robert E. Lee

Jefferson Davis

....

....

Rebuilding the Nation

President Lincoln had wanted to heal the nation after the war but was killed before he could try. After his death, Congress controlled Reconstruction. **Reconstruction** was the period of time when the South was rebuilt. Congress made rules for the Southern states to follow. The government also worked to help newly freed African Americans in the South.

Three amendments to the Constitution helped African Americans. The Thirteenth Amendment made slavery against the law. The Fourteenth Amendment gave equal rights to former slaves. The Fifteenth Amendment granted African American men the right to vote. The amendments helped make the nation stronger and freer.

Still, times were hard for African Americans. Slavery was gone, but discrimination was not. Discrimination is treating someone unfairly because of race or other qualities. In the North, African Americans faced discrimination when looking for housing and jobs.

Southern states passed Jim Crow laws. These laws kept African Americans and white people apart. This separation is called **segregation**. Some white people even formed organizations to scare African Americans. One was called the Ku Klux Klan. It would be another 100 years before the nation began to repair the damages caused by segregation.

During Reconstruction, the first African Americans were elected to Congress. Blanche Bruce was elected to the Senate in 1874. He represented Mississippi.

4. **Cause and Effect**
Write the missing cause and effect using facts about the Civil War and Reconstruction.

Causes and Effects of the Civil War

Causes	Effects
Southern states secede from the Union.	
	Reconstruction begins.

Changes for Native Americans

In the 1860s, many Americans were moving west. They settled in the Plains. Many Native American groups including the Cheyenne, the Lakota, the Comanche, and the Nez Percé already lived there, however. The cultures of these Native American groups were very different from the culture of the white settlers. The two peoples fought constantly over land.

During the next 30 years, the government forced Native Americans to move. The government set up reservations. A **reservation** was an area set aside for Native Americans. Native Americans did not want to move. To avoid the reservation, Nez Percé leader Chief Joseph led his people from their home in Oregon across many miles to Montana. United States troops pursued him and his people. Finally, the Nez Percé gave up. Chief Joseph gave a moving speech, saying, ". . . I will fight no more forever."

Chief Joseph and the Nez Percé lived in the Pacific Northwest. When white settlers wanted to take their land, Chief Joseph and his people resisted.

Got it?

5. ◉ **Main Idea and Details** Jim Crow laws show conflict between white Americans and African Americans. Write an example of cooperation between them from the 1800s.

....

....

6. ❓ Many Americans moved west in the 1800s. **Write** about how your (my) Story Ideas family or a family you know has been shaped by moving or relocating.

....

....

⬜ **Stop!** I need help with ....

⏸ **Wait!** I have a question about ....

▶ **Go!** Now I know ....

The United States Becomes a World Power

Envision It!

When European immigrants arrived in New York Harbor, they saw the Statue of Liberty.

The railroad owner lifted his hammer and hit a golden spike. The news went out across the nation. "DONE," the telegraph said. It was May 10, 1869. The transcontinental railroad linked the East Coast and the West Coast.

Transcontinental means "crossing a continent," such as North America. Now, a traveler could cross the country in a week. Before, such a trip would take about six months. The new railroad changed more than travel time. It was a key part of an even larger change in the nation.

An Industrial Nation

Between the Civil War and 1900, the United States became the world's leader in manufacturing. **Manufacturing** is making goods by machines, usually in factories. These factories depended on railroads. Trains carried resources to factories where certain goods were produced. Those goods could then be carried all across the country by railroad for sale. Railroads helped American businesses of all kinds to grow.

Just as businesses and factories were growing, so were cities. Cities were the home to many big businesses, which provided jobs for people. By 1900, four out of every ten Americans lived in a city. The nation was changing.

1. ◉ **Cause and Effect** As railroads grew, what effect did that have on where people lived and settled?

....

....

Thousands of children worked in American factories and mines. They worked long hours in dangerous jobs. As a result, people demanded laws that would protect all workers.

Write what the Statue of Liberty might mean to people both then and now.

UNLOCK THE BIG ?

I will know that the United States became one of the world's most powerful nations after the Civil War.

Vocabulary

transcontinental   diverse

manufacturing   depression

entrepreneur   fascism

Inventions Bring Change

Inventions of the late 1800s changed people's lives. We use them all the time today: electric lights, elevators, telephones, automobiles, and more. Thomas Edison was one of the most important inventors. In 1879, he invented an electric light bulb that stayed lit for a long time. Edison worked on more than 1,000 inventions. Most were related to electricity.

Edison was not the only inventor changing American life. Alexander Graham Bell invented the telephone in 1876. Later, Henry Ford made a successful automobile with a gasoline engine. The first typewriters changed the way businesses worked. The first sewing machines changed the way that clothes were made. With the invention of elevators, tall buildings were more practical.

American entrepreneurs built many big businesses. An **entrepreneur** risks money to start a new business. Some entrepreneurs became very rich. Big business was part of the reason why the nation was growing.

2. What invention made this "sky scraper" department store practical?

....

A Diverse Nation

The growing United States was a "land of opportunity" for people living in other countries. A large group of immigrants arrived in the 1840s. Later, many more came. There were 9 million newcomers from 1880 to 1900 alone. The nation was becoming more **diverse,** or varied, as people came to the United States from different places.

Industries needed workers. Many immigrants found jobs in the nation's cities. As a result, the populations of cities grew. Chicago grew more than five times bigger between 1870 and 1900. Other newcomers worked to build railroads. Still others started farms on the inexpensive farmland west of the Mississippi River.

Some "old" Americans were afraid that these "new" Americans would steal their jobs. They were nervous about people whose religion or culture was different. Immigrants faced discrimination. During this period the United States passed laws to limit the number of immigrants.

Many new immigrants were families with children.

3. ◎ **Compare and Contrast Look** at the two graphs and compare them. **Circle** the region that had the biggest increase in immigrants between 1840 and 1900.

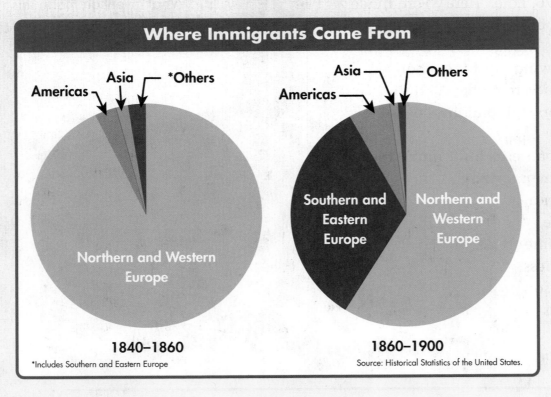

Where Immigrants Came From

1840–1860

Americas — Asia — *Others

Northern and Western Europe

*Includes Southern and Eastern Europe

1860–1900

Americas — Asia — Others

Southern and Eastern Europe

Northern and Western Europe

Source: Historical Statistics of the United States.

Depression and the New Deal

In the early 1900s, America's economy grew rapidly. By the 1920s, the economy was booming. Businesses were expanding. People were making and spending a lot of money. Things were going so well that people called the period "the Roaring Twenties."

Then all of a sudden, in 1929, the Roaring Twenties came to a halt. As people began to lose money, they panicked. Banks closed and businesses failed. People lost their jobs. The economy slowed down so much that it went into a depression. In a **depression,** the economy goes into a deep and serious slowdown. Jobs are very hard to find in such a period. This depression was so bad that it is called the Great Depression.

The United States elected a new president in 1932. His name was Franklin D. Roosevelt. He offered a "New Deal." An important goal was to give people jobs. After his election, President Roosevelt and Congress created programs to make the economy stronger.

One program was the Civilian Conservation Corps (CCC). Several million people were paid to help care for the environment. The Works Progress Administration (WPA) put artists to work creating art for the public. For example, artists painted murals, or large paintings, on the walls of public buildings.

Some New Deal programs still exist today. Social Security is one of them. Social Security helps support people when they cannot work or are retired.

By the end of the 1930s, the economy was stronger. Still, the Great Depression did not end until 1942. By then, the world was at war.

4. ◎ Sequence **Underline** in the text the dates when the following events happened: the Great Depression began; Roosevelt elected president; the Great Depression ended.

One successful New Deal program was the Tennessee Valley Authority (TVA). TVA workers like these built dams and electrical power lines in southern states.

Two World Wars

In 1914, the nations of Europe went to war with each other. The conflict was called World War I. By its end, more than 37 million people were dead or wounded. Many people in the United States wanted to stay out of the war. For several years, it did. But the United States had become a world power. When American ships were sunk, the nation declared war against Germany.

Germany lost the war. Afterward, many Germans were angry. Some followed a leader named Adolf Hitler. Hitler led the Nazi Party. In the 1930s the Nazis gained control in Germany. Soon they were invading other European countries. By 1939, Europe was at war again.

At first, the United States stayed out of the new war. But on December 7, 1941, Japanese planes attacked Pearl Harbor, an American naval base in Hawaii. Japan was on Germany's side. The next day, the United States entered World War II.

"Rosie the Riveter" told women they could play an important role in the effort to win World War II. Many women had never worked in a factory before.

5. **◎ Categorize** Americans worked in different ways to win World War II. **Write** *H* on a picture of people helping at home. **Write** *M* on a picture of people in the military.

Working Together to Win World War II

African Americans served in units like the Tuskegee Airmen.

More than 400,000 women were in the military.

Children collected scrap metal that was used to build guns and bullets.

More than 16 million Americans served in the war.

World War II was fought by millions of American men and women in Europe, Africa, Asia, and the Pacific. It was a horrible conflict. More people were killed in World War II than in any other war. Many cities in Europe and Asia were bombed and destroyed.

Germany was run by a fascist government. Under **fascism** (FASH iz um), a leader like Hitler has complete power over a country. One of Hitler's most horrible acts was his attack on Jewish people. Jewish people were taken from their homes and killed. About 6 million Jewish people died in what is called the Holocaust.

The war came to an end when two powerful atomic bombs were dropped on Japan in 1945. The cities of Hiroshima (heer uh SHEE muh) and Nagasaki (nah guh SAH kee) were destroyed. The worst war in human history was finally over.

People celebrated when Germany surrendered. That day was known as Victory in Europe Day, or V-E Day.

Got it?

6. ◎ **Cause and Effect** What caused America to become more diverse in the late 1800s?

....

....

7. ❓ **Write** about an invention described in this lesson and how your family's life would have been different if it had not been invented.

 my Story Ideas

....

....

◻ **Stop!** I need help with ....

❙❙ **Wait!** I have a question about ....

▷ **Go!** Now I know ....

The United States Since World War II

Envision It!

This is an old telephone. The telephone has changed a lot since it was invented. Today, many people use cell phones.

The end of World War II was a turning point for the United States. The country was a "superpower." That meant it had a strong economy and military. It also had exploded an atomic bomb. The Soviet Union was also a superpower, however. The decades after World War II were years of tension and conflict between these two nations.

Cold War Conflicts

The rivalry between the United States and the Soviet Union was called the **Cold War.** No one wanted to risk a "hot war" that would involve atomic bombs. But people were still afraid. The Cold War lasted for more than 40 years.

The leaders of the Soviet Union believed in **communism.** In a communist country, the government controls the economic and political systems. The Soviet Union wanted to expand communism to other countries. The United States, however, did not want communism to spread. Wars were fought in two Asian countries, Korea and Vietnam, over this issue.

Then in 1962, the Soviets put missiles in Cuba. Cuba is very close to Florida. The United States demanded that the missiles be removed. This conflict was called the Cuban Missile Crisis. Because of diplomacy, it ended peacefully. Diplomacy is when nations solve their problems without going to war.

The United Nations, or UN, also helps countries avoid war. The UN is dedicated to preventing another world war. The United States helped create the United Nations.

This soldier is being awarded a medal for heroism in the Korean War. The Korean War lasted from 1950 to 1953.

1945   1950

Korean War
(1950–1953)

Write what old telephones and cell phones still have in common. Then write what is new about the cell phone.

Vocabulary

Cold War	boycott
communism	terrorist
high-tech	interdependent
civil rights	

Technology Takes Off

The Cold War was also fought over science and technology. The United States was a leader in these areas in many ways. For example, the nation produced some of the world's most **high-tech**, or advanced, computers.

Americans led the way with another high-tech invention: television. In 1950, about 4 million American families had the new machines. Just 10 years later, more than 50 million families had TVs. American technology such as computers and television was helping to change the world.

The Soviet Union was leading the way in the race into outer space, however. The Soviets put a man into space before the Americans did. The next goal was to put a man on the moon. America won that race. In 1969, two American astronauts walked on the moon.

1. **Underline** in the text two high-tech inventions that made America a leader in technology.

An American astronaut walked on the moon on July 20, 1969.

Vietnam War (1954–1975)

Cuban Missile Crisis (1962)

Moon Walk (1969)

1955   1960   1965   1970

The Civil Rights Era

Equality is an American value. The Declaration of Independence says "all men are created equal." But African Americans have not always had equal rights. For example, Jim Crow laws led to segregation in the South.

In 1954, the Supreme Court made a decision. It would lead to huge changes. The decision was called *Brown* v. *Board of Education*. The court said segregation in public schools was against the law. Soon, Americans of all races were cooperating in the civil rights movement. **Civil rights** are the rights to freedom and equality.

In Montgomery, Alabama, Rosa Parks was the cause of a protest. Parks was African American. She refused to give up her seat on a segregated city bus to a white passenger. She was arrested and sent to jail. African Americans in Montgomery called for a boycott of city buses. A **boycott** is when a group of people stops doing something in order to protest. Dr. Martin Luther King Jr. was a leader of the boycott.

Although many people worked to end segregation, others fought to keep it. The conflict was violent at times and people died defending African Americans' rights. Eventually, the government passed civil rights laws. The Civil Rights Act of 1964 did much to end segregation and guarantee equal rights. It also helped change the way people viewed people of different races.

Dr. Martin Luther King Jr. led people in nonviolent, or peaceful, protest. In this photo, Dr. King and the other people are marching for voting rights. In many places, African Americans were prevented from voting.

2. ◎ **Draw Conclusions Look** at the photo and **read** the text. Then **write** what life was like for African Americans in segregated places during the 1950s.

....

....

....

....

....

....

Greater Diversity

The 1960s were a time of great change. Like African Americans, many other groups fought for equality. For example, women struggled for equal rights. A little more than half of all Americans are women, but their opportunities often were more limited than men's. Women often earned less pay than men for the same work. The Civil Rights Act of 1964 said that it was illegal to discriminate based on a person's gender. Gender refers to whether a person is male or female.

The civil rights movement affected immigration, too. After World War I, Congress had limited immigration. Only a certain number of people were allowed to come from certain countries. This was called the quota (KWOH tuh) system. In 1965, Congress changed those laws. They got rid of quotas. That way, no country would be discriminated against.

In the mid-1960s, about 9.5 million immigrants lived in the United States. By 2009, the number was nearly 37 million. Under the new laws, many people from Asia, Africa, and Central and South America came to the United States. This new wave of immigration made the United States more diverse.

3. ⊙ **Main Idea and Details**
Conflict occurs when two groups don't agree on an issue. **Write** an example of conflict over the issue of immigration.

....

....

....

....

....

....

Working for Rights

Latino Rights
César Chávez organized a union of farmworkers. Most were Mexican American.

Native American Rights
Wilma Mankiller was the first woman to be chief of the Cherokee Nation.

Women's Rights
Betty Friedan was a writer and leader of the women's movement.

A New Era

By the end of the twentieth century, the Cold War had ended. The Soviet Union was no longer a communist country. But the United States faced a new threat. On September 11, 2001, terrorists attacked the nation. A **terrorist** is a person who uses violence for political reasons. Terrorists try to make governments do what they want by making people afraid.

On 9/11 (as the event is called), terrorists took over airplanes flying in the United States. Two crashed into and destroyed the World Trade Center towers in New York. Another hit a government building near Washington, D.C. A fourth plane crashed in Pennsylvania. Thousands of people were killed.

The terrorists were part of a violent group, al Qaeda, that threatened the United States and other nations. After 9/11, President George W. Bush led the nation into a "war on terror." Many countries cooperated in this effort. President Barack Obama continued to make decisions about the conflict.

Continuity and Change

The United States faces challenges in the twenty-first century. As a superpower, it plays a key role in world events. Transportation and communication move faster than ever. Nations are **interdependent**. This means they rely on one another for goods, services, or resources.

The world has changed, but there is also continuity in the basic values of the United States. Continuity is the way things stay the same. For example, the nation believes in the ideas of freedom, equality and improving conditions for all people.

In 2010, Haiti experienced a horrible earthquake. People from the United States and all over the world cooperated to help the Haitians recover.

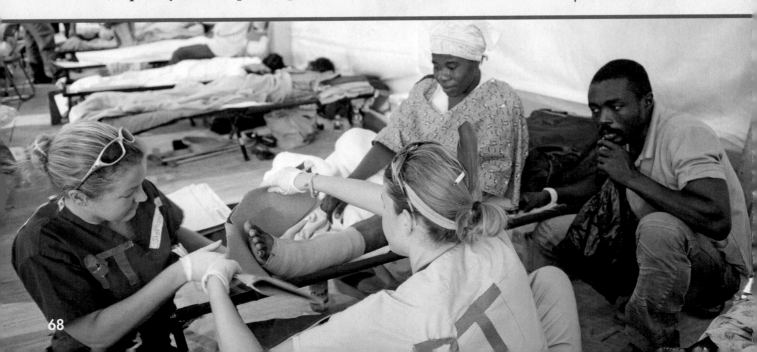

4. Write two examples of continuity and two examples of change from Lesson 5.

Continuity and Change Since World War II

Continuity	Change

Got it?

5. ◉ **Sequence** Number these events from 1 to 4 in the order in which they happened.

	U.S. astronauts walk on the moon		School segregation outlawed
	Cuban Missile Crisis		Start of the Korean War

6. ❓ **Think** of something that has stayed the same in America during your lifetime. **Explain** why you think that is a good or a bad thing.

my Story Ideas

....

....

⬜ **Stop!** I need help with ....

⏸ **Wait!** I have a question about ....

▶ **Go!** Now I know ....

Lesson 1

America and Europe

- Archeologists study artifacts to learn about ancient people.
- Native American groups developed cultures that were affected by their environment.
- Europeans explored and settled the Americas.

Lesson 2

A New Nation

- The United States began as 13 colonies that fought for and won independence from Britain.
- The new nation wrote a Constitution that still guides our nation today.
- The United States doubled in size as a result of the Louisiana Purchase.

Lesson 3

Growth and Civil War

- The nation grew as Americans moved west and as inventions led to the Industrial Revolution.
- The nation's deep divisions over slavery led to the Civil War.
- African Americans gained rights during Reconstruction.

Lesson 4

The United States Becomes a World Power

- With the help of new inventions and new immigration, the United States became a powerful industrial nation.
- The Great Depression was a deep economic slowdown in the 1930s.
- The United States fought in World War I and World War II.

Lesson 5

The United States Since World War II

- The United States opposed the Soviet Union in the Cold War.
- Americans worked to gain civil rights for African Americans and others.
- In the twenty-first century, the United States faces both change and continuity as it moves forward.

Review and Assessment

America and Europe

1. **Write** the letter of the place next to the name of the explorer who explored it.

   _____ Columbus   a. Florida

   _____ de Soto   b. St. Lawrence River

   _____ Champlain   c. Southwest

   _____ Coronado   d. Cuba and the Bahamas

2. **Write** a description of the Columbian Exchange. ....

   ....

   ....

A New Nation

3. ◉ **Sequence Write** the correct number next to these events in order they happened.

   _____ Victory at Yorktown

   _____ Fighting at Lexington and Concord

   _____ Declaration of Independence

   _____ Louisiana Purchase

   _____ Constitutional Convention

Growth and Civil War

4. What was Manifest Destiny?

   ....

   ....

   ....

5. **Write** a short description of each person.

   Abraham Lincoln ....

   ....

   Jefferson Davis ....

   ....

   Robert E. Lee ....

   ....

   Ulysses S. Grant ....

6. What was Reconstruction?

   ....

   ....

   ....

Lesson 4

The United States Becomes a World Power

7. Match the event with its cause.

_____ U.S. enters World War II

_____ America can be crossed in a week

_____ Great Depression begins

_____ America becomes more diverse

a. Millions of immigrants arrive

b. Pearl Harbor attacked

c. Banks close and businesses fail

d. Transcontinental Railroad built

Lesson 5

The United States Since World War II

8. What was the Cold War?

....

....

....

....

9. Describe one person who worked to gain civil rights.

....

....

....

10. How have we changed and how have we stayed the same during our history?

Use this photograph of the Constitution to think more about this chapter's Big Question.

a. How did the Constitution change the nation?

....

....

....

....

b. What has stayed the same?

....

....

....

....

Go online to write and illustrate your own **myStory Book** using the **myStory Ideas** from this chapter.

How have we changed and how have we stayed the same during our history?

You have learned about how the lives of Americans have changed throughout the nation's history. You have also learned about continuity, or ways in which things can stay the same.

Write about something you would like to change in the future. It could be something big that would change the whole country. Or it could be something that would change your own life in some way.

....

....

....

....

Now **draw** a picture to illustrate your writing.

While you're online, check out the **myStory Current Events** area where you can create your own book on a topic that's in the news.

Government in the United States

What is special about American government?

Governments make rules, so does your school. Who makes the rules in your school? **Write** why those rules were put into place.

....

....

....

....

....

Washington, D.C., is the capital of the United States. Shown is the Capitol, the building where Congress meets.

Thurgood Marshall
Supreme Court Justice

my Story Video

Thurgood Marshall was one of our nation's most respected Supreme Court judges. The United States Supreme Court is the nation's highest court. It's the part of our government that makes important decisions about whether laws agree with the Constitution.

Even before Thurgood Marshall joined the Supreme Court, he fought for justice and the belief that all people are equal. In his life's work, he set an example that a single American has the power to change our government.

In 1908, when Thurgood Marshall was born, the United States was different from today. Segregation was common. Segregation means keeping people apart because of their race or ethnic group. Many states had laws that kept whites and blacks apart. They couldn't live in the same neighborhoods, learn in the same schools, or eat in the same restaurants.

At the time, the Supreme Court said that segregation was legal. In an 1896 court case, the Supreme Court had decided that "separate but equal" things for blacks and whites were acceptable. Thurgood Marshall grew up in this segregated world in Baltimore, Maryland.

Marshall wanted to make sure United States laws supported freedom for all Americans.

75

Thurgood Marshall first learned about the law by watching trials with his father.

Thurgood Marshall couldn't go to his first-choice law school because the school didn't admit African Americans.

As a lawyer, Marshall won 29 of the 32 cases that he argued before the Supreme Court.

As he grew older, Marshall became interested in the law. The interest was sparked by his father. William Marshall often took his young son down to the local courthouse to watch trials. From his father, Marshall also gained the belief that all people were equal. From his mother, Norma, he learned never to accept unfair treatment from anyone, black or white.

After college, Marshall decided to become a lawyer. He wanted to go to the University of Maryland School of Law. However, the school refused to take black students. Instead, he went to Howard University Law School in Washington, D.C., and graduated at the top of his class.

One of his first big cases as a lawyer was against the University of Maryland School of Law, the school he had hoped to attend. Marshall convinced a Baltimore, Maryland, court that not accepting black students was against the law because Maryland did not have a "separate but equal" law school for African Americans. The school was ordered to admit African Americans.

In 1936, Marshall began working with the National Association for the Advancement of Colored People (NAACP). The NAACP was a group that worked to obtain fair treatment for African Americans and others. Marshall realized he could use the law to accomplish this.

After Marshall won the 1954 case *Brown* v. *Board of Education*, the Supreme Court made segregation illegal in public schools.

Thurgood Marshall served as a Supreme Court justice from 1967 to 1991. He ruled on many important cases during that time.

In case after case, Thurgood Marshall argued that discrimination was against the law. He won many rights for African Americans. Then, in 1954, he took on his most important battle. It was a Supreme Court case called *Brown* v. *the Board of Education of Topeka.*

At the time, many states had separate schools for white and black children. The schools were segregated because the law said that "separate but equal" was legal.

Marshall argued that this idea was wrong. He told the Supreme Court that separate could never be equal. Separate schools meant that white and black students weren't getting the same education. Only the same education could be equal. The Supreme Court agreed with Marshall. He won the case. School segregation was no longer legal in America.

In 1967, Thurgood Marshall became a member of the Supreme Court. He was the first African American to serve as a Supreme Court justice. During his time as a justice, the Court made many important decisions.

Thurgood Marshall believed in equality and justice. He believed in working with others to solve problems. Most importantly, he believed in the power of law to make changes to government and society. Marshall served on the Court for 24 years. He died in 1993 at the age of 84.

Think About It Based on this story, do you think that law has the power to create change in this country? As you read the chapter ahead, think about what Thurgood Marshall's story tells you about law and government in the United States.

Principles of Our Government

Envision It!

I'm a citizen of the United States and Pittsburgh, Pennsylvania.

People can live in three places at once: their nation, their state, and their community.

The United States has a special type of government. This government serves and protects the people who live here.

What Is Government?

Our government is the system that makes the rules and laws that guide our country. Government includes the people who make the laws and those who make sure the laws are obeyed. We are governed under the rule of law. This means that all people are equal under the law.

Around the world there are different types of government. In the United States we have a republic. In a **republic,** citizens have the power to elect the leaders who make the country's laws and rules. A **citizen** is an official member of a country.

Our republic is a democracy. In a **democracy,** the power of the government comes from the support of the people. Elected leaders represent the people. If people become unhappy with the government, they can choose new leaders at the next election.

On the Fourth of July, we celebrate American independence. This holiday honors the birth of our nation.

My Town/City _____

My State _____

My Country _____

Write the names of the places where you live.

UNLOCK THE BIG ?

I will know the principles upon which our government is based.

Vocabulary

republic   self-evident
citizen   unalienable
democracy   liberty
sovereignty

Part of our government's job is to make laws and rules for the common good of the people. These rules and laws create safe conditions for people to work and live. Traffic laws, for example, make our roads safe. Laws against pollution mean we can breathe cleaner air. Without these laws, individuals might feel freer to act in ways that hurt others.

The government also provides public services and goods. These services include mail delivered by a postal worker. When a park employee fixes a swing on a public playground or when your public-school teacher instructs you about history, they are providing government services, too. Government goods include highways, space ships, and planes for the military.

Families, clubs, and charities serve people in our country as well. The families in a neighborhood often help each other when one family is in need. A community group might gather signatures to get a traffic light at a busy corner. A local charity might collect money or clothes for people hurt by an earthquake or flood.

1. List three types of workers who provide a government service.

....

....

....

The military serves the nation by protecting the country from major threats.

The Declaration of Independence

Not all governments are alike. Each one has different rules. Each is based on different principles, or ideas and beliefs. Some of the principles that guide our government are set down in the Declaration of Independence.

The Declaration of Independence was written by Thomas Jefferson and other Founding Fathers. They were the men who worked to gain independence from Great Britain and form a new republic. The approval of the Declaration by the Continental Congress on July 4, 1776, marked the first moments of the United States of America. Before that, the American colonies had been ruled by the British.

The Declaration says that the American colonies no longer accepted Great Britain's **sovereignty,** or right to rule, in America. Instead, Americans would rule themselves. The Declaration explains what the Founding Fathers believed the purpose of government should be.

Thomas Jefferson wrote the Declaration of Independence. The artist painted John Adams and Benjamin Franklin reading it to show how other Founding Fathers reviewed his work.

Our Founding Principles

The Declaration of Independence says that "all men are created equal." It says that everyone is born with basic rights that require no proof, which means they are **self-evident.** Because no one, including the government, can take away these rights, they are **unalienable.** These rights include "Life, Liberty and the pursuit of Happiness." **Liberty** is the freedom to govern oneself. Protecting these rights is the very reason for government to exist. People consent, or agree, to giving the government power so it can protect these rights. The Declaration suggests that if a government fails to protect these rights, people are free to create a new government.

These ideas are important. They inspired Americans who were fighting for independence from Great Britain. Later they were also used to create a system of government for a new nation, the United States.

2. **List** two ideas that are found in the Declaration of Independence.

....

....

....

....

....

John Hancock, the president of the Continental Congress, signed the Declaration first. The delegates then signed the document based on their region. Northern state representatives signed first. Southern state representatives signed last.

The Constitution of the United States

After the American Revolution, American leaders met in 1787 to form a new government. They created the Constitution. This document was the plan and laws for a national government.

The Constitution has an introduction called the preamble. The preamble explains that the Constitution was written to help Americans establish and run their government. Its first three words are "We the People." These words state the most important idea about our government. In the United States, we govern ourselves. American citizens determine how the government is run.

The main sections of the Constitution describe how our government works. They explain how the country's leaders will be elected. They define and limit the powers of the national government. These powers include things as different as creating post offices, collecting taxes, and declaring war.

Our country was young when the Constitution was written. The Founding Fathers understood that the Constitution might need to change as the nation grew. They came up with a process by which amendments to the Constitution could be made. An amendment is an official change. Amendments must be approved by Congress and the states. Since the Constitution was first written, there have been 27 amendments to the Constitution.

To become the law of the land, the Constitution needed the approval of 9 of the 13 original states. There were many debates. By 1790, all 13 states had approved it.

The Bill of Rights

The first ten amendments to the Constitution are called the Bill of Rights. These amendments list the basic rights of every person in the United States. These rights include freedom of speech, freedom of religion, and the right of the press to publish freely. The amendments also set limits on the power of government.

This plan for government has proven to be both strong and flexible. Our Constitution has kept our republic healthy for more than 200 years.

3. ◉ **Summarize** What is the purpose of the first ten amendments to the Constitution?

....

....

....

The First Amendment guarantees that people can assemble, or gather together, peacefully to protest.

Got it?

4. ◉ **Sequence** Which document was written first, the Declaration of Independence or the Constitution?

....

....

5. ⦿ **Describe** how the principles in the Constitution affect you today.

....

....

....

▢ **Stop!** I need help with ....

▯ **Wait!** I have a question about ....

▶ **Go!** Now I know ....

Identify Primary and Secondary Sources

A **primary source** is an eyewitness account, an observation of an event, or a document from a particular time in history. Primary sources can be letters, speeches, documents, diaries, or interviews. They can be photographs or drawings made during an event. The Declaration of Independence is a primary source. It's an actual document from a time and place in history.

"*We hold these truths to be self-evident, that all men are created equal, that they are endowed by their Creator with certain unalienable Rights, that among these are Life, Liberty and the pursuit of Happiness.*"

A **secondary source** is a secondhand account of history. The words were not from the time that an event took place. A history textbook or a biography is a secondary source. The writer collects information about an event or a person and describes it in his or her own words. Here is an example:

> Writing the Declaration of Independence was one of Thomas Jefferson's greatest accomplishments. He was one of a group of men who were given the task of writing it in 1776. Later, Jefferson became our nation's third president.

Primary and secondary sources both teach you about history. A primary source can bring you closer to an event. A secondary source can make events easier to understand.

Learning Objective

I will know how to identify primary and secondary sources.

To identify whether a text is a primary or secondary source, ask yourself questions such as the following:

- Is this a document, photo, or other item from the event itself? Was the writer or photographer at the event? Does the writer use words such as *we* or *I*? If you answered yes to these questions, then the material is probably a primary source.

- Does the writer use words such as *he* or *she* to talk about events? Does the writer draw conclusions about an event from the past? If you answered yes to these questions, then the material is probably a secondary source.

1. How is the second document on the facing page different from the first?

....

....

2. What word or words in the first document hint that it is a primary source?

....

3. Can you find the words *he* or *she* in either of the two documents? What does that tell you? What other clue words can you find?

....

....

....

....

4. Apply Look back at Lesson 1. **Find** an example of words from a primary source document other than the Declaration of Independence.

....

How Our Government Works

Envision It!

Most games have rules that give the players a fair and equal way to play the game.

Kelly Ayotte is a Republican senator from New Hampshire. There are two major political parties in the United States: Republicans and Democrats.

The Constitution describes how the federal, or national, government of the United States is set up. The government has three different branches, or parts. They are the legislative branch, the executive branch, and the judicial branch.

The Three Branches and Their Responsibilities

The **legislative branch** of the federal government makes laws, or rules that Americans must obey. This branch, called Congress, has two parts. One is the House of Representatives, known as the House. The other is the Senate. The House and the Senate work together to create and pass laws.

The nation's citizens elect all members of Congress. Elections are held in each state. All states elect two representatives, called senators, to the Senate. Each state also elects representatives to the House. The number of House representatives that each state elects depends on the state's population. So California, which has a large population, elects more than 50 representatives to the House. States with a smaller population elect fewer representatives. Alaska, for example, elects 1.

The president is the head of the **executive branch.** This branch is in charge of carrying out the laws that are written by Congress. The president is also the head of our country's armed forces. Citizens vote for the president in a national election.

The executive branch includes the vice president and a group of officials called the Cabinet. The Cabinet advises the president on education, health, and the economy. It also gives advice on international issues, such as foreign trade and wars.

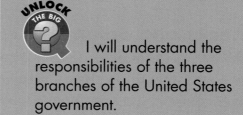

I will understand the responsibilities of the three branches of the United States government.

Vocabulary

legislative branch

executive branch

judicial branch

checks and balances

Write what would happen if games had no rules to limit the players.

The **judicial branch** makes sure that our nation's laws agree with the Constitution. The highest level of the judicial branch is the Supreme Court. Nine judges make up the Supreme Court. Supreme Court justices are not elected. They are selected by the president and then approved by the Senate. Once they are approved, Supreme Court judges can serve for their entire life.

1. **Underline** in the text on the opposite page the number of senators in each state and the group that advises the president.

The Three Branches of Government

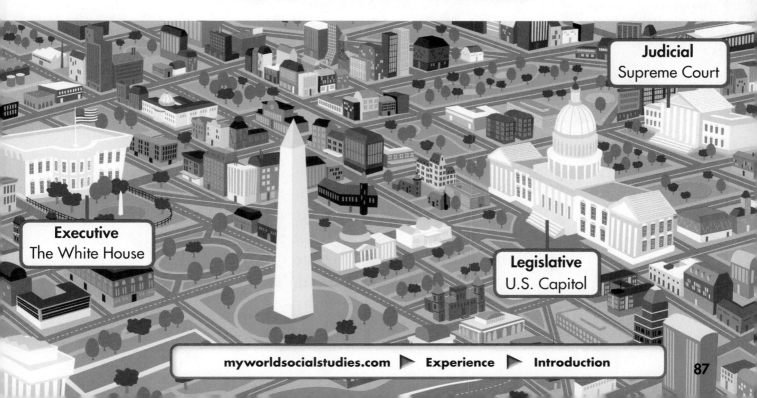

Judicial
Supreme Court

Executive
The White House

Legislative
U.S. Capitol

Checks and Balances

Why did the writers of the Constitution decide to separate the government into three branches? They thought that the government could become too strong and threaten people's rights, especially if one part of the government grew much stronger than other parts. To prevent this from happening, they came up with a system of **checks and balances.**

By dividing the government into three branches, the power was balanced. In addition, each part could check, or limit, the actions of the other two parts. These checks would keep any one branch of government from gaining too much control.

The checks and balances work for each branch of government. Congress, the legislative branch, has to pass all laws. Without the power to make laws, the president cannot act like a king. However, laws that are passed by Congress cannot go against the Constitution. If they do, the judicial branch can declare the laws unconstitutional. The judicial branch can also declare a president's orders unconstitutional.

The system of checks and balances prevents any one branch from gaining too much power.

Checks and Balances

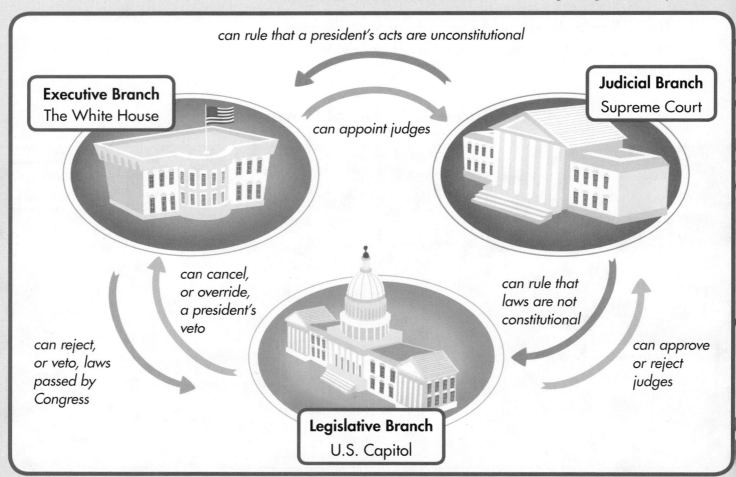

can rule that a president's acts are unconstitutional

Executive Branch
The White House

can appoint judges

Judicial Branch
Supreme Court

can cancel, or override, a president's veto

can reject, or veto, laws passed by Congress

can rule that laws are not constitutional

can approve or reject judges

Legislative Branch
U.S. Capitol

The president has the right to veto, or reject, laws that Congress passes. In turn, Congress can override, or cancel out, the veto if two thirds of its members vote for the law. Although the president can pick Cabinet members and federal judges, which include judges for the Supreme Court, the Senate must approve the president's selection. This provides a check against the president's power.

There are even checks and balances inside a single branch of government. You can see them in the way a law is approved. Before Congress sends a law to be signed by the president, both the House and the Senate must vote to approve the law.

All these checks and balances are known as the separation of powers. For more than 200 years, the system has served us well.

The Constitution says the president must report to Congress on the nation's condition. Presidents, such as Barack Obama, use the State of the Union speech to persuade Congress and the public about issues he or she supports.

2. **Write** how Congress can check, or limit, the power of the president.

....

....

....

State and Local Government

The federal government is just one of three levels of government in the United States. The other two are state government and local government.

Each state has a state government. State governments follow their own state constitutions as well as the Constitution of the United States. Like the federal government, a state government has three branches. States also have a capital where the state government is located. The governor is head of the executive branch. For most states, the legislative branch includes a state senate and a state house of representatives. State courts and judges make up the judicial branch.

Local government includes the government of villages, towns, cities, and counties. Often, a mayor or a group of elected officials runs the government and makes local laws. A local government might also have its own courts.

State and local governments create many of the laws we follow every day. The state government gives local governments the power to make and enforce laws. These include laws about speed limits, littering, and how your school is run. State and local governments collect taxes, just as the federal government does. These taxes are used to pay for services such as police, fire department, schools, and libraries.

3. **Look** at the chart below. **Circle** the head of the state executive branch. **Underline** the national legislative branch. **Add a star** next to the judicial branch of local government.

It is required that the United States flag be flown higher than any other flag, such as the Illinois and Chicago flags shown here.

Levels of Government

Branches of Government	National	State	Local
Executive	President	Governor	Mayor
Legislative	Congress	State Legislature	City or Town Council
Judicial	Supreme Court	State Courts	Local Courts

Some of the Founding Fathers didn't want all the government's power to be at the federal level. They wanted to ensure that the states would have a say in the government as well. Therefore, the tenth amendment to the Constitution says that all the powers that are not given to the federal government in the Constitution are reserved for the states and the people. This sharing and division of power is known as federalism.

4. (●) **Summarize Write** how the Constitution shares power between the federal government and the states.

....

....

....

....

The Kansas State Capitol is in Topeka. This is where the state legislature meets.

Got it?

5. (●) **Sequence Write** what happens after two thirds of Congress votes to approve a bill that the president has vetoed.

....

6. (?) Your family is opening a new restaurant in your town. They have questions about garbage collection. What level of government could provide your family with answers? Why?

my Story Ideas

....

....

....

(■) **Stop!** I need help with ....

(❚❚) **Wait!** I have a question about ....

(▶) **Go!** Now I know ....

Our Rights and Responsibilities

This is the symbol for Wisconsin. The symbol includes the state motto, or saying, and a badger, the state animal.

Thomas Paine was a writer who supported American independence. Later, in 1794, he wrote,

"I have always . . . supported the right of every man to his own opinion, however different that opinion might be to mine."

The federal government protects the rights and freedoms of United States citizens. A person born in the United States is a United States citizen. Many people who move to this country can become citizens. They must follow a process and pass a test. The Constitution makes sure that citizens are treated fairly and that their rights are protected.

Citizens and Their Rights

The Constitution says that the United States government cannot pass any laws that would prevent Americans from expressing their opinions and ideas. Americans also have the right to their own religious beliefs. They have the right to travel freely. People who are accused of a crime have the right to a lawyer and a fair trial by a jury.

A **jury** is a group of citizens who are called on to make a decision in a court of law. A jury listens to facts that are presented by lawyers. A jury's decision is based on these facts and the law.

Some rights, such as freedom of speech, freedom of the press, and freedom of religion, were guaranteed by the Bill of Rights. Other rights have become law over time because of Constitutional amendments.

Vocabulary

jury   petition
candidate
patriotism
symbol

Think about what is important to your community. Then draw a new symbol for your city or town.

Amendments Expand Citizens' Rights

When the Constitution was written, slavery was legal in the United States. On December 6, 1865, the Thirteenth Amendment ended this practice. This amendment said that no American could be enslaved. The Fourteenth Amendment gave all citizens equal protection under the law. The Fifteenth Amendment gave African American men the right to vote.

Women didn't have the right to vote when the Constitution was written. In 1920, women gained that right with the Nineteenth Amendment. Young people have gained rights, too. In 1971, the Twenty-sixth Amendment gave all citizens eighteen years and older the right to vote. Before this, the voting age was twenty-one in most states.

1. **Circle** each example of a person exercising a right in the picture.

Our Responsibilities

In a democracy such as the United States, people have responsibilities as well as rights. To operate effectively, schools, communities, and government need everyone's participation.

Voting is both a right and a responsibility. People cannot choose representatives unless they take the time to vote. Voters should learn about the candidates. **Candidates** are the people who run for a position in government. By reading newspapers, searching the Internet, or watching television, citizens can learn about the issues and how the presidential candidates, for example, view them. Voters can then elect a candidate they agree with on those issues.

Getting elected to public office is just one way to take part in government. A person can serve in government by being appointed, or selected, for a specific job, such as an employee of a government agency.

Americans also have a responsibility to obey laws. When people do not obey the law, our communities become more dangerous and disorderly. Adult citizens meet another responsibility when they serve on a jury. The right to a jury trial in America means that most adults must serve on juries.

Paying taxes is another responsibility. A tax is money that the government collects to pay for services such as roads, parks, schools, police, and the courts. Federal law requires us to pay income tax on the money we earn. Some state and local government laws add a sales tax on things we buy, such as clothes, and a property tax on our homes and land.

2. **Fill in** the citizenship to-do list with ways you can improve your community and your school.

My Citizenship To-Do List

When I'm 18, my responsibilities include	When I'm older, I can keep my community strong by	I can help others in my community by

People also have a civic responsibility to take part in their community by solving problems and making decisions. Civics is the study of the rights and responsibilities of citizens. By being active in their community, people make sure their homes, towns, and cities are good places to live. For example, when it snows, people should shovel the sidewalk in front of their homes. They can also volunteer at a church or raise money for the school library.

Like adults, young people have responsibilities, too. They are required to obey the law. Some laws are aimed especially at children. For example, the law requires children to go to school or be educated at home. Children also have a responsibility to learn about United States history and government. That way, when they grow up, they will be active, informed citizens.

At school, students can take part in making the rules for their school. For example, groups of students have helped start recycling programs. To keep your school a safe and pleasant place to learn, you can help students who are being bullied, or pushed around. If you feel safe, you might ask the bully to stop. You could ask the student who is being bullied to join your table in the lunchroom. Or you might report the bullying to your teacher.

All people, whatever their age, have a responsibility to treat others with respect. This includes people who are different from you. In a strong, healthy democracy, all people benefit from a society that they themselves work to create and improve.

3. Underline a law that applies to young people.

Volunteering at an animal shelter is one way that people can help their community.

Schools work best when people feel like they are part of a team. You can do your part by learning to identify bullying and help prevent this behavior.

National Pride

Americans are proud of their nation, their people, and their government. This pride and support is called **patriotism.** We celebrate this pride each Independence Day. On Veterans Day and Memorial Day, we honor those soldiers who have served our country in war. On Martin Luther King Day and Presidents' Day, we honor important people in our nation's history.

Americans have symbols to display their pride. **Symbols** are images, designs, or things that stand for ideas. For example, the American flag, a symbol of our nation, has 50 stars and 13 stripes. The stars stand for today's 50 states. The stripes stand for the country's original 13 states.

The Great Seal of the United States, shown below, appears on the one-dollar bill. The motto, or saying, on this symbol is *E Pluribus Unum,* which is Latin for "Out of Many, One." This means that many states joined together with the federal government to form one union. Americans also honor their country when they recite the Pledge of Allegiance. In the Pledge, people state their loyalty to the nation and its symbol, the flag.

4. **Look** at the Great Seal. **Write** how this symbol is similar to the American flag.

   ....
   ....
   ....
   ....
   ....

The number 13, which stands for the original 13 states, is shown in the 13 stars, stripes, arrows, and leaves on the olive branch of the Great Seal.

States have symbols, too. There are state flags and seals, which are official symbols. Many states have state animals. The ladybug is New York's insect. Pennsylvania has its own state toy, the Slinky, which was invented in Pennsylvania.

State symbols may show up on official state papers, Web sites, and license plates. License plates often display a state's motto, or saying, as well. Illinois plates say "Land of Lincoln." They point out the state's pride in the famous president from Illinois.

Citizens often take part in choosing state symbols. In 2005, for example, the orca became Washington State's official marine mammal because of students at Crescent Harbor Elementary School. The students created a petition to convince state officals. A **petition** is a formal request. Eventually, the Washington State legislators agreed with their choice and made the orca an official symbol of the state.

The New Mexico license plate is decorated with a Zia Sun, a Native American symbol for the sun.

Got it?

5. ◉ **Summarize Write** how constitutional amendments have changed our nation.

....

....

....

....

6. ❓ You are designing a United States postage stamp to show what is special about this country. What symbol would you put on the stamp? Why?

my Story Ideas

....

....

⬛ **Stop!** I need help with ....

⏸ **Wait!** I have a question about ....

▶ **Go!** Now I know ....

Lesson 1

Principles of Our Government

- Government is made up of the laws, people, and organizations that run a country. The government protects and serves all Americans.
- The founding principles of the United States government can be found in the Declaration of Independence and the Constitution.

Lesson 2

How Our Government Works

- Our government has three branches: legislative, executive, and judicial.
- Each branch works with the other branches and also limits the power of the other branches through a system of checks and balances.
- Government has three levels: federal, state, and local.

Lesson 3

Our Rights and Responsibilities

- All Americans have rights, such as freedom of speech and religion.
- Citizens have responsibilities, which include obeying the law.
- Americans are proud of their country and honor its people, history, and ideas with symbols and holidays.

Review and Assessment

Lesson 1

Principles of Our Government

1. **Circle** which person works at the national level of government?

    A. fire-fighter

    B. governor

    C. mayor

    D. senator

2. **Fill in** the blanks. The principles that shaped the U.S. government can be found in documents such as the .... and the ....

3. **Write** one principle about our government that comes from the Declaration of Independence.

    ....
    ....
    ....
    ....
    ....
    ....
    ....
    ....
    ....

Lesson 2

How Our Government Works

4. **Match** each branch to the right group or place.

    _____ White House   A. legislative branch

    _____ Congress   B. executive branch

    _____ Supreme   C. judicial branch
          Court

5. **Write** why states elect different numbers of representatives to the House of Representatives.

    ....
    ....
    ....
    ....
    ....

6. ◉ **Sequence Write** what happens after the president picks a judge for the Supreme Court.

    ....
    ....
    ....
    ....

Lesson 3

Our Rights and Responsibilities

7. ◉ **Summarize** How did the Nineteenth and Twenty-sixth Amendments affect the rights of Americans?

....

....

....

....

....

....

8. Which of the following are citizens required to do by law? **Circle** the answer.

   A. volunteer at a hospital

   B. volunteer at a school

   C. run for office

   D. pay taxes

9. How many leaves, arrows, stars, and stripes are on the Great Seal? What does this number represent?

....

....

....

....

10. ❓ **What is special about American government?**

Use the document and question to think about this chapter's Big Question.

How do documents that are more than 200 years old affect American government today?

....

....

....

....

....

....

....

....

Go online to write and illustrate your own **myStory Book** using the **myStory Ideas** from this chapter.

What is special about American government?

The government of the United States is based on a set of principles, or basic ideas, from our Founding Fathers. They believed that government existed to serve the people and to protect their rights. These rights include "Life, Liberty and the pursuit of Happiness."

Think about these ideas and how they are reflected in our government.
Write how these ideas affect your life today.

....

....

....

....

Draw a new symbol to represent one of the ideas our Founding Fathers had about how government should work.

While you're online, check out the **myStory Current Events** area where you can create your own book on a topic that's in the news.

The Nation's Economy

How does the economy meet our needs and wants?

Think about the things you and your family have in your home. Which do you need? Which could you do without? **List** three things for each category.

....

....

....

....

Dog walking is one way for kids to earn money.

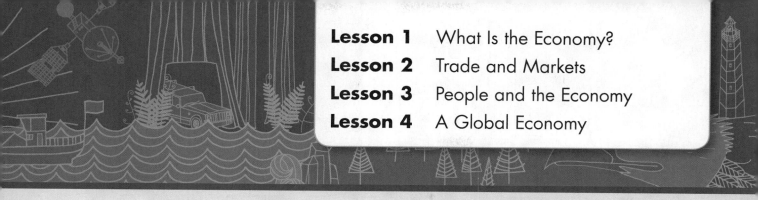

Bill Gates
Filling a Need

my Story Video

Is there a computer in your home? If there is, it probably runs a program created by the Microsoft Corporation. Microsoft is the company started by Bill Gates, an American businessman. Gates is a computer programmer, or someone who designs and writes instructions for computers. Over the last 30 years, Gates's company has become the largest personal computer software company in the world.

William Henry "Bill" Gates was born in Seattle, Washington, in 1955. When he was growing up, computers were rare and not many people used them. Computers were huge, expensive machines that could take up an entire room. They were used mainly by large companies, the government, and universities.

From the age of 13 on, Bill Gates went to a school that had a computer. Gates and a few friends spent every available hour on the computer. He read as much as he could about computers and then wrote his first computer program. The program was a computerized version of the game tic-tac-toe.

When Bill Gates was 13, he and his friends spent many hours in the school computer lab.

103

Gates began creating and selling computer software while he was still in high school.

While attending Harvard University, Gates continued to focus on programming computers.

Gates got better and better at computer programming. While still in high school, he and two friends created a company. They sold computer software to businesses. Software is a set of programs that a computer uses to complete certain tasks.

After graduating from high school, Gates went to college at Harvard University in Massachusetts. However, he sometimes had a hard time thinking about his schoolwork. All he thought about was computer programming. So, Gates and his friend Paul Allen formed a company called Microsoft. The two men began creating software for a new type of computer. This new, smaller computer was made to be used in homes and offices. It was called the personal computer, or PC.

At the time, PC makers needed a type of software called an operating system. This is the basic program a computer needs to run. Without an operating system, a computer is not that useful. With an operating system, however, a computer can do all kind of amazing things.

Small personal computers were developed in the mid-1970s. Bill and his friend Paul Allen decided to create software for them.

Gates's company, Microsoft, grew quickly, and hired many employees.

Microsoft became the biggest supplier of software for personal computers.

Operating systems were the first need that Microsoft sought to fill. In 1981, the company made an operating system for IBM, one of the world's biggest computer makers. Other companies began using Microsoft's operating system as well.

By the 1990s, Microsoft had become an enormously successful company. Microsoft software was on millions of computers all over the world. The company provided jobs for thousands of people, including computer programmers, designers, and accountants. The company also began to make different kinds of software, creating new programs. Microsoft Word helped people to write text on the computer. Internet Explorer allowed users to search for information on the Internet. Of course, the company also kept creating and improving operating systems.

Today, Microsoft's products are used on every continent. They fill the needs of people and businesses everywhere. The company's success has made Bill Gates one of the world's wealthiest men. He uses this wealth to try and fill some basic needs for people. Bill Gates and his wife, Melinda, started an organization whose goal is to help others. The organization is called the Bill and Melinda Gates Foundation. Their foundation looks for ways to provide food, clothing, shelter, and healthcare to poor people all over the world.

Think About It Based on this story, do you think that Bill Gates filled a need? As you read the chapter ahead, think about how Gates's story relates to what you learn about the economy.

What Is the Economy?

Envision It!

In an economy, resources such as these are used to make goods.

Needs
• drinking water
•
•
•

Wants
• lemonade
•
•
•

1. Classify the following items as either needs or wants by adding them to the correct place on the chart: a backpack, a home, shoes, a vacation, food, dance class.

When you buy something or use it after you bought it, you are taking part in our economy. The economy is how the resources of an area or country are produced, delivered, and used. Every town, region, and state has an economy. Economies around the world may vary, but they all have things in common.

Needs and Wants

Economies are set up to satisfy both needs and wants. Needs are the things you must have to survive, such as food, clothing, and shelter. Wants are things you would like to have but can do without, such as a skateboard or a ticket to a movie.

There are two types of needs and wants that are called goods and services. Goods are actual products that you can buy, such as a car, apples, or shoes. Services are things that other people do for you, such as cutting your hair or giving you music lessons.

Making Choices

All economies produce, or make, goods and services for people to buy and use. A person or a company who makes a good or service to sell to others is known as a **producer**. A person or a company who buys a good or service is known as a **consumer**.

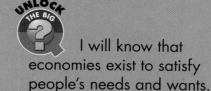
UNLOCK THE BIG ?

I will know that economies exist to satisfy people's needs and wants.

Vocabulary

producer

consumer

free enterprise system

market economy

command economy

private property

Write some things that you could make with a hammer, wood, and nails.

In this country there are many different producers. That means that consumers have many choices of products and places to shop. If you decide to buy something for yourself, you could look in a store or you could shop online. Because you have choices, you might spend time deciding what to buy. Maybe you would end up buying a video game instead of a soccer ball.

Being part of an economy involves choices. By buying the video game, you fulfilled one of your wants. But now you have no money left to purchase a soccer ball. Buying the video game may mean that you have lost the chance to play soccer. Consumers must weigh their needs and wants before spending their money.

2. **Identify** the producer, products, and consumer in the photos.

....

....

....

....

....

In a market economy, businesses decide what to manufacture, or produce. These factory workers are removing tennis balls from a machine.

Types of Economies

All types of economies answer three basic questions: What goods and services should be produced? How should they be produced? For whom should they be produced?

Around the world you will find different answers to these questions. In the United States, the economy is based on the free enterprise system. A **free enterprise system** is one in which producers have the right to create any goods or services they want. The government does not tell producers what they can create or sell. Producers also set the prices and quantities for their goods and services.

Another name for a free enterprise system is a **market economy.** A market in this sense is not like a store. Instead, it refers to an entire area or country in which things are bought and sold freely.

Not every country has a market economy. Some have a command economy. In a **command economy**, the government decides what goods and services can be made and sold. The government tells people and businesses how much of something to produce. Often it is the government, not the producers, that sets prices.

3. Fill in the blanks below to complete the details about each type of economy.

Types of Economies

Market Economy

- .... decide what to produce.
- The government does not decide how much of a product should be made.

Command Economy

- The government tells producers what to produce.
- .... decides how much of a product should be made.

Parts of the Economy

In every economy producers use resources to create goods and services. These may be natural resources, such as trees, or human resources, such as truck drivers. They may even be capital resources, which are human-made products used to make goods and services. For example, the oven in a bakery is a capital resource.

Different parts of the United States economy use these resources to produce a variety of goods and services. Our giant economy is divided into important parts, or sectors.

The agricultural part, or sector, grows much of the food you eat, while the mining part provides materials such as coal for electricity. The manufacturing sector makes many of the goods your family buys. The transportation portion gets people and goods from place to place in cars, trains, and planes. The services sector includes all the people who provide services for others, such as teachers, doctors, and the person who sells you a movie ticket. The entertainment sector includes the companies and people who make the songs and films you enjoy.

Certain parts of the economy are more important in different regions. In the West, entertainment is important to California's economy. In the Southwest, ranching, or raising livestock, plays a large role in the Texas economy.

In the Midwest, manufacturing and transportation contribute to Michigan's economy. In the Southeast, mining provides many jobs in West Virginia.

Tourism, which is part of the service sector, is important in Florida. In the Northeast, services are important in places like New York. The chart shows full-time employment in some parts of the economy.

4. **Look** at the chart. **Write** which part of the economy provides the most jobs.

....

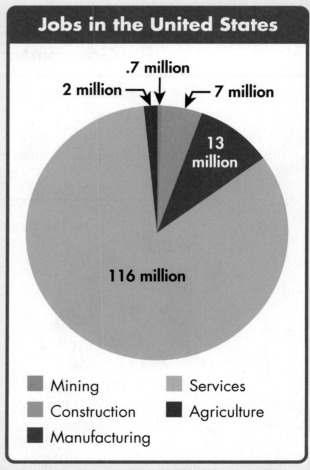

Jobs in the United States

.7 million

2 million → 7 million

13 million

116 million

- Mining
- Services
- Construction
- Agriculture
- Manufacturing

*Fulltime Employment Only, Source: U.S. Bureau of Labor Statistics

Government and the Economy

Even though the United States government does not run the economy, it still has important economic responsibilities. A market economy needs certain rules. The government provides these rules. For example, people want the things they own to be protected, or secure. So the government makes stealing against the law. This is one of the ways in which the government protects **private property,** or the land, homes, stores, and goods that people or companies own. This is important in a free enterprise system, since the system is based on the buying and selling of private property.

The government also takes part in our economy as a producer and consumer. Most goods and services a government produces are public. This means everyone can use them, including those who cannot pay. Public goods include things like roads or schools. Public services include education and mail delivery. Citizens pay for public goods and services with taxes.

5. **Write** what the government's activities are as a producer. Put your answers in the boxes below.

The Government's Role in Our Economy

The Government Makes Laws	The Government as Consumer
The government makes rules and protects private property.	The government buys goods, such as computers and paper.

The Government as Producer

....

....

....

The government is also a consumer. As a consumer, the government buys goods and services from companies and individuals. For example, the government may buy planes for the navy or police cars from a private company. Or the government may buy the services of a teacher to teach at a public school.

In the United States, both the people and the government take part in the economy. Both are producers and consumers. Both provide goods and services that we need in our daily lives.

6. **Underline** a good and a service that the government buys.

The government agrees to pay private companies to make planes for the military.

Got it?

7. ◎ **Main Idea and Details** What is the main purpose of an economy?

....

....

....

8. ❓ You want to start your own business. **Write** what product or service you would provide. Would it fill a need or a want for your customers?

my Story Ideas

....

....

....

⬜ **Stop!** I need help with ....

⏸ **Wait!** I have a question about ....

▶ **Go!** Now I know ....

Graph Skills

Compare Line and Bar Graphs

Information about the economy usually involves lots of data, or numbers and information. Two ways to present data clearly are line graphs and bar graphs.

A **line graph** represents data in a way that shows change over time. The horizontal axis on the line graph to the right shows decades, or periods of ten years. The vertical axis shows the number of people working in construction. The line in the middle of the graph connects the data points on the graph. This line shows how the number of people working in construction changed over 30 years, or three decades. The line graph presents data about the period from 1970 until the year 2000.

Like a line graph, a **bar graph** is a way of showing data. But bar graphs are better at comparing and contrasting information than at showing change over time.

A bar graph uses bars to compare different information. In the bar graph to the right, you can compare the number of Americans who worked in construction, manufacturing, and mining and logging in 2009. The graph compares groups of people working in certain jobs.

Number of People Who Work in Construction

Source: U.S. Bureau of Labor Statistics

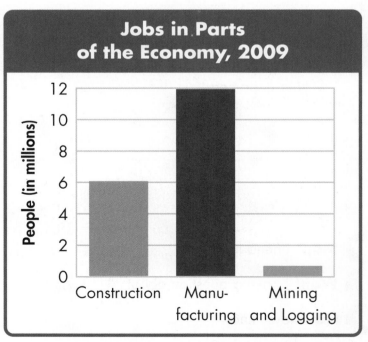

Jobs in Parts of the Economy, 2009

Source: U.S. Bureau of Labor Statistics

To gather information from a line graph, first read the title. It tells you what type of data the graph displays. Next, read the labels for each axis. Then, look at the line that connects the data points on the graph. Does it go up or down? To gather information from a bar graph, you should first read the graph title. Next, read the label for the vertical axis. Then, look at the labels for each bar on the graph. Compare the information by comparing the heights of the bars.

1. **Look** at the line graph on the opposite page. About how many people worked in construction in 1970 and 2000?

   ....

2. Did the number of people who worked in construction go up or down during that time?

   ....

3. **Look** at the bar graph. About how many people worked in construction and manufacturing in 2009?

   ....

   ....

4. Which of the jobs on the bar graph was a larger part of the economy in 2009? Why?

   ....

   ....

5. **Apply** **Compare** the data in the two graphs. Both show data about jobs in construction. Did the number of jobs in construction grow or decrease between 2000 and 2009?

   ....

   ....

Trade and Markets

Money and credit cards are used to purchase goods and services.

Long ago, items such as seashells and pieces of metal served as money. Today, paper bills and metal coins are the most common forms of currency. **Currency** is the type of money used in a particular place. In the United States, our currency is the United States dollar.

Trade and Money

People have been exchanging things to get the goods and services they need and want since ancient times. Before the development of money, people would barter. To **barter** means to trade one type of good or service for another type. Animal furs, for example, might be traded for food.

Today, bartering is still used. A music teacher might trade guitar lessons to a baker. In return, the baker might give the teacher fresh bread. Both get what they need.

Bartering, however, has problems. What if the person who has what you need isn't interested in what you have to trade? That would make it impossible for you to get what you need. For this reason, modern economies use money to trade. Money can be traded for anything. Money is also easy to carry, can be divided into smaller quantities, and it is uniform, which means each piece of money is like another.

The pictures to the right show how the price of a video game changed during the year.

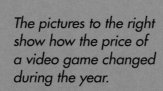

Price of Video Game Before Inflation: January

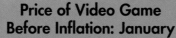

UNLOCK THE BIG ?

I will understand that businesses supply goods and services to match demand.

Vocabulary

currency	income
barter	supply
inflation	demand
profit	

List at least three ways that people can pay for the things they buy.

Prices and Inflation

The buying power of our currency can change as the prices of things change. Sometimes, prices go down—an MP3 player that cost $50 last year might cost $40 this year. Sometimes, prices go up. Next year, the MP3 player might cost $60. A rise in the usual price of many goods and services is called **inflation.**

Inflation means you can buy fewer things for the same amount of money. MP3 players are a want, not a need, so the rising price of one wouldn't threaten people's lives. However, inflation can cause serious problems when it causes the price of needs to rise. When the cost of food, shelter, or basic clothing rises, it can be hard for families to buy the things they need. This is especially true if the money a family earns decreases or stays the same.

1. **Write** how much you think the video game will cost in August if inflation continues at the same rate.

$

Price of Video Game After Inflation: June

Businesses and Markets

When you buy something, your goal is to satisfy a want or a need. The goal of the business you buy from is to make a profit. **Profit** is the money a business has left over after it pays all its costs.

It might cost a bakery about $370, for example, to make bread each day. This cost includes expenses, such as the price of flour, rent on the building, and the money paid to employees. Employees are the workers who bake and sell the bread. If the bakery makes $470 a day in sales, then the difference, or profit, is $100. The profit that a business earns over a period of time, such as a year, is called **income.**

Businesses want to make a profit. They try to keep costs down, since they can't always raise prices. Competition is the reason. If a business sells a product at a high price, another business may open and sell the same product at a lower price. If the first business does not lower its prices or make its product better, it may lose customers. Businesses that can't match the prices or quality of their competitors often close down.

2. This chart shows the monthly income and costs of a bakery. **Calculate** the monthly profit and add it to the chart.

Nelson's Bakery

Monthly Costs	
Rent	$3,500
Worker (Employee) Pay	$4,200
Ingredients and Packaging	$2,100
Equipment Rental	$800
Electricity and Gas	$425
Total Costs (Expenses)	$11,025
Total Sales	$14,100
Profit (Sales − Costs)	$ ....

Entrepreneurs

There are many reasons businesses fail. Competition is just one of them. Opening a new business means taking a risk. You have to spend money to rent a workspace, pay for materials, and hire employees. If the business fails, all this money will be lost.

A person who takes a risk and opens a business is called an entrepreneur. An entrepreneur believes that his or her ideas for a business can make money and are worth that risk. Many of our country's most important companies have been started by entrepreneurs. Some entrepreneurs borrow money from a bank or from investors to start their business. An investor is someone who loans money in the hopes of making a profit when the new business has grown.

Kids can be entrepreneurs, too. Suppose you decided to create a comic book business. You might spend money on paper, art supplies, and printer ink. If you didn't sell many comic books, you wouldn't make this money back. However, if your comic books sold well, you would make this money back plus a profit. Entrepreneurs have good ideas. They are willing to take risks for the chance to see their business succeed.

3. Underline some costs of opening a new business.

Cecilia Cassini is a fashion entrepreneur. When she was six, Cecilia asked her mother for a sewing machine. Today, at age 11, her clothes are sold in several stores.

Supply and Demand

A free enterprise system like the one in the United States is based on supply and demand. **Supply** is the amount of a product that businesses have available to sell. **Demand** is the amount of a product that consumers are willing to buy. Entrepreneurs have to be good judges of both to succeed.

The most successful businesses create products or services that have high demand. For example, if there is a product in great demand in your community, people are more likely to pay a high price for it. A business can charge a price well above what it costs to produce the item. This will result in larger profits.

If there is low demand for a product or service, the situation is reversed. People will not be willing to pay a high price for the item. A business will be forced to lower prices to attract customers. The business's profits may be small.

Supply will usually respond to demand in a pattern.

4. **Write** why the store on the left is having a sale.

....

....

....

Demand: Low

This store is having a sale on clothing.

Demand: High

Customers came to this store to buy supplies before a big storm.

If the amount supplied is low and the amount demanded is high, the price of an item will rise. Since large profits can be made by selling the item, businesses will increase the amount that is supplied. An entrepreneur, for example, may expand his or her business to make more of a product. Then the amount supplied may increase too much, and prices will likely fall.

These people are lining up for a sale. A sale can increase the demand for goods.

5. **Underline** the sentence that tells what happens if the amount supplied is low and the amount demanded is high.

Got it?

6. ⊙ **Main Idea and Details** **Write** why entrepreneurs are willing to take the risk of putting their money into a new business.

....

....

....

....

7. ❓ **Think** about the product for the business you would like to start. **Explain** why there would be a demand for your product. **Describe** the kind of customers who might buy it.

my Story Ideas

....

....

....

⬛ **Stop!** I need help with ....

⏸ **Wait!** I have a question about ....

▶ **Go!** Now I know ....

People and the Economy

Envision It!

You promised your friend you would go to the movies, but your soccer team has a game at the same time.

Our economy offers us many choices. Which sunglasses will these girls choose to buy?

The economy provides you with needed goods, such as food and clothing, and also extras like movies and recorded music. Every day, you and your family take part in the economy by consuming or producing.

The Economy and You

When you get dressed in the morning, the clothes you wear are the result of economic activity. The clothes are produced by a business. You or someone you know made the choice to buy them. When you sit down at the kitchen table, your breakfast is also the result of economic activity and choice. Someone worked to get money to pay for the food. Someone also chose one food, such as a favorite cereal, over another food.

Economic choices are personal. You make choices all the time about your food or clothing. Should you buy the expensive pair of shoes? Maybe you should buy the cheaper pair? After all, you might outgrow them in a few months, and it would be good to save the money.

As you grow older, you will be making choices about more important economic questions. How will you pay for your basic needs? What kind of job will you have to earn money? What kind of home will you live in?

1. List an item your family buys that you help choose.

....

....

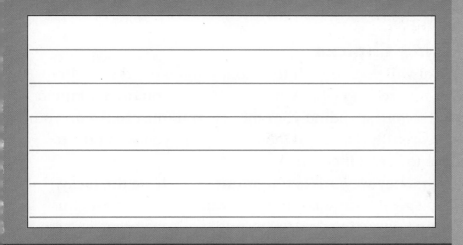

UNLOCK THE BIG ?

I will understand that both individuals and families make economic decisions.

Vocabulary

scarcity   advertising

opportunity   interest
  cost

incentive

How will you spend your day? Will you skip soccer or the movies? Explain your choice.

The Things We Want

Because of scarcity, we can never satisfy all our needs and wants. **Scarcity** means that the amount of a resource is limited. For example, water is scarce in a desert. You may be thirsty and want to fill your water bottle, but the water available to you is limited.

Labor can be scarce, too. During spring planting a farmer may hire three workers to help him. Come fall, those same workers may not be available to help him with the harvest.

What if your favorite team was in the Super Bowl? Because there are a set number of seats in the stadium, and many thousands of fans who want to attend the game, those seats are scarce. The scarcity of those seats can make them costly, too.

For many consumers, the resource that may be scarce is money. You may come up with an endless list of things you want to buy, but the money to buy those things is limited, or scarce. If you earned money shoveling snow, how would you spend it?

2. Shoveling snow is one way to earn money for things you want. **List** one other way to earn money.

....

....

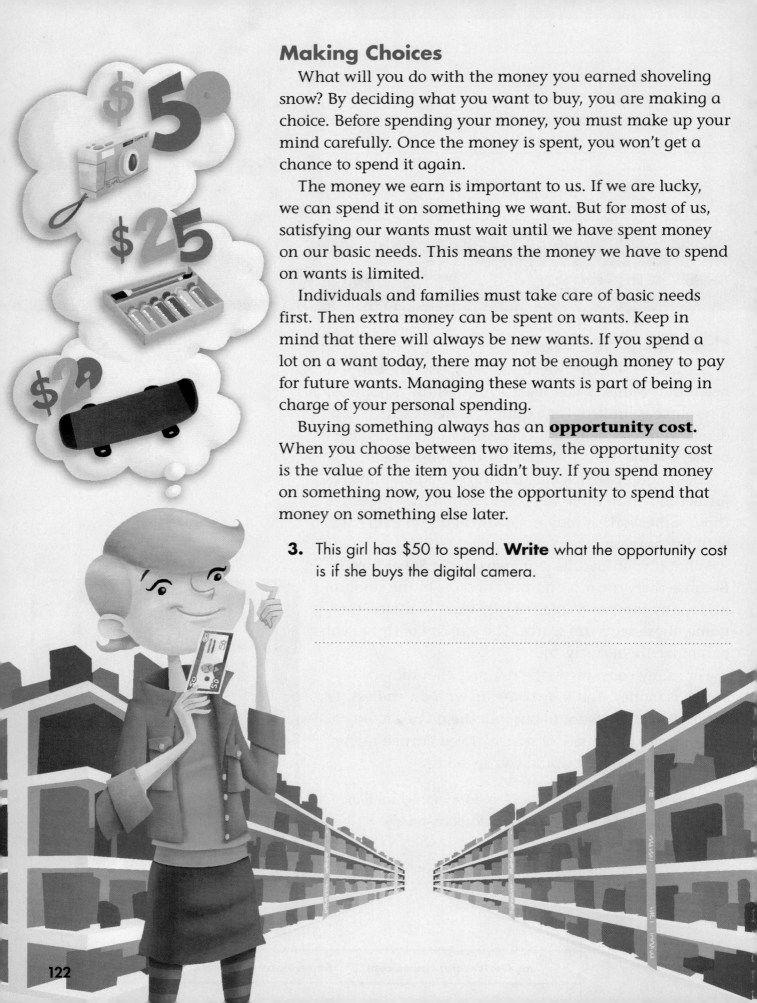

Making Choices

What will you do with the money you earned shoveling snow? By deciding what you want to buy, you are making a choice. Before spending your money, you must make up your mind carefully. Once the money is spent, you won't get a chance to spend it again.

The money we earn is important to us. If we are lucky, we can spend it on something we want. But for most of us, satisfying our wants must wait until we have spent money on our basic needs. This means the money we have to spend on wants is limited.

Individuals and families must take care of basic needs first. Then extra money can be spent on wants. Keep in mind that there will always be new wants. If you spend a lot on a want today, there may not be enough money to pay for future wants. Managing these wants is part of being in charge of your personal spending.

Buying something always has an **opportunity cost.** When you choose between two items, the opportunity cost is the value of the item you didn't buy. If you spend money on something now, you lose the opportunity to spend that money on something else later.

3. This girl has $50 to spend. **Write** what the opportunity cost is if she buys the digital camera.

....

....

122

Incentives

Why do we choose one product or service over another? Incentives play a big part in our decision. **Incentives** are things that encourage us to take an action, such as making a purchase. Sales and coupons are incentives. A low price on an item is a monetary incentive for people to buy it. Monetary means having to do with money. A negative incentive might be a fine on an overdue library book.

People usually learn about sales through advertising. **Advertising** is the use of public notices to bring attention to a product or service. Ads may appear in newspapers and magazines, on posters and billboards, or on the radio, television, and the Internet.

Advertising also uses nonmonetary incentives to make a product seem attractive or cool. Some ads try to convince consumers that a want is really a need. Ads can appeal to your emotions, making you think that you'll feel good if you purchase a product or service. Eye-catching packaging can make one product seem more attractive than another.

Location is an incentive, too. A restaurant owner may choose a street with convenient parking as an incentive to attract customers. Manufacturers try to get their products into good spots in stores, such as in displays near the cash registers. This location would make it easy for shoppers to see and buy the items at checkout.

4. **Look** at each type of incentive shown in the photos below. **Label** each incentive as *monetary* or *nonmonetary*.

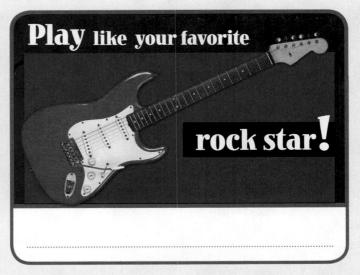

Studying and learning new skills can help students find a job.

ATM machines print out a receipt. This can help you to keep track of the money you save and take out of the bank.

Making a Living

To provide for their wants and needs, most people must have an income, which is money people make from work or from property or businesses they own. Without an income, most people would suffer. The need for money is an incentive to find work.

Incentives play a role in job choice, too. The location of the job is one. Many people prefer jobs that are close to home. Income is another incentive. People usually prefer jobs that pay more money. However, the income a person can earn depends on many things. High-paying jobs often require special skills and education. Doctors, for example, need many years of college and training to learn their skills. Students who continue to study and learn new skills can increase their chances of finding employment, or a job, after they finish school.

Banking and Saving

Most people keep the income they earn in a bank. Banks are a safe place for people to save money. Banks are also businesses that lend money. Banks take the money people save and give it out as loans to borrowers, who must pay it back over time. This borrowed money may be used to purchase a home or pay for education.

Since banks need money from savers to loan out, they provide an incentive. When you keep money in a bank, the bank pays you extra money called **interest.** Interest is added to your account regularly, usually once a month. This can make saving money a better choice than spending it.

Some people use their savings to buy stocks, or portions of a company. Stocks are risky as their value can change. Stock owners can make money if they sell their stocks when the value is high, but lose money if they sell at a low value.

Savings

Loans

BANK

Interest

Loan Payments
and
Interest

SAVER

BORROWER

5. **Write** how banks benefit savers, bankers, and borrowers.

....

....

....

....

Got it?

6. ◎ **Main Idea and Details** What do nice packaging and store sales have in common?

....

....

7. ❓ **Think** of the product or service your new business will offer.
What incentives could you use to encourage customers to buy?

my Story Ideas

....

....

....

■ **Stop!** I need help with ....

❚❚ **Wait!** I have a question about ....

▶ **Go!** Now I know ....

Lesson 4

A Global Economy

Each of these musicians has learned to play one instrument well.

In the past, many goods were transported on barges, or boats with a flat bottom. Mules would pull the barge.

Some of the goods that your family uses probably come from your community. The milk might come from a local dairy or the bread from your neighborhood bakery. Most goods, however, come from other places. Your community is connected to the whole world in a web of trade.

Trade Then and Now

Transportation is what makes trade and services between different places possible. Agricultural products from the countryside can be brought to the city. Goods from city factories can be brought to the countryside. Georgia peaches can be bought in Illinois. A package from Texas can be delivered to a business in Michigan. No single place can provide everything that the people who live there need. Each region depends on the others.

Today, many goods are shipped in huge containers on large cargo ships.

Vocabulary

innovation	specialization
import	productivity
export	outsourcing
division of labor	

Would it be better if each musician learned how to play all these instruments or a single instrument?

Trade has existed for many thousands of years. However, while it once took barges, wagons, and stagecoaches weeks and months to make a delivery, a jet plane can now cross those same distances in hours. Today's cargo ships can hold more goods than ever before. They can transport those goods far more cheaply, too. More goods are shipped and received around the world than at any other time in history.

New Technologies

Supersized boats, jumbo jets, and high-speed trains are all transportation **innovations,** or new inventions or ways of doing things. These innovations have helped bring the world closer together.

Innovations have changed communications, or the sharing of information, too. Computers, the Internet, and e-mail have made global communication faster and cheaper. Information from one place can move to another place almost instantly.

Both communication and transportation innovations allow companies to do business in countries around the world. They can buy resources in different places. Businesses can have factories in different nations. In the past, bosses may have spent long hours traveling to their company's factories. Now, they can run those factories using a video camera.

These innovations affect your life every day. Your computer may have been made in China, with parts from the United States. You can snack on strawberries in winter because they were grown in a part of the world where it is summer.

1. **List** two communication innovations that have increased globalization.

....

....

....

....

Globalization and Interdependence

The process through which goods and ideas spread between different countries is called globalization. Recently, the import and export of goods and services around the world has made trade grow. **Imports** are goods that are brought in from another country to be sold here. **Exports** are goods that are shipped to another country to be sold there. For example, bananas and figs might be imported into the United States, while wheat and apples may be exported to other countries.

Globalization makes the consumers and producers of different countries more connected to one another. A company can use parts or services from all over the world to create a product, such as the car in the map below.

To do this, the company can have factories and workers in many places making the product. It can then sell this product to consumers almost anywhere. Through globalization, the world has become one giant market. This economic connection between countries is called interdependence. It means that one country's economy relies upon the economies in other countries to succeed.

2. ◉ **Main Idea and Details** The map shows a car being made in Michigan. **Write** how the car is an example of globalization.

....
....
....
....
....
....

Car Manufacturing

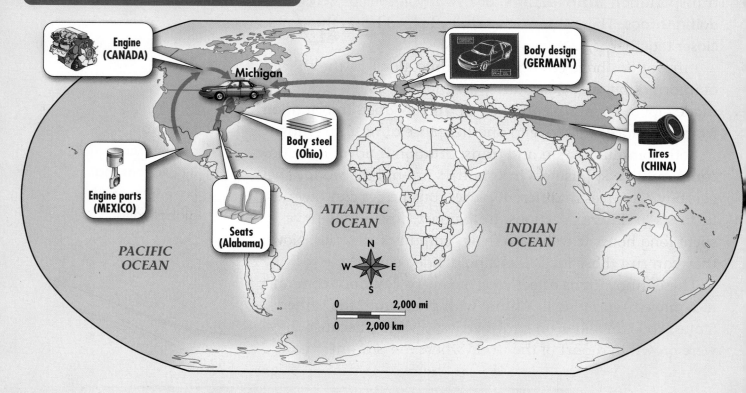

Engine (CANADA)

Michigan

Body design (GERMANY)

Body steel (Ohio)

Engine parts (MEXICO)

Seats (Alabama)

Tires (CHINA)

PACIFIC OCEAN

ATLANTIC OCEAN

INDIAN OCEAN

N W E S

0   2,000 mi
0   2,000 km

Specialization and Productivity

The map of car manufacturing is also an example of the **division of labor,** or the separation of a work process into a number of different jobs. In a car factory, one group mounts the car's engine while another paints the body. The task of building the car has been split into different steps.

Division of labor is what allows for **specialization.** Specialization is the ability of a company, group, or person to focus on a single task. Focusing on a single job helps make people faster and more skilled at what they do. The people who mount car engines don't have to learn how to paint the car properly. Specialization often leads to innovation. Someone who is an expert at something is more likely to figure out ways to improve the product or process.

Specialization and the division of labor can also lead to greater **productivity.** Productivity is the amount a company can produce with a certain amount of labor. A person who only paints cars can paint more cars faster than a person who does other jobs as well.

Greater productivity can bring economic growth. A car company that increases productivity can supply more cars in the same amount of time. This means that the cars are probably cheaper to produce. The cost savings get passed on to consumers, which increases demand for the cars. It also means that consumers have more money to spend on other goods, such as food and clothes.

3. **Look** at the photo. Then **circle** the different jobs that the division of labor creates.

The Benefits and Costs of Globalization

Globalization has many benefits. For the consumer, globalization means more choices. At the mall, you can choose from a vast selection of clothes and electronics. Because of globalization's division of labor, you can often buy these goods for less than you would if they were made entirely in the United States. If a part can be made more cheaply in another country, that lowers the cost of the entire product for you.

Globalization can also increase the number of jobs. If consumers in other countries can afford to buy American goods, it means American companies need to hire more workers to create, sell, and ship these goods.

Globalization has costs, too. It increases competition for sales and jobs. For example, strawberry farmers in the United States must compete for sales with strawberry farmers in Mexico. Although some jobs are gained, others are lost. If workers in another country will work for less money than workers in the United States, American companies may move jobs to that country. This process of hiring people to work outside of a company is called **outsourcing**. Globalization has led to competition among different countries for a share of the world's jobs. Globalization has environmental costs as well. For example, jet fuel, which is used to fly goods across the ocean, pollutes the air.

4. **Look** at the map. **Circle** the number one trading partner of the United States.

The Top United States Trading Partners, 2010

ARCTIC OCEAN

GERMANY 5
UNITED KINGDOM 6
FRANCE 8
CANADA 1
UNITED STATES
MEXICO 3
ATLANTIC OCEAN
PACIFIC OCEAN
BRAZIL 10
CHINA 2
JAPAN 4
SOUTH KOREA 7
TAIWAN 9
INDIAN OCEAN

Source: U.S. Census Bureau

The map shows key U.S. trading partners. In 2010, the United States imported and exported the greatest number of goods with these nations.

5. List some benefits and costs of globalization.

Globalization

Benefits	Costs

6. ◉ **Cause and Effect** How does specialization lead to better-quality products?

....

....

....

....

7. ？ **Think** about your new business. What materials and workers do you need to create your product or service?

my Story Ideas

....

....

....

□ **Stop!** I need help with ....

❚❚ **Wait!** I have a question about ....

▶ **Go!** Now I know ....

Study Guide

What Is the Economy?

- The economy satisfies people's needs and wants.
- Every economy answers three questions: What should be produced? How should it be produced? For whom should it be produced?
- The United States has a market economy.

Trade and Markets

- In the modern economy, money is traded for goods or services.
- Businesses satisfy the demand for goods and services.
- Entrepreneurs take risks by starting new businesses in the hope of making a profit.

People and the Economy

- Individuals and families make economic decisions every day.
- Our choices are shaped by our wants and needs, as well as scarcity.
- Banks fill an important role in our economy by connecting savers and borrowers.

A Global Economy

- Innovations in transportation and communication have increased trade between countries.
- Specialization and the division of labor have increased productivity.
- Globalization has both benefits and costs.

Review and Assessment

Lesson 1

What Is the Economy?

1. **Underline** each want in the list below. **Circle** each need.

   - food
   - movie tickets
   - shelter
   - skating lessons

2. **Write** the names of five parts, or sectors, of the economy and the states where they are especially important.

   ....

   ....

   ....

   ....

   ....

3. **Circle** the letter of the statement that is true about a free enterprise system.

   A. The government decides what goods can be sold.

   B. The government decides what services can be offered.

   C. Producers can decide what goods or services to sell.

   D. Producers cannot decide how much to produce.

Lesson 2

Trade and Markets

4. **Fill in** the blanks. An .... is willing to take .... in the hope that his or her new business will earn a profit.

5. 🎯 **Main Idea and Details** **Write** about a problem with the barter system that the use of currency solved.

   ....

   ....

   ....

   ....

   ....

   ....

   ....

6. **Match** each word with its definition.

   _____ inflation   A. a rise in the prices of many goods and services

   _____ currency   B. the amount of a product that businesses have to sell

   _____ supply   C. the type of money used in a particular place

133

Lesson 3

People and the Economy

7. Fill in the blanks. A _____ pays interest to savers. It makes _____ to borrowers.

8. Circle the letter of the answer that is a monetary incentive.

A. clever packaging

B. a 50% off sale

C. a television commercial

D. a highway billboard

Lesson 4

A Global Economy

9. Write F if a statement is a fact. **Write O** if a statement is an opinion.

- Because of innovations in transportation, goods can be delivered more quickly today than in the past. _____

- All products made locally are better than those made thousands of miles away. _____

10. Write how specialization might help a worker improve his or her skills.

....

....

....

....

11. How does the economy meet our needs and wants?

Describe how the picture shows the economy meeting a need or want.

....

....

....

....

....

Go online to write and illustrate your own **myStory Book** using the **myStory Ideas** from this chapter.

How does the economy meet our needs and wants?

The United States economy helps families and individuals meet their basic needs and satisfy many of their wants. Taking part in this economy means making choices about your spending, your career, and your skills.

Think about your future role in the United States economy. **Write** how you can prepare yourself to take part in it.

....

....

....

....

Draw a picture that shows you taking part in the economy.

While you're online, check out the **myStory Current** Events area where you can create your own book on a topic that's in the news.

Regions: The Northeast

How does where we live affect who we are?

Beginning in the 1600s, people from Europe came to the Northeast to make new lives for themselves. What changes when a person moves to a new home far away?

....

....

....

....

Central Park is in the center of Manhattan.

New York City
A City of Sights and Variety

my Story Video

Ten-year-old Alpha is a proud New Yorker. He lives on Staten Island, which is one of the five boroughs, or parts, that make up New York City. Alpha thinks it is one of the best cities to live in. "You know why I love this city?" Alpha asks. "Because it's so exciting. Every neighborhood has history, and there are fun things to see and do around every corner."

Alpha visits some of the neighborhoods in the borough of Manhattan. Manhattan is famous for its many tall buildings. More than 1 million people live here, and many more come each day to work. There are also dozens of museums, including the Metropolitan, or the "Met." "The Met is really cool," he says. "Inside they have mummies, knights in armor, and, oh yeah, a lot of paintings." Manhattan also has famous performing arts centers, such as the Apollo Theater.

Alpha explores New York City's many museums.

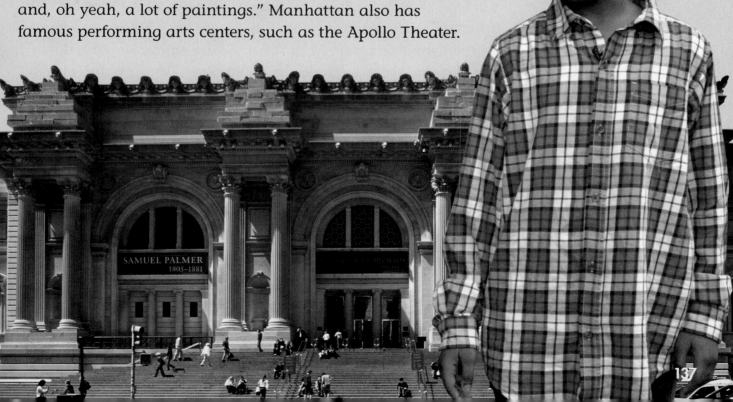

SAMUEL PALMER
1805–1881

137

In Little Italy, many stores and restaurants serve foods that you would find in Italy.

Many people visit Chinatown to shop and eat.

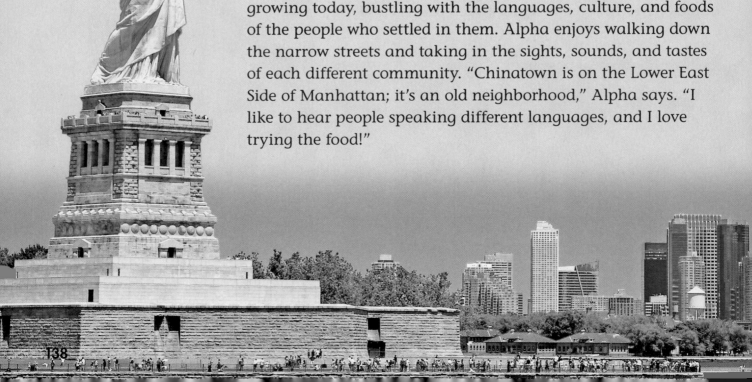

The Statue of Liberty is a symbol of hope to many newcomers.

In some ways New York is like no other city in the world, but in other ways it is similar to many cities in the Northeast. Like other cities in the region, including Philadelphia, Pennsylvania, it was founded as a port city. It is known for its history and culture, too, just as Boston, Massachusetts, is.

In the 1800s, New York was an entryway for people who wanted to move to the United States. Many of these immigrants came to this country though the Ellis Island Immigration Station in New York Harbor. At the tip of Manhattan, looking out over the water, Alpha can't miss the sight that millions of immigrants first saw when their ships sailed toward New York: the Statue of Liberty. "You've probably seen the Statue of Liberty in pictures, but it's even more incredible in person," Alpha says.

Many immigrants stayed in New York and built communities such as Little Italy and Chinatown. These communities are still growing today, bustling with the languages, culture, and foods of the people who settled in them. Alpha enjoys walking down the narrow streets and taking in the sights, sounds, and tastes of each different community. "Chinatown is on the Lower East Side of Manhattan; it's an old neighborhood," Alpha says. "I like to hear people speaking different languages, and I love trying the food!"

Wall Street has been a center of banking since the 1800s.

Alpha rides the subway to get around New York City.

Not far from Chinatown is Wall Street. It's the heart of New York's banking industry, and one of the largest banking centers in the world. "Millions of dollars change hands here every day," Alpha says. It is home to the New York Stock Exchange and part of the Federal Reserve, the central banking system of the United States.

With all the people working and living in the city, getting around New York can be a challenge. Taking some of the traffic underground helps, and New York has the largest subway system in the United States. More than 5 million people take the subway every day from Monday to Friday. "It's a little crowded sometimes," Alpha admits. "But it's a lot faster than sitting in traffic."

Traveling north up Manhattan, Alpha is happy to enjoy the quiet of Central Park. Central Park includes more than 800 acres of open space. "This isn't just an ordinary park," Alpha says. "Sure, it has swings and slides and ponds. It also has an ice-skating rink, an outdoor theatre, and my favorite—a zoo."

New York is not only home to many famous sights, but also home to millions of people. Like Alpha, people here can enjoy different cultures, walk through history, and relax or play at the center of the action.

Think About It Based on this story, how is where Alpha lives similar to or different from your own city or town? As you read the chapter, think about how where we live affects who we are.

The Land of the Northeast

Envision It!

Niagara Falls in New York is one of many unique landforms to see in the Northeast region.

In parts of Pennsylvania, the land is used for farming.

Many people choose to live in the Northeast region of the United States. What makes this region so special? Is it the land? The people? The history? In fact, it is all of these things.

Welcome to the Northeast

The Northeast is a diverse region. The region is known for the beauty of its land. It has rolling hills, mountains, farms, and thick forests. It has large busy cities and small quiet villages. Beach towns line the coast. The region has fast-running rivers, lakes, and the roaring waters of Niagara Falls. It also has trees with blazing colors in the fall. In winter, storms often cover the land in snow. All this variety is found in the smallest region of the United States.

I will know that the Northeast has mountains, a long coast, and large lakes and rivers.

Vocabulary

lighthouse   glacier
peninsula
sound

Write the name of a place that you might like to visit in the Northeast.

The Northeast is made up of 11 states: Maine, New Hampshire, Vermont, Massachusetts, Rhode Island, Connecticut, New York, New Jersey, Pennsylvania, Maryland, and Delaware. Eight of these states are among the smallest states in the country. To the east of the region is the Atlantic Ocean. To the north is Canada. The Northeast is also bordered by two of the five Great Lakes.

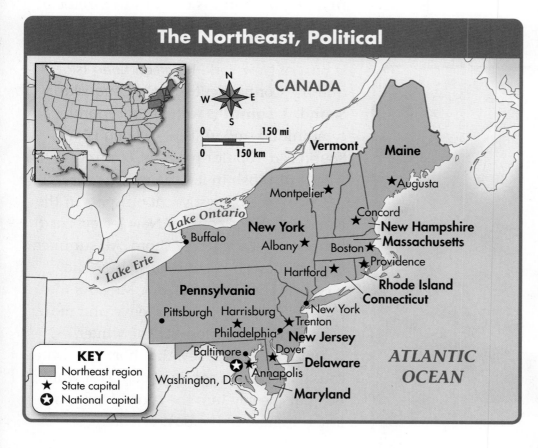

The Northeast, Political

CANADA

N W E S

0   150 mi
0   150 km

Vermont   Maine

Montpelier ★   ★ Augusta

Lake Ontario

Concord
★

Buffalo   New York   New Hampshire
  Albany ★   Boston ★   Massachusetts

Lake Erie

Hartford ★   ★ Providence

Pennsylvania   Rhode Island
Connecticut

Pittsburgh   Harrisburg   New York
★   ★ Trenton
Philadelphia ●   New Jersey

Baltimore ●   Dover
  ★ Delaware   ATLANTIC
Washington, D.C.   Annapolis   OCEAN

Maryland

KEY
☐ Northeast region
★ State capital
✪ National capital

1. **Circle** the northern and western borders of the region. Then **write** the names of the lakes that form part of the region's northwest border.

....

....

....

....

The Atlantic Coast

All but two of the states in the Northeast, Pennsylvania and Vermont, are bordered by the Atlantic Ocean. The Atlantic coast is long and jagged as bays carve into the land. Islands lie just off the coast in many states, including Maine.

The coast of Maine is known for its rugged beauty. It is also known as the home to the easternmost point in the nation, Quoddy Head State Park. At Quoddy Head and other places on the Atlantic coast, waves crash against the rocks and cliffs. Dozens of lighthouses line the coast. A **lighthouse** is a tower with a bright light at the top called a beacon. The beacon shines to guide ships at sea during the night.

Some of the ships that travel along the Atlantic coast dock at one of the harbors in Massachusetts. People also come to the state to visit Cape Cod. The Cape, as it is often called, extends out into the Atlantic Ocean. It is a **peninsula**, or land that is almost surrounded on all sides by water.

Farther south along the coast is Long Island. You can see on the map on the next page that it has this name because of its long, thin shape. Long Island is part of New York. Between Long Island and the Connecticut coast is Long Island Sound. A **sound** is water that separates a mainland and an island. Long Island Sound is a popular place for boating. People also fish in its waters.

One of the busiest vacation spots in the Northeast is the coast of New Jersey. Local people call it the Jersey shore. All summer, visitors fill its hot, sandy beaches. They visit Atlantic City and Cape May. As the weather cools, the visitors leave and many of the businesses close for the winter.

South of New Jersey, the short Delaware coast is a strip of sandy beach. Delaware Bay cuts deeply into the coast. Marshes line the shore of the bay.

In winter, storms called nor'easters hit the coast of the Northeast. The storms are named for the northeasterly winds that blow during the storms. The storms often bring winds, strong waves, and heavy snow.

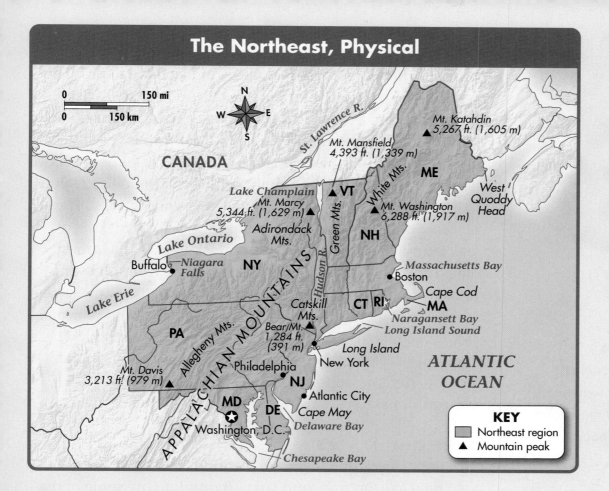

The Northeast, Physical

0 150 mi
0 150 km

CANADA

St. Lawrence R.

Mt. Katahdin
5,267 ft. (1,605 m)

Mt. Mansfield
4,393 ft. (1,339 m)

ME

Lake Champlain
Mt. Marcy
5,344 ft. (1,629 m)

VT

White Mts.

West
Quoddy
Head

Adirondack
Mts.

Green Mts.

Mt. Washington
6,288 ft. (1,917 m)

NH

Lake Ontario

Buffalo
Niagara
Falls

NY

Hudson R.

Massachusetts Bay

Boston

Cape Cod

Lake Erie

Catskill
Mts.

CT RI

MA

Naragansett Bay
Long Island Sound

PA

APPALACHIAN MOUNTAINS

Allegheny Mts.

Bear Mt.
1,284 ft.
(391 m)

Long Island

New York

ATLANTIC
OCEAN

Mt. Davis
3,213 ft. (979 m)

Philadelphia

NJ

Atlantic City

MD

DE

Cape May

Washington, D.C.

Delaware Bay

KEY

Northeast region
Mountain peak

Chesapeake Bay

The Appalachian Range

Some of the oldest mountains on Earth are found in the Northeast. They are the Appalachian Mountains. This mountain range stretches nearly 2,000 miles from Alabama, in the Southeast region, north into Canada.

The Appalachian range is made up of several smaller mountain ranges. In the Northeast, they include the White Mountains in New Hampshire, the Green Mountains in Vermont, the Catskill Mountains in New York, and the Allegheny Mountains in Pennsylvania.

The White Mountains include Mount Washington, the tallest mountain in the Northeast. This mountain is also considered to have the worst weather in the region and nation. Its high elevation and its location in the path of storms often cause high winds on the mountain. In fact, in 1934 the winds reached more than 200 miles per hour!

The Green Mountains run north and south through Vermont. They were named for the evergreen trees that cover much of the slopes. Heavy winter snowfall in both the Green Mountains and White Mountains make them popular for winter sports.

2. **Find** the mountain peaks. **Circle** the tallest mountains in New York State and New Hampshire.

143

A black bear in the Adirondacks

3. ⊙ **Make Generalizations** **Finish** the sentence. People visit mountains in the Northeast

....

....

The Catskill Mountains are north of New York City. These mountains have steep, rocky valleys and wooded slopes. The beautiful views are popular with hikers and skiers. Artists also visit the area to take photographs or paint pictures.

Another major mountain range in New York is the Adirondack Mountains. Long ago, **glaciers,** or huge sheets of ice, carved these and other mountains throughout the region. As the glaciers began to melt, lakes and ponds formed. Forests also grew. A large part of the land in the Adirondacks is a protected state park. In fact, Adirondack Park is the largest state park in the United States. Visitors come from all over to camp, swim, hike, and even ice-skate. People also come to see the wildlife, which includes moose, black bears, and bobcats.

Many people also travel to the Allegheny Mountains. These mountains stretch from Pennsylvania south into Virginia. They, too, are known for their majestic views. Visitors can cross-country ski, hike, fish, and see white-tailed deer there.

Lakes and Rivers

Streams, rivers, and lakes are plentiful in the Northeast. Lake Erie, Lake Ontario, and Lake Champlain are some of the largest lakes in the Northeast. These and other lakes in the region are valued not only for their beauty and recreational opportunities, but also as natural resources. Lakes provide fresh drinking water.

The region's four largest rivers, including the Hudson River, drain into the Atlantic Ocean. Like lakes, the rivers in the Northeast are used for swimming and boating. Some rivers are also used for white-water rafting.

White-water rafting is popular in the Northeast.

The rivers of the Northeast have been used for transportation for many years. In the 1600s and 1700s, rivers were the main transportation routes for settlers. Many cities, such as New York City, New York, and Baltimore, Maryland, were built at the mouths of rivers. The mouth is where a river flows into a larger body of water, such as a bay or ocean. These cities were important ports for people and goods that crossed the Atlantic Ocean, traveling to or from Europe.

Today, people still move goods on the rivers of the region. Large cargo ships carry vehicles, oil, fruit, and other goods on rivers such as the Delaware River and the Hudson River.

The Hudson River

Got it?

4. ◉ **Make Generalizations** **Write** a generalization about the Northeast.

....

....

....

5. ❓ You and your family decide to take a trip to the Northeast. **Choose** one place to visit on your trip and describe it. Why did you choose that place?

my Story Ideas

....

....

....

⬛ **Stop!** I need help with ....

⏸ **Wait!** I have a question about ....

▶ **Go!** Now I know ....

Resources in the Northeast

Envision It!

These pictures show natural resources and products from the Northeast region.

Vermont and New York are the top two maple-syrup-producing states. In one year, the two states produced over 1 million gallons of maple syrup.

Just as people everywhere do, people in the Northeast depend on natural resources to live. Luckily, this region has many resources to offer. Many of its resources come from the Northeast's forests.

Forest Resources

People have used forest resources in many different ways. Long ago, Native Americans used the wood from trees to build homes and fences. They also carved wooden boats. In the 1600s, settlers built with wood, too. They also cleared forests to start farms.

Maine, New Hampshire, and Vermont are the most thickly forested states in the region. The forest industry is important in these states. Workers in the industry cut down trees to make into lumber, paper, and other products.

Sugar maple trees are another forest resource. These trees grow throughout the Northeast. They are used to make maple syrup. To make syrup, people drill holes and put spouts in the tree trunks. People collect the sap that drips out. Then they boil the sap in large tubs. After many hours the water evaporates, leaving behind maple syrup.

1. ◎ **Sequence** **Write** the steps in the correct order.

.... Collect tree sap in buckets.

.... Drill holes and put spouts in tree trunks.

.... Boil the sap until only maple syrup remains.

146

1. trees _____

_____

2. dairy cows _____

_____

3. apples _____

_____

Write a product that can be made from each of the examples.

UNLOCK THE BIG ?

I will know that the Northeast is rich in natural resources and makes many products.

Vocabulary

mineral	bog
quarry	tourist
overfishing	

Resources in the Earth

Some of the most valuable natural resources in the Northeast are found in the earth. For example, Pennsylvania has underground deposits of coal. Coal is used as fuel. The region also has valuable minerals. A **mineral** is a nonliving material that is found in the earth. Most stone or rocks, such as granite and marble, are a mix of minerals. These materials are often used for building.

New Hampshire is famous for its rock quarries. A **quarry** is a place where stone is dug, cut, or blasted out of the earth. In fact, the state nickname is the Granite State.

Vermont also has large amounts of granite. Vermont has marble, too. The first marble quarry in Vermont opened in Dorset, in 1785. Vermont marble has been used on well-known landmarks. It was used on the New York Public Library and the United Nations building in New York City.

The two narrow sides of the United Nations building are covered with marble from Vermont.

Water Resources

The Atlantic Ocean is another important resource in the Northeast. For hundreds of years, fishing has been a way of life along the coast. Over time, people improved fishing gear and boats. This allowed them to stay out in the ocean for longer periods and catch more fish. In the 1970s, the fish populations dropped in many areas in the Northeast. One of the main reasons for this drop was that people were overfishing the waters. **Overfishing** is when people catch fish faster than natural processes can replace them. Because there were fewer fish, fewer people could make a living by fishing. Today, people work to find solutions to overfishing. They often limit the amount of fish that people can catch.

People in the Northeast also catch other sea life such as shellfish and crabs. Maine is famous for its lobsters. Many lobster fishers have been fishing the same way for many years. The fishers lower a baited trap into the water. Days later, the fishers haul up the traps and collect the lobsters. Maryland, on the Chesapeake Bay, is famous for its blue crabs. People use nets and baited cages or traps to catch blue crabs.

Blue crab from Maryland

Rivers are another resource. Many rivers in the Northeast are used as sources for drinking water. Others, such as the Niagara River, near Niagara Falls, are used by power plants to make electricity. The Niagara River provides electricity for much of New York.

2. ◉ **Cause and Effect** **Fill in** the missing effect.

Overfishing in the Northeast

Cause

People were overfishing the waters.

Effect

smaller fishing industry in Northeast

Agriculture in the Northeast

The states in the Northeast with the most farms are New York and Pennsylvania. In fact, about one third of the open land in both states is farmland. Farms in New York produce a variety of crops, including apples and grapes. New York also has many dairy farms. In Pennsylvania, farmers raise dairy cows, beef cattle, hogs, chickens, and sheep.

There are many farms in New Jersey, New Hampshire, and Vermont, too. Farmers in New Jersey grow many different fruits and vegetables. Most farms in Vermont are dairy farms. In fact, Vermont is a leading producer of milk in the Northeast.

In some parts of the region, such as Maine, the soil is rocky and not fertile enough for most crops. The climate is also cooler. However, certain crops, such as potatoes and blueberries, grow well there.

In Massachusetts, cranberries are a leading crop. These tart red berries grow in wet, marshy areas called **bogs**. The bogs near Cape Cod are perfect for growing them.

Farmers harvest cranberries by flooding the bogs.

3. **Study** the map and the map key. **Circle** the crops that grow in cooler climates or in wet marshes.

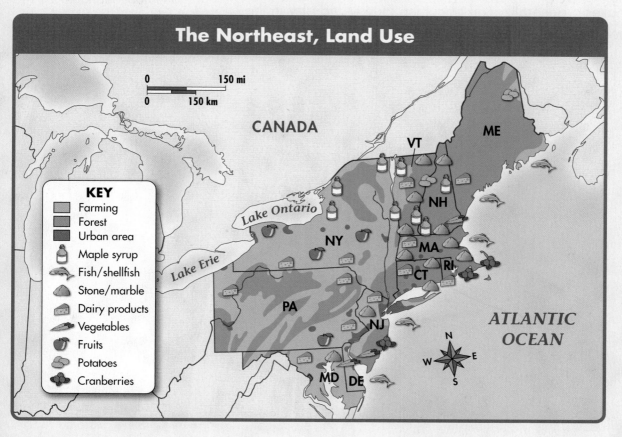

The Northeast, Land Use

KEY
- Farming
- Forest
- Urban area
- Maple syrup
- Fish/shellfish
- Stone/marble
- Dairy products
- Vegetables
- Fruits
- Potatoes
- Cranberries

CANADA

Lake Ontario

Lake Erie

VT
ME
NH
NY
MA
RI
CT
PA
NJ
MD
DE

ATLANTIC OCEAN

149

Visitors to the Northeast

Vermont is a state with many mountains and plenty of snow. In fact, the average yearly snowfall in parts of the Green Mountains is around 10 feet. In some states, that much snow might be a problem. In Vermont, it is a resource. Snow attracts **tourists,** or visitors, to ski. Skiers help support the state's tourism industry. This industry includes resorts, hotels, and restaurants. These places are busy summer and winter, serving skiers, hikers, and other visitors.

The tourism industry is important in other states in the Northeast, too. The Adirondack Mountains and the mountains and lakes of New Hampshire attract tourists all year. So do cities such as Boston, Massachusetts, and New York City, New York. Coastal communities from Maine to Maryland attract many tourists in the summer.

Many people across the Northeast depend on tourism to earn a living. Workers in the tourism industry do many different jobs. They clean hotel rooms and serve food. They run ski lifts and give guided tours. They also sell T-shirts and rent bicycles.

4. ◎ **Make Generalizations** **Underline** a sentence that makes a generalization about the tourism industry in the Northeast region.

In Rhode Island, tourists take guided tours of historic homes.

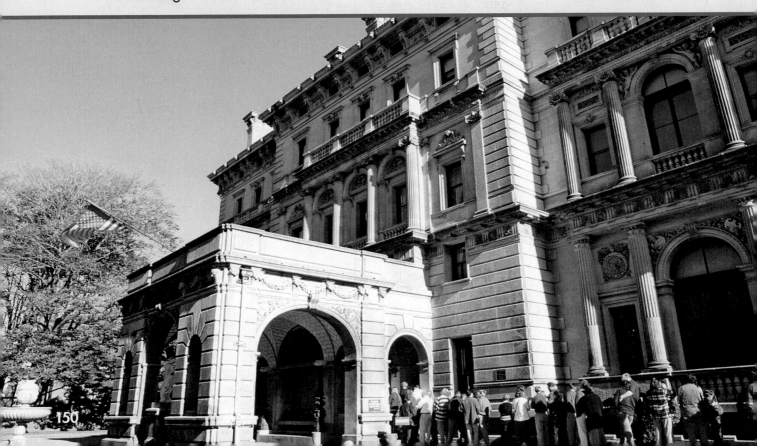

150

5. This picture shows snowboarders in the Northeast. **Write** a caption that explains how they help the industries in the region.

....

....

....

....

....

....

6. ◉ **Make Generalizations Make** a generalization about overfishing in the Northeast.

....

....

....

7. ❓ Big news! Your family is moving to the Northeast because your parents have found work there. Where will you live and what jobs will your parents be doing?

my Story Ideas

....

....

....

◻ **Stop!** I need help with ....

❙❙ **Wait!** I have a question about ....

▶ **Go!** Now I know ....

Birthplace of the Nation

Envision It!

These pictures show how Wampanoag Native Americans and English settlers dressed in the 1600s.

Many of the events that led to the beginning of the nation took place in the Northeast. In fact, one of the first colonies was in what is now Massachusetts. In 1620, people from England arrived on the coast. They built a settlement they called Plymouth. Soon after, a cold, hard winter hit. Many of the settlers survived only with the help of the nearby Wampanoag (wahm puh NOH ag) people, a Native American group.

Native Americans of the Northeast

Long before English settlers came to Plymouth, many different Native American groups lived in the region. They lived in the forests and along the coast. Each group had its own beliefs, language, way of governing, and way of life.

The Wampanoag built their villages in forests. Each village had its own chief, or **sachem** (SAY chum). Families lived in **wetus** (wee TOOZ) made of poles covered with tree bark or reed mats. People wore clothing made of deerskins and fur. The Wampanoag hunted, fished, and grew corn and other vegetables.

The Wampanoag taught the settlers their ways of planting, fishing, and cooking. These skills helped the settlers adapt to the land. The English settlers brought with them goods from Europe. The goods included guns, metal tools, and cloth. These items were new to the Wampanoag.

Plimoth Plantation is a re-creation of an early English village. It shows how the settlement may have looked in 1627. It also shows a re-created Wampanoag wetu (above).

UNLOCK
THE BIG
?

I will know that many
of the events that led to the
formation of the United States
took place in the Northeast.

Vocabulary

sachem

wetu

suffrage

What differences do you see? Write them in the box.

At first, the Wampanoag and the English settlers helped each other and traded items. In time, more settlers came to the area. Many of them settled on land where the Wampanoag lived and hunted. In 1675, a war broke out. In a year of fighting, thousands of Wampanoag, Narragansett, and other Native Americans were killed or forced out of their villages.

Farther inland lived the Mohawk, Oneida, Onondaga, Cayuga, and Seneca Native Americans. Around 1600, these five groups joined together. They formed the Iroquois (IHR uh kwoi) Confederacy. This helped the groups live in peace. It also made them stronger in battles against the settlers from England and other European countries. For many years, the Iroquois were able to keep others off of their land.

1. **Draw** an X where the Wampanoag lived. **Circle** the five groups that made up the Iroquois Confederacy.

Native Americans of the Northeast

KEY
Northeast region
Map shows present-day borders.

Penobscot
Abenaki
Pennacook
L. Ontario
Seneca
Cayuga
Onondaga
Oneida
Mohawk
Mohican
Pocomtuc
Massachuset
Lake Erie
Pequot
Wampanoag
Narraganset
Susquehannock
Montauk
Delaware
ATLANTIC OCEAN
Conoy
Nanticoke

0   150 mi
0   150 km

The Colonies Gain Independence

Settlers from England continued to set up colonies in North America. By the late 1700s, thirteen English colonies lined the Atlantic coast. Eight of them were in what is now the Northeast. Each was formed for a different reason. Rhode Island, Connecticut, and New Hampshire were settled by colonists from Massachusetts. New York was a Dutch colony that was taken over by English settlers. Pennsylvania was founded by William Penn. Penn wanted a colony where people had religious freedom. Delaware split off from Pennsylvania. New Jersey and Maryland were given to leaders by the king of Great Britain.

The colonies belonged to Great Britain. However, the colonists followed the tradition of self-government that the first settlers had learned. Colonists held town meetings to discuss and vote on issues. In time, British leaders passed laws that the colonists were not allowed to vote on. Many colonists felt the laws were unfair and protested against them. Some of the first protests came from colonists in the Northeast. In Boston, Massachusetts, Samuel Adams wanted the colonists to oppose the laws.

Tensions between the colonists and British leaders grew. Soon, British soldiers were sent to Boston to keep order. In a clash between soldiers and colonists, five people were shot and killed. The first to die was Crispus Attucks. The fight was called the Boston Massacre. This fight led to even more protests and anger against Britain.

2. These paintings show key people from the colonies. **Write** a sentence for each missing caption.

Samuel Adams	**Crispus Attucks**	**Abigail Adams**
		Adams wrote letters in support of freedom and liberty.

In 1775, the first battle of the American Revolution took place in the Northeast region. It was fought at Lexington, a town near Boston, Massachusetts. A year later, colonial leaders met in another area of the Northeast, in Philadelphia, Pennsylvania. There, they wrote the Declaration of Independence. This document marked the beginning of the United States of America.

A New Plan of Government

In 1787, after the American Revolution was over, leaders from the states met again in Philadelphia. This time they met to make the states in the nation more united. They spent three months writing the United States Constitution. Benjamin Franklin from Pennsylvania played a key role. At 81, he was a respected leader. He helped settle disagreements between the states.

After the new United States government was formed, the nation's first capital was in the Northeast, in New York City. Here, George Washington was sworn in as the first president. In 1790, the capital moved to Philadelphia. It remained there until 1800, when it moved to the newly built city of Washington, D.C.

3. ◉ **Make Generalizations**
Write a generalization about the events that took place in the Northeast.

....

....

....

....

....

....

....

....

Joseph Brant	Benjamin Franklin	Phillis Wheatley
Brant was a Mohawk leader. He fought against the Americans during the American Revolution.		Wheatley was a Boston poet who grew up in slavery. Her poetry celebrated the birth of the new nation.

The Abolitionists

Just as the Northeast region played an important role in the start of the nation, it played an important role in Americans' struggle for equal rights. The Declaration of Independence states that "all men are created equal." It says that all people have rights, including the right to "life, liberty and the pursuit of happiness." Yet when the Declaration was written, many Americans were not free. Africans had been working as slaves in the colonies since the early days of settlement. In 1776, slavery was allowed in all 13 states.

Between 1777 and 1827, most of the states in the Northeast, except Maryland and Delaware, passed laws to end slavery. Many people in the Northeast also wanted to abolish, or end, slavery throughout the United States.

William Lloyd Garrison was a leading abolitionist. In 1833, he helped start the American Anti-Slavery Society in Philadelphia. Garrison was outspoken and fearless. He wrote, "I will not retreat a single inch—AND I WILL BE HEARD."

Stanton spoke to close to 300 people who gathered at the Seneca Falls Convention.

Many free African Americans and former slaves were part of the movement. Frederick Douglass and Sojourner Truth both had been slaves. They traveled and spoke about what life was like for a slave. Their speeches convinced many people to join the fight to end slavery. In 1865, the Thirteenth Amendment was added to the United States Constitution. The amendment made slavery illegal in the United States.

Women's Rights

Many people who worked to end slavery also worked so that women could have equal rights. In the 1800s, women did not have the same rights as men. Women could not vote, and in most states they could not own property.

In 1848, Elizabeth Cady Stanton and Lucretia Mott organized a public meeting to talk about women's rights. It was to be a large convention held for this special purpose. It took place in Seneca Falls, New York. It was the first women's rights convention held in the United States.

156

The Seneca Falls Convention started the women's rights movement. Susan B. Anthony was a key leader in the women's rights movement. She led the struggle for women's **suffrage,** or the right to vote. An amendment to grant women suffrage was first introduced to Congress in 1878. However, the Nineteenth Amendment to the United States Constitution, which granted women the right to vote, did not pass until 1920.

4. ◉ **Sequence** Which came first, the end of slavery or women's suffrage?

....

Like many abolitionists, Frederick Douglass supported women's rights at Seneca Falls.

Got it?

5. ◉ **Main Idea and Details** In the history of the Northeast, there are examples of conflicts and examples of how people worked together. **Write** an example of each.

....

....

....

....

6. ❓ The Northeastern town where you live is near a Revolutionary War battle site. **Describe** what you might see in your town that shows its history. **my Story Ideas**

....

....

....

◻ **Stop!** I need help with ....

⏸ **Wait!** I have a question about ....

▶ **Go!** Now I know ....

Lesson 4

Growth and Change in the Northeast

The Statue of Liberty, in New York Harbor, signaled to newcomers that they had arrived in the United States.

Immigrants have been coming to the United States for hundreds of years. The settlers who started the colonies were immigrants. After the United States became a nation, many more immigrants came.

Immigrants Come to the Northeast

Beginning in the early 1800s, immigrants came to the Northeast from many parts of Europe. From 1820 to 1860, most immigrants came from Ireland, Germany, and Great Britain. Newcomers from a part of northern Europe called Scandinavia came from 1860 to 1890. Many of them moved to the Midwest. Then from 1890 to 1910, immigrants came from countries in southern Europe and eastern Europe.

1. Draw an X on the map arrow showing the most recent wave of immigration.

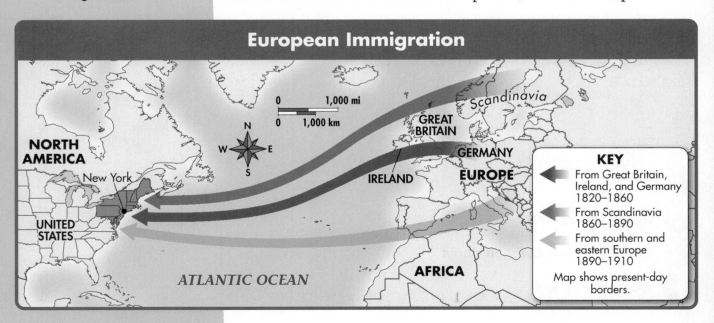

European Immigration

0 | 1,000 mi
0 | 1,000 km

NORTH AMERICA

New York

UNITED STATES

ATLANTIC OCEAN

Scandinavia

GREAT BRITAIN

GERMANY

IRELAND

EUROPE

AFRICA

KEY

From Great Britain, Ireland, and Germany 1820–1860

From Scandinavia 1860–1890

From southern and eastern Europe 1890–1910

Map shows present-day borders.

158

UNLOCK THE BIG ?

I will know that immigrants and growing industries brought change to the Northeast.

Vocabulary

steamboat
patent
sweatshop
labor union

Like today, immigrants came to the United States for many different reasons. Some came to find work. In the fast-growing cities in the Northeast, jobs in factories were plentiful. Others came to farm their own land. Still others came to escape war or a difficult life in their home country. Hope for a better life inspired them all.

Many immigrants came to the large port cities of the Northeast, such as Boston and New York City. New York was the busiest of these ports. In 1892, an immigration station opened on Ellis Island in New York Harbor. Millions of immigrants passed through its doors. At the station, government workers checked people's identification and other records. They examined eyes and throats to make sure the newcomers were healthy. Many of the newcomers were free to start their new lives. Those who did not pass the health checks were sent back to their home country.

2. 🎯 **Make Generalizations** **Make** a generalization about why immigrants came to the United States.

....

....

....

Ellis Island

The Contributions of Immigrants

Immigrants have made many contributions to both the Northeast region and the rest of the nation. In the 1800s and 1900s, immigrants worked in factories and laid railroad tracks. Immigrants also planted and harvested crops.

Other immigrants made contributions to the study of science, to businesses, and to the arts. One well-known immigrant is Albert Einstein, a scientist from Germany. Irving Berlin came from Russia. He wrote songs. Alexander Graham Bell, the inventor of a telephone, was from Scotland.

Inventions and the Rise of Industry

The telephone was just one of many new inventions that changed the way Americans lived and worked. In 1807, Robert Fulton started the first steamboat service in the Northeast. A **steamboat** is a boat powered by a steam engine. Steamboats allowed people to travel more quickly from place to place.

In 1879, Thomas Edison invented an electric light bulb. In Menlo Park, New Jersey, Edison and his workers spent more than two years working with light and electricity. After many failed experiments, they had success. Edison applied for a patent. The **patent** gave him the right to make and sell the invention. Lewis Latimer, an African American inventor, found a way for light bulbs to last longer. Soon, light bulbs lit homes and city streets.

Fulton, Edison, and Latimer were not the only inventors to change the world. The first gasoline-powered automobile in the nation came out in 1893. Not long after, new roads linked cities. These and other new inventions helped bring the nation into the modern age. Together, they changed Americans' way of life.

3. Fill in inventions that brought America into the modern age.

Edison's light bulb

Thomas Edison

1807
First steamboat service

1800

1793
Cotton gin

160

New inventions and advances in technology helped industry grow. This change came first to the Northeast region, where there were already many factories and mills. In Massachusetts, Francis Cabot Lowell built a textile mill. His mill was one of the first to use a power loom to weave cloth.

In Pennsylvania, Andrew Carnegie, an immigrant from Scotland, used the Bessemer process to make steel. This led to rapid growth in the steel industry. Steel was used to make cars, railroad tracks, and bridges. Steel beams were also used to make tall buildings. After Elisha Otis of Vermont invented the brake for elevators in 1853, buildings could reach new heights. People could now use elevators to easily get to the upper floors. The tallest of these buildings were called skyscrapers.

A worker at a Lowell mill

The growth of industry had both helpful and harmful effects. Factories and mills provided jobs for immigrants and Americans. Workers turned natural resources into goods. As the amount of goods grew, many goods became less expensive.

However, industrial growth also created problems. Immigrants poured into the cities to find work. Cities grew so fast that there was not enough housing. Most newcomers lived in poorly built and unsafe buildings. Whole families were often crowded into one or two rooms. Some lived with no heat or hot water. In these poor conditions, diseases spread easily.

4. ◎ **Cause and Effect** **Write** one helpful and one harmful effect of industrial growth.

....

....

Inventions from the Northeast

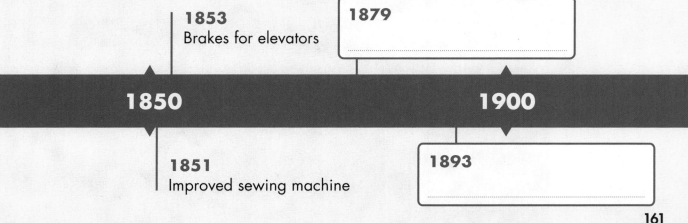

1853
Brakes for elevators

1879

1850

1900

1851
Improved sewing machine

1893

161

The firefighters in New York City tried to rescue the Triangle Shirtwaist Factory workers.

Movements for Reform

Working conditions in most mills and factories were poor. In New York City, most clothing factories were so crowded, dirty, and unsafe that they were known as **sweatshops.** Workers were often paid very little and worked long hours. Wages were so low that even children worked to help their families. Child workers were not able to go to school, and they were often hurt by the machines they worked with.

On March 25, 1911, dangerous conditions at a garment, or clothing, factory led to a tragedy. At the Triangle Shirtwaist Factory in New York City, a fire broke out. It raced through the top floors of the ten-story building. Many workers couldn't get out because the doors were locked. They went to the windows, hoping for rescue, but the firefighters' ladders were too short. Many people died, most of them young immigrant women.

The deadly fire angered many people in the Northeast region and across the country. People who wanted to reform, or improve, society worked together. These people were often called reformers. Reformers called for laws to protect workers. Groups of workers also banded together to form labor unions. A **labor union** is a workers' group that tries to gain better pay and working conditions. After the fire at the Triangle Shirtwaist Factory, many people joined the International Ladies' Garment Workers Union (ILGWU) and supported its demands for safer workplaces.

Workers joined labor unions.

As industry grew in the Northeast, reformers continued to solve the problems that came with this growth. They pushed for laws to end child labor. In Massachusetts, the reformer Horace Mann worked to improve public schools. In New York City, reformers started community centers in poor immigrant neighborhoods. The centers offered child care, classes to teach English, and other help to immigrants.

5. 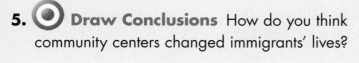 **Draw Conclusions** How do you think community centers changed immigrants' lives?

....

....

....

Immigrants could learn English at school.

Got it?

6. ● **Cause and Effect Choose** one invention or industrial development of the 1800s. **Write** about its effects.

....

....

....

7. ❓ You have made a new friend. Your friend's grandparents came to the Northeast as immigrants from Europe. What questions would you like to ask them about their experience?

my Story Ideas

....

....

....

⬛ **Stop!** I need help with ....

⏸ **Wait!** I have a question about ....

▶ **Go!** Now I know ....

Work in Teams

A team is a group of people who work together to reach a goal. Many people in the United States have worked as a team to make changes to the nation. Women's groups, labor unions, and reformers have all worked as teams to reach their goals.

Being part of a team can be fun, but it can be a challenge, too. School projects, team sports, nature groups: all these activities are more successful when the people in them work together. The following steps will help you work in a team.

1. Identify the team's goal. Make sure all team members agree on the goal.

2. Discuss what actions need to be taken. Take turns talking and listening. Make a list of tasks or jobs that need to be accomplished.

3. Decide who will complete each task. Try to divide the responsibilities equally.

4. Check in with each other as you work. Ask questions, give each other helpful ideas, and keep each other on schedule.

5. Meet to make sure all jobs have been accomplished.

At school, students often work as a team.

Suppose you have been given the assignment below. **Read** the assignment. **Add** your name to the team. Then **answer** the questions.

> Work as a team to create a newspaper about well-known people and events in the history of the Northeast. Be creative! Due in three weeks.
>
> Team members: _____, Katie, Vanessa, Brad

1. What is your team's goal?

....

....

....

2. Vanessa suggests brainstorming a list of topics for articles. Then you can each choose one you like. Why is this a good idea?

....

....

3. Brad tells the group he doesn't want to write any articles. He says he's doesn't write very well. What might you say?

....

....

....

4. Members of the team check in with Katie the day before the newspaper is due. She hasn't even started her article. What can your team do?

....

....

The Northeast Today

This photograph of the United States was taken at night from space. Find the Northeast region and circle it.

Since the 1900s, cities in the Northeast have continued to grow. Today, when people think of the region, they often think of big cities. They picture tall buildings, crowded sidewalks, and busy streets. The Northeast is known for its cities because it has some of the largest, oldest cities in the country.

The Growth of Cities

The three biggest cities in the Northeast are New York City, Boston, and Philadelphia. All three began as port cities in the colonies. Trade with Europe was important to the colonies. Ships brought people and goods to the colonies and took furs, wood, and other natural resources to other countries. The cities became centers of commerce. **Commerce** is the buying and selling of goods. The smaller port cities of Providence, Rhode Island, and Baltimore, Maryland, also grew from trade.

As settlers moved west, they started cities on inland waterways. Buffalo, New York, is a port city on Lake Erie. Pittsburgh, Pennsylvania, is located where three rivers meet. Boats brought people, animals, and goods to these cities, helping them grow.

The Northeast is not made up only of cities. It has rural areas as well. **Rural** areas have fewer people. In rural parts of the Northeast, there are small towns and farms. Most people live in houses with yards. They use cars or trucks to get where they want to go.

The Port of New Jersey

UNLOCK
THE BIG
?

I will know that cities in the Northeast are centers of commerce and culture.

Vocabulary

commerce   population
rural   density
urban

Urban areas are different. **Urban** areas are in or near cities. In urban areas, most people live in apartment buildings or houses with little or no land. Many people use public transportation systems to get around the city. Children play in parks and might take the bus or subway to school.

1. ◎ **Make Generalizations** **Finish** each sentence with a generalization about how people live in rural and urban areas.

In urban areas ....

In rural areas ....

Public transportation in Boston

Centers of Population and Commerce

In urban areas, people live close together. The closer together people live, the denser the population is. The number of people in an area of land is the area's **population density.** In places with a high population density, each square mile of land has many people living on it.

The population density of the Northeast varies from place to place. As the map shows, the most densely populated area is along the Atlantic coast. It is an area that includes Boston, New York City, Philadelphia, and Washington, D.C. The nation's capital has strong ties to Northeastern cities. It adds to the population density of the region.

Many people live in the Northeast because its cities are centers of activities. New York City is a center of shipping. In fact, it is the busiest port on the East Coast. Each year, imports and exports worth billions of dollars pass through the port. Imports are goods that are brought into a country for sale. Exports are goods that are sent to other countries for sale. Buffalo, New York, is also a key port. Many of the goods that travel to and from Canada go through Buffalo.

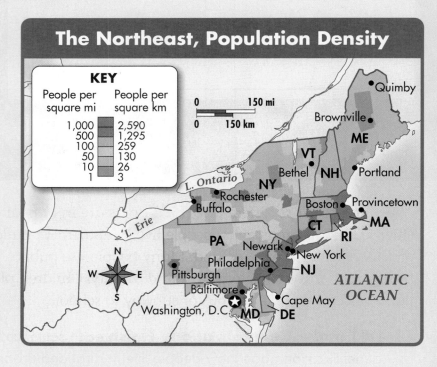

The Northeast, Population Density

KEY

People per square mi	People per square km
1,000	2,590
500	1,295
100	259
50	130
10	26
1	3

0   150 mi
0   150 km

Quimby
Brownville
ME
Bethel   NH   Portland
L. Ontario
NY
Rochester
Buffalo   Boston   Provincetown
L. Erie   CT   MA
PA   Newark   RI
Philadelphia   New York
Pittsburgh   NJ   ATLANTIC OCEAN
Baltimore
Washington, D.C. MD   Cape May
DE

2. **Circle** the area along the Atlantic coast where population density is high. Then **Draw** an X on the city in the area with the lowest population density.

Camden Yards

168

Northeastern cities are hubs for other businesses as well. Wall Street, in New York City, is home to the world's leading financial companies and banks. Many high-tech businesses, such as computer software companies, are located in urban areas of the Northeast, too. Philadelphia is a leader in medical and health research. Boston is a leader in higher education. It has many colleges and universities.

City Sights and Landmarks

Each city in the Northeast has landmarks that make it unique. In Boston, people stroll on the Boston Common, or the Common, as it is often called. The Common is the oldest public park in the nation. From the Common you can walk the Freedom Trail to tour historic sites from the American Revolution.

In Maryland, Oriole Park at Camden Yards is a favorite place to visit. This baseball stadium is located in downtown Baltimore. Nearly 50,000 people can fit in the ballpark at one time!

In New York City, visitors ride an elevator to the top of the Empire State Building. People also visit Central Park or see a show on Broadway, the city's famous theater district.

In Philadelphia, many people visit Independence Hall. It is where the Declaration of Independence and the Constitution were signed. Nearby is the famous Liberty Bell.

3. **Label** each picture with the first letter of the city in which it is found. For example, write N next to a sight in New York.

Empire State Building

Independence Hall

Changing Times, Changing Cities

The cities of the Northeast have changed over time. One of the biggest changes has been economic. Manufacturing has become less important than it once was. Service industries have become more important. Banking and healthcare are examples of service industries. High-tech industries are also growing. They are built around technologies that were unknown a century ago.

Pittsburgh is a good example of how cities in the Northeast have changed. In the early 1800s, the city produced so much iron that it was known as the Iron City. Coal mining in the region provided the fuel for the furnaces used to make iron. Iron ore was brought by boat and railroads from the Midwest.

Then Pittsburgh turned to making steel. Steel brought money and jobs to the city for about 100 years. It also brought heavy pollution. Smoke dirtied the air and darkened the skies. Some say that men working in the city had to change their white shirts once a day because of the soot that dirtied them.

This is how Pittsburgh looked in the 1800s. The smoke came from factories.

Pittsburgh today

After World War II, the demand for steel began to drop. The city passed laws to clean up the air. Pittsburgh changed once again. Today the city's steel industry is gone. Instead, it has high-tech industries, including businesses that make computer software, robots, and medical equipment. Service industries are important, too. Like all the Northeast's cities, Pittsburgh has changed with the times.

4. ◉ **Cause and Effect** **Fill in** the missing cause to show how Pittsburgh has changed.

Effects of Industry

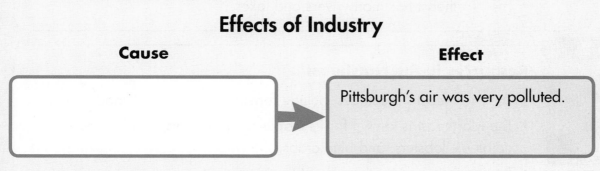

Cause

Effect

Pittsburgh's air was very polluted.

Got it?

5. ◉ **Make Generalizations** **Write** a generalization about rivers in the region.

....

....

6. ❓ One of your parents has been offered a new job working for a high-tech company. It will mean moving from your rural home to Pittsburgh. **Describe** your feelings about the move. Do you want to live in a city? Why or why not?

my Story Ideas

....

....

....

⬛ **Stop!** I need help with ....

⏸ **Wait!** I have a question about ....

▶ **Go!** Now I know ....

Lesson 1

The Land of the Northeast

- The Northeast region includes 11 states.
- The Northeast has a long Atlantic coastline. It has several mountain ranges inland.
- The Northeast has many rivers and lakes.

Lesson 2

Resources in the Northeast

- The Northeast's resources include forests, soil, minerals, and water.
- The Northeast is known for its maple syrup, apples, cranberries, potatoes, lobsters, and blue crabs.
- Tourism is important throughout the Northeast.

Lesson 3

Birthplace of the Nation

- Long ago, many Native American groups lived in the Northeast.
- People and places in the Northeast played an important part in the American Revolution and the writing of the Constitution.
- The Northeast was the birthplace of equal rights for many.

Lesson 4

Growth and Change in the Northeast

- Between 1820 and 1910, millions of immigrants came from Europe to the Northeast. They came to have a better life.
- Northeastern industries grew rapidly throughout the 1800s.
- Many immigrants lived and worked in unsafe conditions.

Lesson 5

The Northeast Today

- The largest cities in the Northeast are New York, Philadelphia, and Boston. Buffalo and Pittsburgh are also important cities.
- Trade helped the cities of the Northeast grow.
- Cities in the Northeast are centers of commerce and culture.

Review and Assessment

Lesson 1

The Land of the Northeast

1. **Match** each mountain range to its state.

   _____ Adirondack   a. New Hampshire
         Mountains

   _____ White   b. Pennsylvania
         Mountains

   _____ Green   c. New York
         Mountains

   _____ Allegheny   d. Vermont
         Mountains

2. ◉ **Make Generalizations** **Finish** the sentence. The Northeastern coast is

   ....

   ....

Lesson 2

Resources in the Northeast

3. What three products do people make from the forest resources in the Northeast?

   a. ....

   b. ....

   c. ....

4. How are some rivers used as a resource in the Northeast?

   ....

   ....

Lesson 3

Birthplace of the Nation

5. **Explain** how each place was important to the history of our nation.

   a. Plymouth, Massachusetts

   ....

   ....

   ....

   b. Lexington, Massachusetts

   ....

   ....

   c. Philadelphia, Pennsylvania

   ....

   ....

   ....

   ....

   ....

   d. Seneca Falls, New York

   ....

   ....

   ....

Lesson 4

Growth and Change in the Northeast

6. **Circle** the best answer. Most immigrants to cities in the Northeast

   A. became inventors and scientists.

   B. worked in factories and mills.

   C. moved on to the Midwest to become farmers.

   D. came to this country against their will.

7. Which industry grew rapidly as a result of the Bessemer process?

   ....

8. **Fill in** the missing effect of the fire at the Triangle Shirtwaist Factory.

Cause
Many workers died as a result of the fire.

Effect

Lesson 5

The Northeast Today

9. Manufacturing is less important than it once was in cities in the Northeast. What two industries have become more important?

   ....

   ....

10. **How does where we live affect who we are?**

    Immigrants still come to the Northeast from countries around the world. How do you think the experience of immigrant children today compares to the experience of immigrant children in the 1800s? **Write** one similarity and one difference.

Go online to write and illustrate your own **myStory Book** using the **myStory Ideas** from this chapter.

How does where we live affect who we are?

People are affected by where they live. Land, climate, and resources affect what people wear, how they play, and what jobs they do. Our surroundings also shape our values and beliefs. Think about living in a place that has a rich history. How might these surroundings affect you?

Choose a place in the Northeast that you have read about. **Suppose** you have moved there. Then **write** about how the move has affected activities you do.

....

....

....

Now **draw** a picture to illustrate your writing.

While you're online, check out the **myStory Current Events** area where you can create your own book on a topic that's in the news.

Regions: The Southeast

How does where we live affect who we are?

The country's first permanent European settlements were in the Southeast. The region's land and climate made it a good place for agriculture. **Write** how the land and climate affect the jobs people do in your region.

....

....

....

....

The Southeast has a rich history and culture. For example, if you visit the region today, you can see magnificent houses that were built many years ago.

Mobile Bay
A Busy Port With Natural Beauty

my Story Video

The Southeast has a long coastline that wraps around much of the region. It starts along the Atlantic, facing east, and runs to the Gulf of Mexico shore, facing south. The city of Mobile (moh BEEL), Alabama, is on the Gulf Coast.

Rosales and his family live in Mobile. They thought it would be fun to explore some of the most interesting places in the Mobile area. Their first stop is the USS *Alabama* museum in Battleship Memorial Park.

The USS *Alabama* is a battleship that served during World War II. "This ship is so big!" says Rosales. He has fun climbing down the ladders to different parts of the ship. He learns about how the sailors lived on board. "This is where the sailors ate," notes Rosales. He sees that there is a bumper along the edge of the counter. That was to keep plates from sliding off when the seas were rough.

At Battleship Memorial Park in Mobile, Alabama, visitors can learn about how soldiers lived on board a huge battleship.

177

The USS *Alabama* served during World War II. Today, it sits at Battleship Memorial Park, where visitors can walk on its decks.

At Weeks Bay Reserve, visitors can see all kinds of plants, trees, animals, and birds. These birds are called pelicans.

At the Weeks Bay Reserve, visitors like Rosales can look at a big map that tells more about the Weeks Bay area.

Mobile is one of the largest ports in the Southeast. It is located on the shore of Mobile Bay. Mobile Bay is an inlet on Alabama's Gulf Coast. An inlet is a narrow opening in a coastline. Several rivers flow into Mobile Bay. Small communities are found all around. The climate is subtropical. That means that winters are mild and the summers are hot and humid.

Rosales and his parents drive down the east side of Mobile Bay. They're going to the Weeks Bay National Estuarine Research Reserve. An estuary is a place where fresh water from rivers mixes with salt water from oceans. An environment like this provides a home for many kinds of plants and animals.

At Weeks Bay, baby fish, shrimp, oysters, and crabs are born and grow bigger. Rosales learns that the fishermen who work on the bay would not have much to catch if the estuary weren't there. He also learns that when he and his dad go fishing, some of the fish they catch come from this estuary.

Rosales explores the path that winds through the trees. "This is a great place to see nature," exclaims Rosales. "There are lots of birds here, too!" Weeks Bay is the perfect place to learn more about the wildlife of the Gulf Coast.

The Bellingrath Gardens and Home was once the personal home of the Bellingrath family. Now it is a place that tourists can visit.

At the Bellingrath Gardens, there is a special Asian American garden. One attraction there is its large, beautiful red bridge.

On the other side of Mobile Bay is Bellingrath Gardens and Home. It used to be a fishing camp. The Bellingrath family bought the land and turned it into a vacation spot. When they built a home for themselves, they wanted it to match the style of the other homes of the region. They reused bricks and metal from old buildings in the area. The house also had balconies and porches like the homes nearby. Rosales's favorite part of the home is the gardens.

Mrs. Bellingrath loved the natural world around the Mobile area and created beautiful gardens. Because of Mobile's mild climate, "there's almost always something blooming here," notes Rosales. He learns that the gardens will give him an idea of plants that could grow in his own garden at home.

Rosales enjoys exploring the Rose Garden and a big space called the Great Lawn. Another favorite spot is the Asian American Garden. There he finds a big red bridge he can walk across. It's called the moon bridge.

There is much more to explore, but Rosales's parents say it's time to go home. "I never knew there were so many fun places to see right here where I live," says Rosales.

Think About It If you wanted to learn more about the natural world where you live, what are some places you would visit? As you read the chapter, think about the way differences in land and climate affect the wildlife in the Southeast. Also think about the way people interact with their environment.

Land and Water of the Southeast

Rivers flow downhill. Where the land drops, river water does, too. It forms a waterfall.

Barrier islands lie between the mainland and the ocean.

Atlantic Ocean

barrier island

mainland

The Southeast region of the United States is made up of 12 states. Virginia, West Virginia, Kentucky, Tennessee, Arkansas, Louisiana, Mississippi, Alabama, Georgia, South Carolina, North Carolina, and Florida are all part of the Southeast. Something that makes the Southeast region unique is that it has two coasts.

Two Coasts

The Atlantic Ocean forms the eastern edge of the Southeast region. The Gulf of Mexico forms the southern edge. Thousands of miles of beaches line the two coastlines. In some areas, however, the coast is made up of wetlands. A **wetland** is an area sometimes covered with water. Swamps, marshes, and bogs are all kinds of wetlands.

The Southeast region has many wetlands. The coast of Louisiana has many wetlands. Another large area of wetlands is the Dismal Swamp. This swamp lies between Virginia and North Carolina.

Groups of long, narrow, islands called barrier islands lie off part of the Southeast's coast. **Barrier islands** lie between the mainland and the ocean. They began as sand dunes along the coast thousands of years ago. Then when glaciers melted, the ocean waters rose, and the dunes became islands.

1. **Fill in** the blanks with the missing landforms: Thousands of miles of sandy .... are found on the Southeast's two coasts. However, some areas of the Southeast's coasts are ...., such as the coast of Louisiana.

UNLOCK THE BIG ?

I will know that the Southeast's geography is varied, from the Appalachian Mountains to the Gulf and Atlantic coasts.

Describe what is happening to the water in the picture. Draw a line where the land drops and the water falls.

Vocabulary

wetland

barrier island

piedmont

fall line

watershed

endangered species

extinct

From the Coast to the Mountains

As you move inland from the shore, the land is flat. This is the Coastal Plain of the United States. It stretches along both the Atlantic Ocean and the Gulf of Mexico. Wetlands such as the Dismal Swamp are found on the Coastal Plain.

As the elevation rises, there are rolling hills covered with forests. This area is called the **piedmont.** *Piedmont* means "foot of the mountain." The piedmont is high land at the foot of the Appalachian Mountains.

Rivers flow down from the mountains to the ocean. There is a drop-off between the higher land of the piedmont and the lower land of the Coastal Plain. In places at the drop-off, rivers tumble down in waterfalls. The falls form a line where the piedmont meets the Coastal Plain. That drop-off line of waterfalls is called the **fall line.** Several cities of the Southeast grew along the fall line, where falling water provided power for factories.

2. **Underline** on the map the names of states in the Southeast region that do not have coastlines.

The Southeast, Political

0   100 mi
0   100 km

West Virginia
★ Charleston   Richmond ★

Frankfort ★
Kentucky   Virginia

★ Nashville   Raleigh ★
Tennessee   North
          Columbia ★   Carolina
Atlanta
Arkansas   ★   South
★   Alabama   Carolina
Little   Montgomery
Rock   ★

N
Louisiana ★ Jackson   Georgia
W   E   Mississippi   ★   ATLANTIC
S   Baton   OCEAN
     Rouge ★   ★ Tallahassee
      ● New Orleans

                    Florida
KEY   *Gulf of*
☐ Southeast region   *Mexico*
— Fall line   ● Miami
★ State capital

The Appalachians

The Appalachian Mountains run through most of the states in the Southeast. Different parts of the range have their own names. The Allegheny, Great Smoky, and Blue Ridge mountain chains are in the Southeast.

The mountains hold rich natural resources. Today, one third of the nation's coal comes from Appalachia, the land in the mountains. The area's forests have long provided wood.

Every year, thousands of hikers follow the Appalachian Trail. The trail is more than 2,000 miles long. It begins in Maine and ends in Georgia. They say it takes 5 million footsteps to walk the whole trail. Many of those steps are in the Southeast.

3. On the map, **find** the Appalachian Mountains. Then **find** the Mississippi River and **draw** a line along its path. Then do the same for the Savannah River. Which river is east of the Appalachians? What body of water does it empty into?

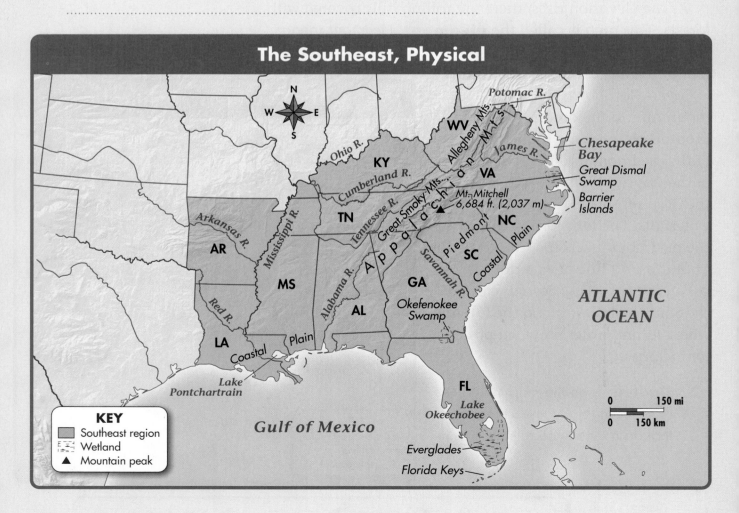

The Southeast, Physical

KEY
- Southeast region
- Wetland
- ▲ Mountain peak

Rivers of the Southeast

The largest river in the United States passes through the Southeast on its way to the Gulf of Mexico. The Mississippi is long, deep, and wide. It is a water highway through the center of the country. Ships and barges carry cargo along the river and out to the ocean.

In the high elevations there are watersheds. A **watershed** is an area where all the water drains in one direction. On the east side of the Appalachians, for example, rivers flow toward the Atlantic. On the other side of the Appalachians, the rivers flow to the west. The Tennessee River, for instance, travels west, from the Appalachians into the Ohio River. The Cumberland River does the same thing. Then the Ohio flows west into the Mississippi. By the time the Mississippi reaches the Gulf, it carries the water of many rivers along its route.

Kentucky Bluegrass

In northern Kentucky, there is a very beautiful area called the Bluegrass region. The region is known for its rich soil. Pastures of bluegrass (which is not actually blue) cover much of the land. Livestock and racing horses are bred there. It is home to Kentucky's biggest cities, like Louisville. It is also home to the state capital, Frankfort.

4. In the text, **underline** the names of two rivers that flow west into the Ohio River.

The Mississippi is one of the busiest rivers in the world.

The Bluegrass region of Kentucky is famous for its horse farms.

Animals and Birds of the Southeast

When you see an alligator, you may think you are in danger. But not long ago, alligators were in danger. In the late 1960s, alligators were an endangered species. An **endangered species** is a kind of plant or animal that is in danger of disappearing.

Back then, people were killing too many alligators for food or for their hides. Alligator hunting is now carefully controlled. Today, there are more than 1 million American alligators. Almost all of them live in the Southeast. Many live in wetlands, rivers, and canals in Florida and Louisiana.

The Southeast is home to many different kinds of birds. Some are endangered. The red-cockaded woodpecker is one. These birds depend on certain kinds of very old pine trees that grew in the Southeast. They make their nests and find their food in trees more than 80 years old. More and more of those trees have been cut down. So the woodpeckers are in danger of becoming **extinct**, or disappearing.

Red-cockaded woodpeckers eat insects that live in old pine trees.

5. ◎ **Compare and Contrast** **Write** a sentence comparing the wildlife of two of the regions in the picture.

....

....

The Southeast is home to many different kinds of plants and animals.

Landforms of the Southeast

bald cypress

Spanish moss

mountains

piedmont

coastal plain

armadillo

alligator

wetlands

manatee

184

Trees, Plants, and Flowers

About 250 different kinds of trees grow in the Southeast. They are a valuable resource. In fact, some farmers grow trees as a crop. Wood from the region's trees is used to make furniture and build houses. Some wood is ground up and used to make paper.

Some trees, plants, and flowers grow especially well in the Southeast. The warm and humid climate is good for Spanish moss, for example. Trees hanging with moss are sometimes a symbol of the region.

Camellias come from warm Asian climates. They grow well in the Southeast. The camellia is Alabama's state flower.

6. ◉ **Fact and Opinion Underline** a fact about the camellia in the photo caption.

Got it?

7. ◉ **Summarize** Summarize the Southeast's major physical features.

....

....

....

8. ? You have been hired to create an advertisement for the Southeast. Your goal is to attract new business. Show why the region's land would be a good place for a business.

my Story Ideas

....

....

....

⬛ **Stop!** I need help with ....

⏸ **Wait!** I have a question about ....

▶ **Go!** Now I know ....

Map Skills

Use a Road Map and Scale

It's fun to explore new places. On a driving trip, a road map is the perfect tool to help you find your way. You can find a road map in an atlas, online, or on a Global Positioning System (GPS). A road map shows highways and other roads, as well as the location of important places. Road maps also show distance.

Suppose your family is visiting Georgia. The road map below could help you on your trip. You start out at Stone Mountain Park. You want to drive to Grant Park. Which road do you take? Find Stone Mountain Park on the map. You decide to take Highway 78 to a larger road, Interstate 285. Then you go south to Interstate 20. Then you take it west to Grant Park.

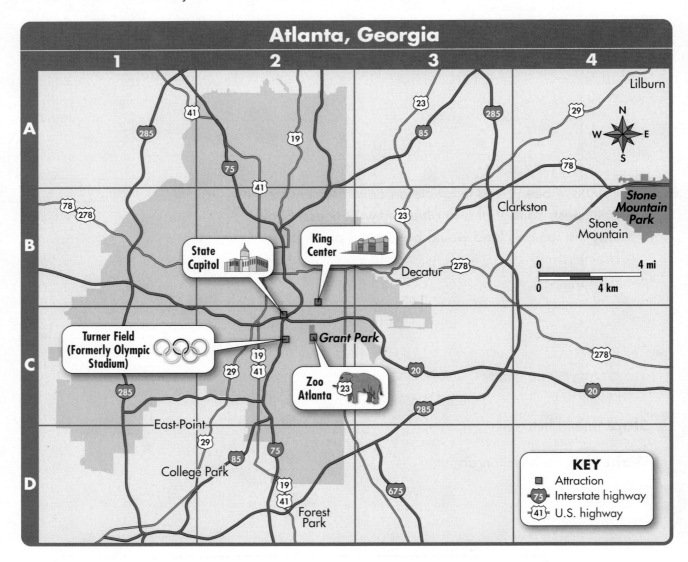

Atlanta, Georgia

To find out distance on a map, you need to use the map scale. On this map, 1 inch on the map equals 4 miles on land. Use a ruler or a piece of paper to measure the distance of your trip from Stone Mountain Park to Interstate 285. You will discover that it is about 21 miles.

Many road maps have grids. A grid is a pattern of squares labeled with numbers and letters. A map index will tell you the number and letter of the square where you can locate a place on the map.

Try it!

In Atlanta, you want to visit many different places. Use the map, the scale, and the grid to answer these questions.

1. **Find** the State Capitol on the map. **Circle** it.

2. You'd like to visit the King Center next. This is a memorial to Dr. Martin Luther King Jr. **Mark** the King Center on the map.

3. **Draw** the route described on p. 186 that your family will take to drive from Stone Mountain Park to Grant Park.

4. Use the map scale to figure out how many miles it is between Turner Field and the King Center. **Write** your answer below.

   ....

5. What grid square is Grant Park located in?

   ....

6. **Apply** Now draw a map of your desk on a separate piece of paper. Use a ruler to measure the length and width of your desk in inches. Create a scale for your map where one inch on your map equals four inches of your desk. Now place two objects on your desk. Measure the objects with your ruler. Then draw them on your map to scale.

Climate of the Southeast

Envision It!

Cameras in space take photographs that show the size of huge storms. This is a photo of a huge storm from 2005.

The Southeast's mild climate makes it a great place to spend time outdoors.

"Heading south" is something many Americans like to do in the winter. A cold January day in Chicago is likely a warm January day in Miami. The Southeast's climate is not all the same, however. It changes from the coast to the mountains. It changes from north to south. And it changes from season to season.

Climate of the Southeast

The climate of the Southeast is mild. In most of the Southeast, average January temperatures are above freezing. A warm climate means a long growing season. A **growing season** is the part of the year when temperatures are warm enough for plants to grow. In some parts of the Southeast, the growing season can be as long as 300 days a year.

1. ◎ **Draw Conclusions** **Circle** the lowest average temperature on the chart. How much colder is it than the average January temperature in Miami?

....

Average January and July Temperatures

	January	July
Charleston, WV	33.5°F	74°F
Little Rock, AR	40°F	82°F
Miami, FL	68°F	83.7°F

Find the bright red center of the storm. Use the scale to measure the size of the storm's center and write it above.

UNLOCK THE BIG ?

I will know that the Southeast's location gives the region a warm climate and varied weather.

Vocabulary

growing season	storm surge
key	levee
hurricane	evacuation

Living in a Mild Climate

Across the Southeast, people can enjoy the outdoors for much of the year. People spend time hunting, fishing, hiking, and playing on sandy beaches.

With its miles of coastline, the Southeast is a perfect place for water sports. Cape Hatteras (HAT ur uhs), North Carolina, was the nation's first national seashore. Visitors swim, camp, and explore about 30,000 acres there. At Virginia Beach, Virginia, surfers compete in surfing competitions every year.

Key West is another favorite. A **key** is a low island. Key West is one of a string of keys off Florida's southern coast. More than 1 million people visit it every year. They come to dive in the warm waters there, eat fish, and find shells.

Climate affects how people build their homes, too. In Florida many houses have a screened porch called a Florida room. You can be inside and outside at the same time. Sometimes it is too hot to be outdoors, however. People turn on the air conditioning to solve that problem.

2. **Underline** your favorite outdoor activity in the text. Then on a separate sheet of paper, draw a picture of yourself doing your activity.

There is a big fishing industry in the Gulf of Mexico, but people also fish for fun.

Hurricanes create the huge waves of a storm surge. Storm surges can cause damage along the coast.

Hurricanes

Sometimes the Southeast's weather can be dangerous. Hurricanes strike the Southeast more than any other region. A **hurricane** is a powerful storm. Hurricanes form in warm areas such as the waters off the Southeast. Warm air rises from the ocean and hits cooler air above. The temperature difference can create strong winds.

Hurricanes begin as tropical storms. The National Weather Service gives each storm a name. When the winds reach 74 miles per hour, the storm becomes a hurricane. About six storms become hurricanes each year. In 2005, there was one particular hurricane that was very severe. It was called Hurricane Katrina.

A hurricane's winds move in a circle. At its center is the eye of the storm. The strong winds can cause a **storm surge.** This is when the ocean's level rises as the water is pushed toward shore. Hurricanes also bring heavy rain and huge waves. The rain, waves, and storm surge often cause flooding.

3. Hurricane centers track the power and path of each hurricane. On this map, **mark** the place where Katrina hit land as a Category 4 storm.

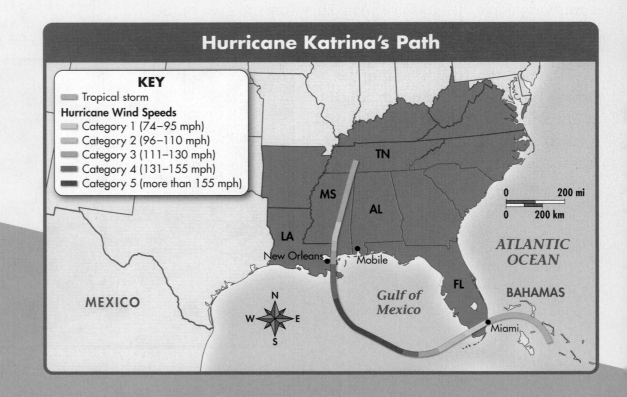

Hurricane Katrina's Path

KEY
- Tropical storm
- **Hurricane Wind Speeds**
  - Category 1 (74–95 mph)
  - Category 2 (96–110 mph)
  - Category 3 (111–130 mph)
  - Category 4 (131–155 mph)
  - Category 5 (more than 155 mph)

TN

MS

AL

LA

New Orleans

Mobile

FL

ATLANTIC OCEAN

BAHAMAS

MEXICO

Gulf of Mexico

Miami

N W E S

0 200 mi
0 200 km

Effects of Hurricanes

The hurricane season lasts from June to the end of November. During this period, hurricanes form in the Atlantic and the Gulf of Mexico. Some are small. Some move in a direction away from the land. Others lose their strength before they hit the land. But some hurricanes cause severe damage when they hit the Southeast.

Every few years a major hurricane strikes the region. Hurricane Andrew hit Florida hard in 1992. It caused more than $26 billion in damages. In 2005, Hurricane Katrina became the costliest natural disaster in American history. When it hit land in Mississippi, the storm surge was more than 26 feet high. In New Orleans, the storm caused terrible flooding. More than 1 million people had to leave the city and surrounding area. Overall, more than 1,800 people died as a result of Katrina. It was a terrible storm.

After Katrina, people across the nation wanted to help. More than 1 million people volunteered to rebuild Louisiana and Mississippi. People came to build houses. Others provided medical care. Many helped by giving money or serving food.

4. ◉ **Cause and Effect Fill in** this graphic organizer with one effect of Hurricane Katrina.

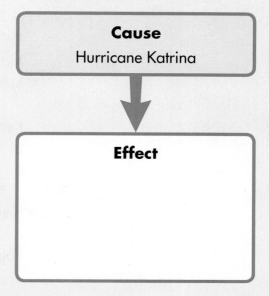

Cause

Hurricane Katrina

Effect

Volunteers gave millions of hours of service after Hurricane Katrina.

Handling Floods

Hurricanes are not the only time when water is a danger. The Mississippi River travels through five states in the Southeast. Sometimes the river floods. When the nation's largest river floods, there can be big problems.

Along the Mississippi River, people have built levees. A **levee** is a dirt or concrete wall. It keeps water from overflowing the riverbanks. When the water gets too high, however, it can overflow or break through a levee.

What causes the high water? Often, heavy rains swell the river. The flood of 1927 was one of the worst floods in the nation's history. Heavy rains began in late 1926. By January 1927, the Mississippi River flooded 27,000 square miles. That May, the river water spread across 70 miles of land near Memphis, Tennessee.

In May 2010, there were terrible floods in Tennessee, Kentucky, and Mississippi. More than 13 inches of rain fell in just two days. The Cumberland River flooded and water spread out over Nashville, Tennessee, causing damage.

Many people take action when a river floods. The National Weather Service alerts people living near the river when it rises. National, state, and local workers and volunteers pile bags of sand to raise the levees. When towns are flooded, groups like the American Red Cross help, too.

5. ◉ **Fact and Opinion** **Read** the statements. **Underline** the opinion.

I think floods are worse than hurricanes.

The flood of 1927 was one of the worst floods in American history.

Being Prepared

Most of the time, people in the Southeast enjoy good weather. When the weather turns bad there, people are prepared.

Today, people can get weather news quickly and easily. Televisions, computers, and even cell phones can give weather alerts. When there is danger, officials may call for **evacuation** of an area. This means that people are moved to safety.

In coastal areas, people need protection from hurricanes. They need houses that can stand up to strong winds or high waves. In Florida and the Carolinas, new houses have special roofs and windows. Whatever the weather, the people of the Southeast are ready.

Houses near beaches have special designs. They may be built high up to avoid damage from a storm surge.

Got it?

6. ◉ **Make Generalizations Write** a general statement about the weather in the Southeast region and how it changes.

....

....

....

7. ❓ You have a new job in the Southeast. You are working at the nation's main weather channel. **Write** a short weather report on a day when a hurricane is forming in the Atlantic.

my Story Ideas

....

....

....

⬜ **Stop!** I need help with ....

⏸ **Wait!** I have a question about ....

▶ **Go!** Now I know ....

Lesson 3

A Land of Many Resources

Envision It!

Peanuts grow in the ground, not on trees. They are a major crop of the Southeast region.

Take a ride around New Iberia, Louisiana. You'll get a picture of the Southeast's many different resources. At nearby Avery Island, you'll see fields of hot red peppers. You can visit a factory where hot sauce is made. Then you can drive down to the nearby Gulf of Mexico. Along the way, you can talk to some people who catch fish for a living and watch workers leave for their jobs on oil rigs in the Gulf. Just like the whole Southeast, New Iberia is rich in resources.

Using the Land and Water

The Southeast's land and water offer valuable resources. These resources vary across the region. On the Coastal Plain, there are wide stretches of good farmland. Trees cover half of most of the states in the Southeast. Coal is mined in the mountains. Oil and natural gas come from the Gulf Coast area. In the Atlantic and the Gulf of Mexico, fishing boats bring up the resources of the sea.

Resources offer more than food and products. They create jobs. The people of the Southeast earn money at these jobs.

1. **Main Idea and Details**
   Underline in the text three resources of the Southeast.

The waters off the Southeast's two coasts hold many fish. The fishing industry is important in the Southeast.

Scientist George Washington Carver found hundreds of uses for peanuts. How many can you think of? Draw one here.

Vocabulary

timber   fossil fuel
pulp   hydroelectric
agribusiness   power
livestock   heritage

Forest Resources

Much of the land of the Southeast is forested, or covered with trees. In most Southeastern states, at least half the land is forested. Forests provide timber. **Timber** is trees that are grown and cut for wood. Much of the Southeast's timber comes from the region's many tree farms.

The forest industry plants millions of acres of trees. Most are pine trees. They grow quickly and well in the region's sandy soil. The forest industry brings thousands of jobs and billions of dollars to the region.

The region's timber is raw material. It is used for making many different products. At mills, trees are turned into lumber used for building homes. Wood is also crushed by machines into pulp. **Pulp** is a mix of ground-up wood chips, water, and chemicals. The pulp is used for products from paper to cardboard to diapers.

The Southeast's trees are important to the environment, too. They give off oxygen and help cool Earth. They provide homes for birds and other animals.

2. **Fact and Opinion** Trees are an important resource. **Write** a fact about what trees are used for.

....

....

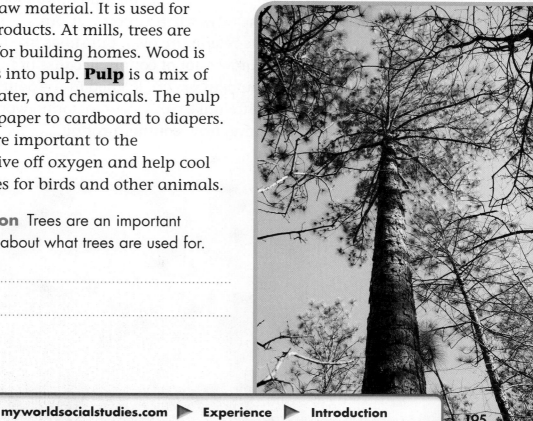

The loblolly pine is a tree that grows all across the Southeast region.

A Great Region for Farming

The Coastal Plain of the Southeast has all the conditions for good farming. The land is flat, temperatures are warm, and there is plenty of rain. In the long growing season, farmers can grow many different crops. Many of these crops, such as cotton and sugar cane, do not grow well in colder regions.

There are many family farms in the Southeast. The region is also a good place for agribusiness. **Agribusiness** is farming as an industry. Some companies own huge farms. They ship agricultural products around the country and the world. Florida produces about 8 million tons of citrus fruit each year, for example. Citrus fruits include oranges, lemons, and grapefruit. That's a lot more fruit and juice than the people of Florida can eat and drink. Companies ship most of it out of the state.

Growing Food

Southeastern states are the leading producers of some crops. Georgia raises more peanuts and pecans than any other state. Arkansas and Louisiana are leading growers of rice. In fact, almost half of all the rice grown in the United States comes from Arkansas.

Other main crops include fruits such as strawberries, corn for grain, and soybeans. Soybeans are used to make food for livestock, vegetable oil, and other foods.

The days when cotton was practically the only crop grown in the region are over. But states like Georgia and Alabama still grow a lot of cotton. Because of this, some textile manufacturers are located in the Southeast. A textile is cloth used to make clothes. In factories, workers produce cloth and clothing from southern cotton.

3. ◉ **Cause and Effect Find** two cause-and-effect relationships in the text. **Circle** the cause. **Underline** the effect. Then **draw** an arrow from the cause to the effect.

Georgia produces more than 130 million pounds of peaches every year.

Raising Animals

The land and climate of the Southeast also make it a good place to raise animals. In Virginia, for example, more than two thirds of the money made from agriculture comes from livestock. **Livestock** are animals raised for sale. Georgia, Arkansas, and Alabama are the nation's leading producers of broilers, or young chickens. North Carolina is a major producer of hogs and turkeys. Beef cattle also are important in several Southeastern states.

Kentucky claims to have more Thoroughbred horse farms than anywhere in the world. Thoroughbreds are the horses used in racing. Kentucky even has an official state horse. As you might guess, it's the Thoroughbred.

These cattle in Virginia are raised for beef.

4. **Find** the states that grow peaches and **circle** them.

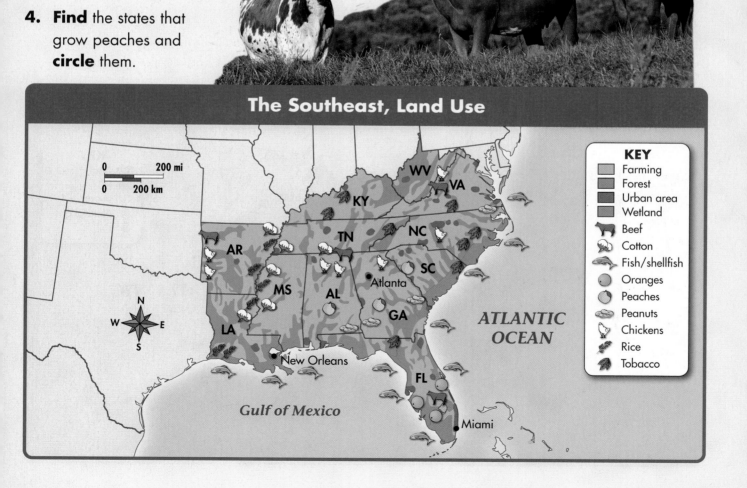

The Southeast, Land Use

0   200 mi
0   200 km

WV
VA
KY
TN
NC
AR
SC
Atlanta
MS
AL
GA
LA
ATLANTIC OCEAN
New Orleans
FL
Gulf of Mexico
Miami

N
W   E
S

KEY
Farming
Forest
Urban area
Wetland
Beef
Cotton
Fish/shellfish
Oranges
Peaches
Peanuts
Chickens
Rice
Tobacco

Building dams is a way that people change their environment to meet their needs. Hydroelectric power plants can be found inside dams like this one.

Energy Resources

Coal is one of the most important energy resources in the United States. Electricity comes from a power plant, and almost half of our power plants get their energy from coal. In the Southeast, coal is mined in Appalachia.

In the Southeast, coal, oil, and natural gas are found both underground and underwater. Each is a **fossil fuel**, formed in the earth from the remains of plants or animals. Fossil fuels are millions of years old. They are a nonrenewable resource.

Another source of energy is falling water. Power plants capture the energy of falling water and turn it into electricity. Electricity that is created by the force of falling water is called **hydroelectric power.**

5. ◉ **Compare and Contrast Pick** two states in the region. Compare and contrast their energy resources.

....

....

....

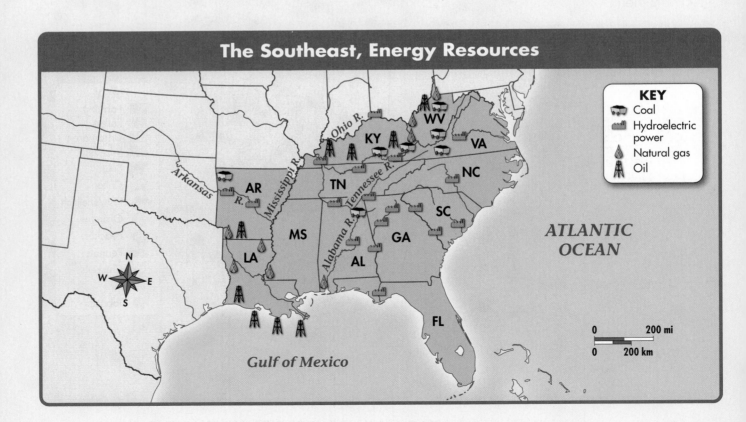

The Southeast, Energy Resources

KEY
Coal
Hydroelectric power
Natural gas
Oil

Tourism and the Land

The land of the Southeast is a resource in another way, too. Its beauty brings tourists to the region. There are national parks in many southeastern states. Some are so special that they are World Heritage Sites. This means that they are preserved as part of the cultural heritage of everyone in the world. Your **heritage** is the beliefs and customs passed down from one generation to another. There are 21 World Heritage Sites in the United States. Four are in the Southeast.

Great Smoky Mountains National Park is in North Carolina and Tennessee. It is a World Heritage Site.

Got it?

6. **◉ Summarize** Choose one resource in the Southeast. Summarize its importance to the region.

....
....
....
....
....

7. **?** You are going to start a business in the Southeast, using one of the region's resources. **Describe** your business. What resources will it use?

my Story Ideas

....
....

■ **Stop!** I need help with ....

❚❚ **Wait!** I have a question about ....

▶ **Go!** Now I know ....

Settling the Southeast

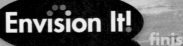

finish

start

Crossing the Appalachian Mountains was difficult. Travelers had to find a path if they wanted to go west.

In the town of Cherokee, North Carolina, you can hear people speaking the Cherokee language, and you can hear storytellers pass on Cherokee traditions. Long before people came from Europe and Africa, this was Cherokee land.

Native Americans of the Southeast

For thousands of years, Native Americans have lived in the Southeast. Even before Europeans came, the Southeast had a large population. Many different groups lived in the region. For example, the Cherokee lived in southern Appalachia. The Powhatan were on the coast of Virginia. These and other groups developed different cultures.

Like others in the region, the Cherokee lived in villages. Their lives were shaped by their environment. They built houses from wood and clay. For food, they hunted, fished, and farmed. They made clothing from the skins of animals they hunted.

Explorers and Settlers

In the early 1500s, the Native Americans' world changed. That's when Europeans began to explore North America. Many of the first explorations began in the Southeast. Juan Ponce de León and Hernando de Soto landed first in Florida. In 1513, Ponce de León claimed Florida for Spain. In the 1560s, Spanish and French explorers settled along the Atlantic coast.

Modern Cherokee people keep their culture alive. This Cherokee woman is weaving a basket.

UNLOCK
THE BIG
?

I will know that the Southeast has a history of crisis and rebuilding.

Vocabulary

indentured servant

plantation

pioneer

emancipation

On the picture, draw the easiest route from start to finish. Then write about what you see along your journey.

About 20 years later, the English settled off the coast of what is now North Carolina. Then, in 1682, French explorer Robert de La Salle arrived. He sailed down the Mississippi River. He claimed the entire Mississippi valley for France. In 1718, the French settled New Orleans.

The Europeans met the Native Americans who lived there. Sometimes the meetings were peaceful. Other times there was conflict. The Native Americans were threatened by these newcomers. The Europeans had guns and steel armor, unlike the Native Americans.

The early explorers mostly passed through the region. Some were interested in settling down. Others kept moving. They left behind something deadly, however: germs. European diseases would kill thousands of native people.

1. ◉ **Sequence Write** these settlements in order of earliest to most recent: *New Orleans, Jamestown, St. Augustine.*

....

....

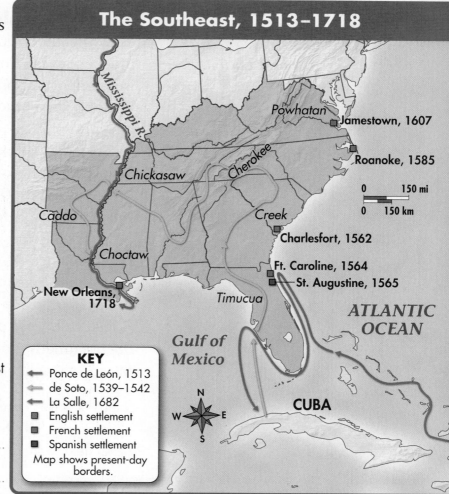

The Southeast, 1513–1718

Mississippi R.

Powhatan
Jamestown, 1607

Roanoke, 1585

Chickasaw

Cherokee

0   150 mi
0   150 km

Caddo

Creek

Charlesfort, 1562

Choctaw

Ft. Caroline, 1564
St. Augustine, 1565

New Orleans, 1718

Timucua

ATLANTIC OCEAN

Gulf of Mexico

N
W   E
S

CUBA

KEY
← Ponce de León, 1513
← de Soto, 1539–1542
← La Salle, 1682
■ English settlement
■ French settlement
■ Spanish settlement
Map shows present-day borders.

The English Colonies

In 1607, a group of 104 English men and boys set up a colony in what is now Virginia. They called it Jamestown, after the English king. The early days of the colony were hard. The Powhatan, a group of Native Americans, helped the colonists. They traded food with the colonists. Jamestown became the first successful English colony in North America.

By the early 1700s, the English had 13 colonies along the Atlantic. Four of them were in the Southeast: Virginia, North Carolina, South Carolina, and Georgia.

The colonies grew as Europeans made new lives in America. Many came as indentured servants. An **indentured servant** signed an agreement in which he or she promised to work for free for a period of time. Others came to America against their will. Many enslaved Africans worked on large farms called **plantations.** They helped build the colonial economy and culture from the beginning.

Three Virginians

By the late 1700s, the colonies were on the road to independence. Women and men from the Southeast were important on that journey. Three men from Virginia were among the leaders in the creation of a new nation.

George Washington led the colonial army in the Revolutionary War. He became the first president of the United States in 1789. As the "Father of His Country," he was an example for later presidents.

Thomas Jefferson wrote the Declaration of Independence. As the third president, he doubled the size of the United States with the Louisiana Purchase.

James Madison is called the Father of the Constitution. He played an important role in creating the document that still guides our nation today. Madison was the nation's fourth president.

The power under the Constitution will always be in the people. ☐

. . . honesty is always the best policy. ☐

2. ◉ **Fact and Opinion** George Washington had a lot to say. **Write** *F* next to the statement that is a fact and *O* next to the statement that is an opinion.

Pioneers Head West

Even before American independence, settlers pushed west. They wanted to find more land. Daniel Boone was an early pioneer. A **pioneer** settles a place, leading the way for others. In 1775, Boone led a group into Kentucky. They went through the Cumberland Gap. This was a gap, or pass, in the Appalachians. They built the Wilderness Road. It became a main route for settlers moving west.

Many settlers moved west to find better land for growing cotton. These were the days when cotton was "king." Plantation owners planted more and more of the crop. To run the plantations, they depended on a growing number of enslaved Africans.

As people moved west, new states were formed. Kentucky and Tennessee became states in the late 1790s. Alabama, Mississippi, and Louisiana joined the Union in the 1810s. By 1845, Arkansas and Florida were states, too.

Conflict with Native Americans increased in these years. Settlers wanted to farm Cherokee land, but the Cherokee did not want to move. The Cherokee fought in the courts but did not win. Then the United States ordered the Native Americans to give up their land. Some Cherokee escaped, but most were forced to move. They went to a territory that is today part of Oklahoma. Their journey was so terrible that it is called the Trail of Tears.

3. ◉ **Cause and Effect** What caused new states to form? **Underline** a reason in the text.

Daniel Boone led others to new settlements. His wife, Rebecca, and his daughter, Susannah, later joined him.

Historians believe that as many as 15,000 Native Americans died during the Trail of Tears.

203

Slavery and the Civil War

On February 4, 1861, men from six Southeast states were meeting in Montgomery, Alabama. They represented South Carolina, Mississippi, Florida, Alabama, Georgia, and Louisiana. They created the government of a new country. They called it the Confederate States of America or the Confederacy.

The six states had already seceded from the United States. In a few months they were joined by Texas, Virginia, Arkansas, North Carolina, and Tennessee. These 11 states were the Confederacy. Only Kentucky and West Virginia among the Southeastern states remained in the Union.

The Civil War between North and South lasted from 1861 to 1865. Conflicts over slavery were the main cause of the war. About 3.5 million enslaved Africans lived in Confederate states. In 1863, President Abraham Lincoln issued the Emancipation Proclamation. **Emancipation** means freeing someone from slavery. It freed all enslaved people in the Confederacy. Many learned they were free only after the Civil War had ended.

The Confederacy lost the war. Much of the Southeast lay in ruins. Almost 500,000 men died or were wounded. Buildings and homes were destroyed. The slave-based economy was also destroyed. The Southeast had to rebuild.

4. **Main Idea and Details** Which states from the Southeast region did not join the Confederacy?

After the Civil War ended, the city of Richmond, Virginia, lay in ruins. Today, 150 years later, it is a thriving city.

The Southeast After Slavery

After the war, the nation had to be joined together again. To rejoin the United States, each Confederate state promised African Americans their civil rights.

Without slavery, people had to learn new ways of living and working together. For almost 100 years, segregation separated African Americans and whites in the Southeast. This changed in the civil rights movement of the 1950s and 1960s. Some people called the civil rights movement "the second Reconstruction."

Many of the leaders of the civil rights movement were from the Southeast. Rosa Parks was born in Tuskegee, Alabama. Dr. Martin Luther King Jr. was born in Atlanta. Today you can visit the King Center there. It is a memorial to Dr. King and the entire civil rights movement.

John Lewis is from Troy, Alabama. Inspired by Martin Luther King Jr., he became a civil rights leader. Today he is a U.S. Congressman from Georgia.

Got it?

5. ◎ **Make Generalizations** Tell how one of the following signficant people influenced the lives of other people in the Southeast: Robert de La Salle, Daniel Boone, Abraham Lincoln.

....

....

....

....

6. ❓ You are going ot take a historical tour of one of the early European settlements in the Southeast. Which one would you choose? Why?   **my Story Ideas**

....

....

....

◻ **Stop!** I need help with ....

❚❚ **Wait!** I have a question about ....

▶ **Go!** Now I know ....

Southern Life

Envision It!

The banjo is a musical instrument that is played like a guitar. It is part of the culture of the Southeast region.

It's May and you are visiting Memphis, Tennessee. You are there for the city's big celebration called Memphis in May. At the Beale Street Music Festival, you hear the best in rock and blues music. Later, you wander over to the World Championship Barbecue Cooking Contest. In one day, you've gotten a wonderful taste of Southeast culture.

The Culture of the Southeast

As in every region, the Southeast has a special culture. We use the word *culture* to talk about things like music, painting, dance, literature, and cooking. Whether you are listening to a banjo player or eating barbecue, you are sharing part of the culture of the Southeast.

The Southeast is famous for its barbecue cooking.

The culture of the Southeast is a rich mix of many traditions. Most people in the region come from English or African American backgrounds. Others have different cultural roots. For example, the Cajuns of Louisiana have French backgrounds. On the Gulf Coast, you may enjoy a Vietnamese meal. In South Carolina, you can hear the Gullah language. The **Gullah** are African Americans in the Southeast who have kept much of their African heritage. All of these are part of Southeastern culture.

UNLOCK
THE BIG
? I will know that the Southeast is home to cultural traditions that have influenced the nation and the world.

Write about how music is part of your own life today.

Vocabulary

Gullah	craft
jazz	port

Music in the Southeast

Many of America's favorite kinds of music have their roots in the Southeast. Rock, blues, gospel, bluegrass, country, and ragtime all began or grew in the region.

One unique kind of music that began in the Southeast is jazz. **Jazz** music was mostly created by African American musicians. The music they played in New Orleans in the early 1900s soon spread to other cities.

Rock and roll music was also born in the Southeast. In the 1950s, both African American and white musicians developed this new form of music. Memphis and Nashville, Tennessee, were centers of rock and roll.

The gospel songs of southern black churches inspired others. Singers like Aretha Franklin made gospel singing popular. Beginning in the 1920s, radio programs broadcast gospel and other music across the nation. Today, the Internet brings it to the world.

Music in the Southeast has changed over time. For example, electronic instruments like keyboards might be heard in jazz bands today.

Louis Armstrong was a jazz trumpeter who was from New Orleans. He helped make jazz popular for millions of people in America and around the world.

1. ⊙ **Fact and Opinion Write** an opinion about jazz, rock and roll, or gospel music.

Cultural Traditions

Writers tell the stories of each region. They help us understand the past and how it shaped the present. Diaries like *Mary Chestnut's Civil War* report one person's view. William Faulkner wrote fiction about life in Mississippi. In her novels, Zora Neale Hurston records the African American experience. Like its music, the region's literature is popular with people all over the world.

The Southeast has a long tradition of crafts. A **craft** is an object made by hand. In Appalachia, for example, people make musical instruments such as banjos. The quilters of Gee's Bend live in Alabama. Their quilts are in museums today.

Sports are an important part of life in the Southeast. One of the most popular is NASCAR racing. NASCAR is the National Association for Stock Car Auto Racing. Millions of fans watch the races. Most of the racing teams are based in North Carolina.

2. The quilters of Gee's Bend sew pieces of cloth together to create their designs. **Draw** a quilt design of your own.

At medical centers like this one at the University of Florida, scientists research new cures for diseases.

The New South

The Southeast has changed a lot in the 150 years since the Civil War. A century ago, most people in the region lived in rural areas. Today, most live in cities. Georgia is a good example: In 1900, more than eight out of every ten people in Georgia lived in the country. Today, about eight out every ten live in cities, and the cities of the Southeast are still growing.

The Southeast moved away from an economy based on agriculture. In Birmingham, Alabama, industry grew quickly. Crowded with steel mills, it was called the Pittsburgh of the South. Like most other southeastern cities, however, Birmingham is no longer an industrial center. Most people in Birmingham work in service industries today. The city is a leader in medical research and banking.

One area of North Carolina called the Research Triangle is also growing quickly. The cities of Raleigh, Durham, and Chapel Hill are there. This area is a center for research in medicine, computers, business, and education.

In Arkansas, too, service industries lead the economy. Especially important are businesses that sell things. Arkansans sell everything from automobiles to groceries.

Some of the world's biggest service providers are in the Southeast. The headquarters of many communications, technology, and Internet companies are in northern Virginia. UPS, one of the world's top package delivery services, is based in Georgia. The Southeast is a busy place.

3. ◎ **Main Idea and Details Write** a sentence that tells one way the economy of the Southeast has changed.

....
....
....
....
....
....

Fast-Growing Cities

Many cities in the Southeast lead the country in population growth. Of the 100 fastest-growing United States cities, 16 are in the Southeast. Two cities in North Carolina, Charlotte and Raleigh, are among the top 10.

New Orleans, Louisiana, is known for its food and its music. Founded in the early 1700s, the city is a busy port on the Mississippi River. A **port** is a place where people or goods can enter or leave a country. Large ships move products up and down the Mississippi between the Southeast and the Midwest. Thousands of ocean-going ships connect New Orleans and the world. In 2005, Hurricane Katrina caused a lot of damage to the city. The people of New Orleans survived many challenges as they rebuilt their city. The rebuilding of New Orleans continues today.

Charleston, South Carolina, is one of the Southeast's oldest cities. It was founded in 1670 by English settlers. It is a mix of old and new. Many tourists come to see the colonial buildings and beautiful gardens. Near Charleston's harbor is the South Carolina Aquarium. There you can see plants and animals from all areas of the state. Also at the harbor is the Fort Sumter National Monument. It marks the place where the first shots of the Civil War were fired. Like the rest of Charleston, it is a good place to see how the Southeast has changed.

Atlanta

Atlanta, Georgia, is one of the leading cities of the Southeast. The capital of Georgia, Atlanta began as a railroad center in the 1830s. Today, Atlanta is still a center of transportation. In fact, it has the world's busiest airport.

Atlanta is growing quickly. Shiny new buildings are going up, and new businesses are moving in. The city is a center of communications and finance. Atlanta is one of the cultural capitals of the Southeast.

The 1996 Summer Olympics were held in Atlanta. This park with fountains was built for visitors.

4. Draw a picture postcard that shows your favorite thing about the Southeast region.

5. ⊙ **Fact and Opinion Write** a fact about southern life. Then **write** an opinion on the same subject.

....

....

....

....

6. ❓ You have a chance to learn more about quilting, jazz trumpet, or barbecue cooking. What would you pick and why?

my Story Ideas

....

....

....

⬛ **Stop!** I need help with ....

⏸ **Wait!** I have a question about ....

▶ **Go!** Now I know ....

Lesson 1

Land and Water of the Southeast

- The Southeast is shaped by two coastlines as well as by rivers.
- The Coastal Plain, the piedmont, and the Appalachian Mountains are the landforms of the region.
- The varied land supports many kinds of animals and plants.

Lesson 2

Climate of the Southeast

- The Southeast's climate is mild, which allows many people to enjoy outdoor activities there.
- Hurricanes can strike the region and cause major damage.
- Floods on rivers also create challenges for Southeast communities.

Lesson 3

A Land of Many Resources

- The Southeast has many different resources.
- Raising food and animals, as well as using forest and energy resources, are important parts of the region's economy.
- The land of the Southeast is a resource for tourism.

Lesson 4

Settling the Southeast

- In the 1500s, European explorers encountered Native Americans.
- English colonists built lasting colonies in the region.
- Colonists moved west and caused conflict with Native Americans.
- The Civil War damaged the region, but eventually it was rebuilt.

Lesson 5

Southern Life

- Artists contribute to the region's culture, which is a rich mix of traditions.
- Changes in the region since the Civil War include less dependence on agriculture and the growth of service industries.
- The Southeast is home to fast-growing cities.

Review and Assessment

Lesson 1

Land and Water of the Southeast

1. **Write** the letter of these features on the map.

A. Atlantic Ocean   C. Coastal Plain

B. Gulf of Mexico   D. Appalachian Mts.

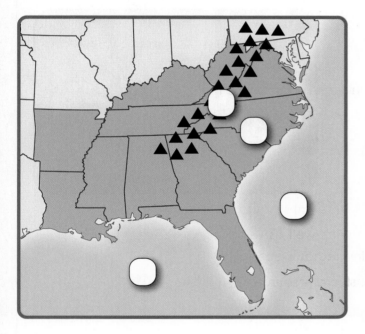

Lesson 2

Climate of the Southeast

2. **Define** these terms.

evacuation

....

levee

....

....

Lesson 3

A Land of Many Resources

3. **Match** the words and phrases.

_____ timber

_____ agribusiness

_____ livestock

_____ hydroelectric power

a. electricity created by falling water

b. animals raised for sale

c. farming as an industry

d. trees grown for wood

4. Why are World Heritage Sites special?

....

....

....

....

5. **Look** again at the map used for question 1. Then **read** the list of resources below. **Write** the number of each resource near an area where you could find it.

1. fish and shellfish

2. coal

3. Thoroughbred horses

4. peaches

5. oil

Lesson 4

Settling the Southeast

6. **Match** the person with his description.

_____ George Washington

_____ Daniel Boone

_____ Robert La Salle

_____ John Lewis

a. Civil rights leader and Congressman

b. Led pioneers west

c. Explored the Mississippi

d. Father of His Country

7. **List** these events in sequence: *Reconstruction, Civil War, secession*

....

....

Lesson 5

Southern Life

8. ◉ **Fact and Opinion Write** one fact and one opinion about the culture of the Southeast.

....

....

....

....

9. ❓ **How does where we live affect who we are?**

Use the photograph and questions below to think more about this chapter's Big Question.

a. How does having two coasts affect the Southeast?

....

....

....

....

....

b. How do cities affect the Southeast?

....

....

....

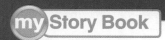

Go online to write and illustrate your own **myStory Book** using the **myStory Ideas** from this chapter.

 ## How does where we live affect who we are?

You have learned about the Southeast's land and water, its weather and climate, and its resources. You have learned about the region's past and present. You have thought about how all of these parts of the Southeast would affect the people who live there.

You are the mayor of a southeastern town. You want to attract businesses from other countries to your region. **Write** an advertisement describing the Southeast. Explain what makes it a great place to work and live.

....

....

....

....

Now **draw** a picture that shows it as a great place to start a business.

While you're online, check out the **myStory Current Events** area where you can create your own book on a topic that's in the news.

Regions: The Midwest

How does where we live affect who we are?

Long ago, the rich farmland and many rivers of the Midwest attracted settlers. Soon, cities grew in the region. Then more people came to work in these cities. **Think** about your community. **Write** about what might attract people to move to where you live.

....

....

....

....

The Midwest region has rich farmland and pastures. Farmers raise food here to sell all over the world.

Nebraska
Great Land for Farming

my Story Video

The Midwest region is known for its prairies, pastures, and fertile farms. It produces large harvests of corn, wheat, and other crops. Nebraska is one of the nation's great agricultural states. Its land rises steadily from the Missouri River valley in the east toward the high, dry Great Plains in the west.

Devin was born and raised in Omaha, Nebraska. Omaha is located on the eastern border of the state. He loves this area. "I don't live on a farm, but there are a lot of them close to me. Tractors are cool," he says. Laura is from Lincoln, Nebraska. Lincoln is southwest of Omaha. She lives out in the country. "It's so wide open, it's like you can see forever!" she says. Today Laura and Devin are going to explore Nebraska.

Devin stands on a tractor on a farm near his hometown of Omaha, Nebraska. Nebraska is in the heart of Midwest farmland.

Omaha is the largest city in Nebraska. It is located on the eastern border of the state.

At Pioneer Courage Park in Omaha, metal sculptures honor the pioneers who came into Nebraska with covered wagons long ago.

Devin enjoys visiting the farms near his home in Omaha, Nebraska.

"Welcome to Omaha," Devin says. Devin lives in Nebraska's largest city. Omaha is located on the Missouri River. "It's the Missouri River that separates Nebraska and Iowa," Devin explains. Its location on the Missouri River makes Omaha an important city.

Rivers such as the Missouri have long been important trade routes. The river provides a transportation route for shipping crops such as corn. Crops grown in Nebraska will be sold in markets all over the world. In fact, all kinds of products from the Midwest are shipped from Omaha on large ships called barges.

Devin walks along an area near the river's edge. It's called the Old Market District. This area was once a major port. Today, people shop in stores, eat in restaurants, and visit the Omaha Children's Museum.

Nebraska has a lot of farmland that is good for growing corn. "Corn is everywhere around here," says Devin. "I even pass a cornfield on my way to school."

Special buildings called grain elevators are filled with crops during every harvest. Farmers store crops in grain elevators before the crops are taken to market. Even though Devin doesn't live on a farm, he helps out on local farms. He shucks, or peels, corn and helps feed the cows.

"There are a lot of safety rules on the farm," Devin says, "and I follow each one carefully!" Devin learns a lot from the farmers every time he comes to help out. Midwestern farmers, known for being hardworking, love the land of the region.

Laura lives in Lincoln. Lincoln is the capital city of Nebraska. It is located to the southwest of Omaha.

Beautiful fields cover the land near Lincoln. Laura loves the wide-open spaces there.

Laura's home in Nebraska's capital city of Lincoln is not very far from Homestead National Monument. Homestead National Monument honors the Homestead Act of 1862. This law allowed United States citizens to own government land. The pieces of land were called homesteads. Thousands of families moved to the Midwest region and built homesteads. More than 270 million acres of government land were given out as homesteads between the 1860s and the 1930s.

Laura is finishing her visit to the Homestead Monument. As she walks home, she looks out at the land of her state. Laura loves the wide-open spaces near her home. She can enjoy the prairies or admire the fields of grain. Above the land, the sky stretches far away in every direction. "Look at all this land," she says. "Isn't it pretty?"

The weather in Nebraska can sometimes change from sunny to snowy in just a few hours. "But that's part of what makes it exciting here," Laura says. "And we wouldn't have it any other way. Nebraska rules!"

Think About It If you could choose one job in your region to help with, what would it be? As you read the chapter, think about the region's resources and economy and the work you might do there.

The Homestead National Monument is a park not far from Lincoln, Nebraska.

In the Heart of the Nation

Envision It!

Pacific Ocean

Rocky Mountains

Plain

The land in the middle of the United States looks different from the land to its east and to its west.

The Midwest region is located in the middle of the country. It stretches from Ohio in the east to Nebraska and Kansas in the west. In the north, it includes states that border Canada, such as Michigan and North Dakota.

Midwestern Land

You can think of the Midwest as the area between two mountain ranges. To the west are the Rocky Mountains. To the east are the Appalachians. Though there are hills and mountains in the Midwest, much of the land is level. The region includes farmland, forests, and open grasslands. In western parts of the Midwest, the land is higher and drier, as it stetches toward the Rocky Mountains. This area is called the **Great Plains.** Much of the Great Plains is prairie. **Prairie** is level or gently rolling land covered in grasses, with few trees. The eastern part of the Midwest is called the **Central Plains.**

Thousands of years ago, glaciers covered much of the region. Glaciers changed the land. They flattened hills and carved out valleys. Some valleys filled with water, creating river valleys. Glaciers also left behind moraines when they melted. A moraine is a mound or ridge of rock and gravel.

1. **Cause and Effect** When ancient glaciers melted, they left behind many lakes. Minnesota is called "the Land of 10,000 Lakes." **Underline** in the text some other effects caused by glaciers.

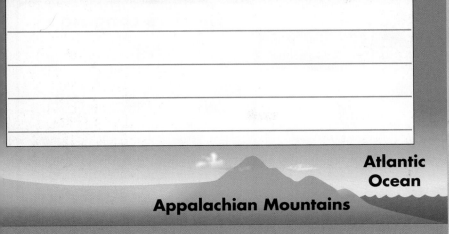

UNLOCK THE BIG ?

I will know that the lives of people in the Midwest are affected by its landforms and bodies of water.

Atlantic Ocean

Appalachian Mountains

How does the land change as you travel from either coast to the middle of the country?

Vocabulary

Great Plains	blizzard
prairie	tornado
Central Plains	Badlands

Great Rivers

Rivers have shaped the Midwest, too. The nation's two longest rivers run through the region.

The greatest river of all is the Mississippi River. The Mississippi carries more water than any other river in North America. It flows from north to south. The river begins in the lakes of Minnesota and travels 2,350 miles. Along its journey, other rivers, such as the Missouri and the Ohio, flow into it. The Mississippi begins as a small stream and grows to be more than 11 miles wide in places. Its waters drain into the Gulf of Mexico.

The Missouri River is the longest in the country. It runs 2,540 miles. The Missouri begins in Montana and runs east and south through the Dakotas. It marks part of the borders between Nebraska and Iowa and between Kansas and Missouri.

The Ohio River is another long Midwestern river. It is more than 1,300 miles long. It flows west out of Pennsylvania along the southern edges of Ohio, Indiana, and Illinois.

2. The Ohio River creates the southern borders of Ohio, Indiana, and Illinois. On the map, **draw** a line along the Ohio River and label it.

The Midwest, Political

North Dakota ★ Bismarck

Minnesota

L. Superior CANADA

N E W S

St. Paul ★

Wisconsin
Madison ★

L. Michigan

L. Huron

Michigan ★
Lansing
Detroit

L. Erie
Cleveland

South Dakota ★ Pierre

Iowa

Chicago ●

Nebraska
Lincoln ★

★ Des Moines

Indiana
Indianapolis ★

Ohio
Columbus ★

Illinois ★
Springfield

Kansas City Kansas City
Topeka ★ ●

St. Louis ●

Kansas

★ Jefferson City

Missouri

KEY
 Midwest region
★ State capital

0 ___ 200 mi
0 ___ 200 km

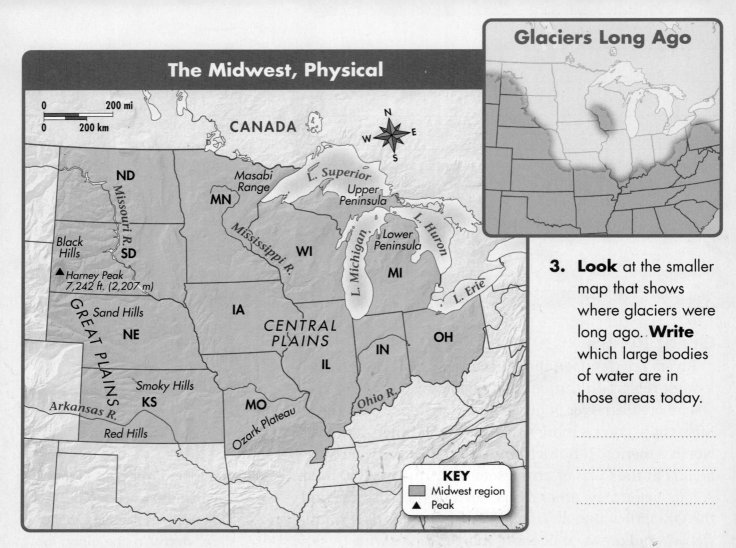

The Midwest, Physical

0   200 mi
0   200 km

CANADA

N
W   E
S

ND
Masabi Range
L. Superior
Upper Peninsula
MN
Mississippi R.
L. Huron
Missouri R.
Black Hills
SD
WI
L. Michigan
Lower Peninsula
▲ Harney Peak 7,242 ft. (2,207 m)
MI
IA
GREAT PLAINS
Sand Hills
NE
CENTRAL PLAINS
L. Erie
OH
IN
IL
Smoky Hills
KS
MO
Ohio R.
Arkansas R.
Ozark Plateau
Red Hills

KEY
Midwest region
▲ Peak

Glaciers Long Ago

3. **Look** at the smaller map that shows where glaciers were long ago. **Write** which large bodies of water are in those areas today.

....

....

....

The Great Lakes

Not only does the Midwest have the country's largest rivers, it also boasts its biggest lakes. There are five Great Lakes: Lake Erie, Lake Huron, Lake Michigan, Lake Ontario, and Lake Superior. All the lakes are connected to each other. All but Lake Ontario are in the Midwest. The Great Lakes hold about one fifth of the world's fresh water. Unlike seawater, fresh water is not salty. Each of the Great Lakes is huge. If you stand on one side of a Great Lake, the opposite shore will be far out of sight. Winds can whip up large waves on the lakes, making them seem like oceans.

The Great Lakes were formed long ago by glaciers. As the glaciers moved across the land, deep pits formed in the earth. When the glaciers melted, water filled the pits.

Though all the Great Lakes are inland, they connect to the Atlantic Ocean. The St. Lawrence River flows out of Lake Ontario and east to the ocean.

Climate of the Midwest

The Midwest is located far from the coasts. This affects its climate. Coastal places are cooled in the summer and warmed in the winter by the fairly steady temperature of ocean water. Oceans moderate the temperatures on land nearby. Inland, temperatures can be extreme. In the Midwest, summers can be very hot and winters very cold.

Winters are especially cold in states like North Dakota, Minnesota, Wisconsin, and Michigan. Snow is common there. Blizzards sometimes sweep through the region. A **blizzard** is a heavy snowstorm with powerful winds. Summers can bring heat waves and hot temperatures.

The western part of the Midwest tends to be much drier than the eastern part. That's because of the Rocky Mountains. The Rockies block moisture-filled air. Rain falls to the west of the Rockies, and then dry air passes into the Midwest. In the Great Plains, less than ten inches of precipitation falls in an average year. Farther east, states like Indiana and Ohio get about 40 inches of precipitation each year. Moist air blows up from the Gulf of Mexico and meets cool Canadian air. This brings rain and snow to these states.

While being inland means Midwesterners don't have to fear hurricanes, they do have to watch out for other kinds of extreme weather. When dry Midwestern air meets hot, wet air coming up from the Gulf of Mexico, big thunderstorms can result. So can tornadoes. Tornadoes are both common and dangerous in the Midwest. A **tornado** is a destructive column of spinning air with winds that can reach more than 300 miles per hour. Part of the Midwest is located in an area called Tornado Alley. Tornadoes are common there in spring and summer.

Midwestern winters can bring blizzards and freezing temperatures. The record low temperature in North Dakota is a frigid −60° F.

4. ◎ **Summarize Write** how the Midwest's inland location affects the region's weather.

....

....

....

....

Wildlife of the Midwest

The Midwest is home to a great variety of wildlife. Deer, sheep, and snakes live in the dry, rocky hills of the Badlands. The **Badlands** is an area of rough land in western South Dakota. Vegetation is light in the Badlands, and few trees grow there. The black-footed ferret, one of North America's most endangered animals, has been brought back to Badlands National Park.

The Midwest's prairie is home to the American bison. Millions of these animals once roamed the plains. Long ago, they were almost hunted out of existence. Today, there are thousands of bison once again. They share the area with pronghorn antelope, prairie dogs, and coyotes. The wide-open grasslands are also perfect for ranching. Ranchers raise cattle across much of this region.

To the north and east, other animals like squirrels, raccoons, and deer are common, especially in forests. The gray wolf, which almost became extinct, is now found in parts of Wisconsin and Minnesota.

The Midwest is home to many species of birds, such as owls and hawks. Bald eagles make their nests along rivers and lakes. There, these birds can find fish to eat. Birds that migrate, or fly long distances when the seasons change, visit the Midwest. Ducks, geese, and cranes can be seen in marshes. A marsh is a grassy wetland.

Many kinds of fish live in the Midwest's rivers and lakes. Lake fish such as pike, perch, bass, and carp fill the waters of the Great Lakes. Huge catfish live on the muddy bottom of the Mississippi River.

Prairie dogs are common in the Midwestern grasslands. They live in holes called burrows that they dig in the ground.

The American bison, or buffalo, is a large animal that feeds on the grasses that cover the prairies.

5. ⊙ **Categorize Write** one animal that lives in each type of land.

Wildlife of the Midwest

prairie	
dry, rocky hills	
forest	
rivers, lakes, and wetlands	

The Midwest is home to many different kinds of birds. This is a cardinal.

Got it?

6. ⊙ **Compare and Contrast** What is the difference in climate between the western part of the Midwest and the eastern part? **Explain** why they are different.

....

....

....

7. ❓ You are planning a summer trip to the Midwest. **Think** about the region's climate. What would be the best and worst reasons for going in summer?

my Story Ideas

....

....

....

◻ **Stop!** I need help with ....

❙❙ **Wait!** I have a question about ....

▶ **Go!** Now I know ....

Give an Effective Presentation

Suppose everyone in your class had to give a social studies presentation. Some of the presentations would be interesting. Others might not be. What is the difference between an effective, interesting presentation and a weaker one? You might guess it is the subject matter. Think again. You can make anything interesting if you know how to prepare. To give an effective and interesting presentation, follow the steps below:

1. **Know your audience.** It is always important to keep in mind the people to whom you'll be speaking. How much do they already know?

2. **Identify your main idea and state it at the beginning and the end.** Your audience needs to know right away what your presentation is about. Otherwise, they may lose interest. It is also good to remind people of your main idea before you close.

3. **Choose your details carefully.** Your audience does not need to know every single detail you found in your research. Choose only the most interesting details that support your main point.

4. **Speak clearly and loudly.** A presenter who mumbles or whispers will quickly frustrate his or her listeners. Audiences lose interest when they cannot hear clearly. Also make sure you look up at your audience from time to time when you make a presentation.

5. **Use visuals.** A visual, such as a map or picture, gives the audience something else to focus on. Using visuals is also a great way to illustrate your point.

6. **Practice before you present.** Effective presenters practice their presentations so that they feel comfortable with their material.

Look at this student's notes for a presentation about the Great Lakes. Then answer the questions.

> ### Great Lakes Presentation
>
> I am doing a presentation about the Great Lakes. My main idea is that the Great Lakes are important to the states that border them, especially Illinois, and to the port of Chicago. I will speak clearly and loudly when I present.

1. Review the steps to an effective presentation. What are three things that the student is missing?

....

2. What do you think is the most important step to an effective presentation? Why?

....

....

....

3. **Apply Choose** a topic about the Midwest for a presentation. **Write** your notes for the presentation below. Remember to include all the steps for giving an effective presentation.

Topic: ....

Notes: ....

....

....

....

Lesson 2

Resources and Farming

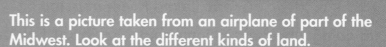

This is a picture taken from an airplane of part of the Midwest. Look at the different kinds of land.

To successfully grow crops, a farmer needs sunshine, water, rich soil, level ground, and a long growing season. In the Midwest, all of these resources are plentiful.

Farming Resources

Successful farms need certain resources. For example, planting crops is easier on level or gently rolling land. With its plains, prairies, and low hills, much of the Midwest is perfect for farming. Deep soil that contains many nutrients is also important. **Nutrients** are substances that help plants grow. Some of the richest soil in the country is found in the Midwest.

Crops also need water. Much of the Midwest gets enough rainfall to raise crops. This is particularly true in the Central Plains. In the drier Great Plains, farms can get water from rivers and underground wells. Using irrigation, farmers bring water to their fields.

Sunshine is the final ingredient for successful farming. With its long growing season and hot summers, the Midwest gets plenty of sun. That sunshine, combined with everything else, makes the Midwest one of the most productive farming regions in the world.

1. **Summarize** Above is a typical Midwestern farm in Iowa. What does the Midwest have that makes it great for farming?

....

....

UNLOCK THE BIG ?

I will understand why the Midwest is one of the world's most important agricultural areas.

Vocabulary

nutrient
arable
crop rotation

Which areas in the picture are not farmed? What conclusion might you draw about the Midwest's land?

A Region for Farming

Farming is important in the Midwest because the region has much more arable land than the other regions in the country. **Arable** means capable of growing crops.

So thanks to the Midwest, the United States is one of the world's leading producers of farm products. For example, each year the United States produces an enormous amount of corn. In fact, it produces more than twice as much corn as China and far more than any other country. The United States is the world's biggest producer of soybeans. More than a third of the world's crop is grown here. Our country is also one of the world's top producers of dozens of other farm products, from blueberries to cheese.

The food that is grown in the Midwest is used and eaten in the United States. It is also sold to other countries. That makes Midwestern agriculture an important part of the nation's economy.

2. The purple parts of these circle graphs show the amount of farmland. The left graph shows that about one fifth of all land in the United States is farmland. **Look** at the right graph. How much of the land of the Midwest is arable?

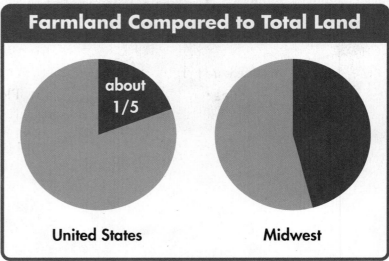

Farmland Compared to Total Land

about 1/5

United States   Midwest

Regions Within a Region

Not every part of the Midwest is the same. Because the region includes different landforms and climates, it produces a variety of crops.

The Central Plains are perfect for growing corn. In fact, the area that includes Ohio, Illinois, Iowa, southern Minnesota, Missouri, Kansas, and Nebraska is known as the Corn Belt. Farmers in this area grow soybeans as well as corn. Often, they switch between the two crops, growing corn one year and soybeans the next. This is called **crop rotation.**

Farms in the Great Plains to the west don't get as much rain as those in the Central Plains. As a result, farmers there grow crops that require less water, such as wheat and oats. They might also use irrigation to grow corn and soybeans.

3. ⊙ **Summarize Write** which area of the Midwest would be best for growing the following crops:

corn ....

wheat ....

soybeans ....

Wheat grows well in the drier Great Plains. Besides being ground into flour for bread, wheat can be used to make animal food, glue, and plastic.

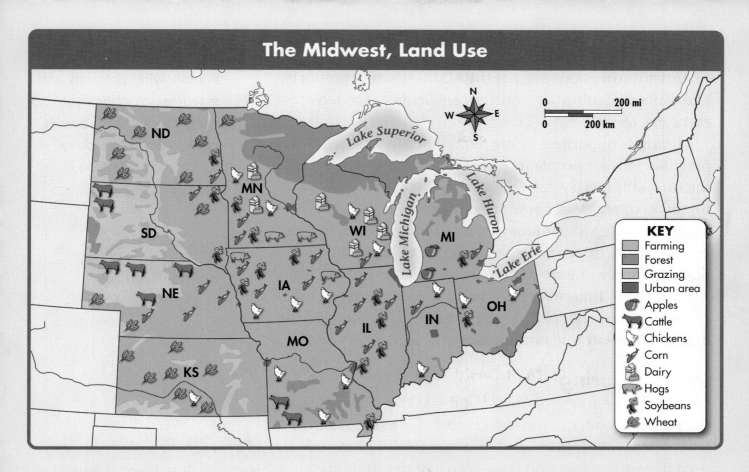

The Midwest, Land Use

KEY
- Farming
- Forest
- Grazing
- Urban area
- Apples
- Cattle
- Chickens
- Corn
- Dairy
- Hogs
- Soybeans
- Wheat

Farm Products

Of course, wheat, corn, and soybeans are just some of what is grown in the Midwest. In the north central region, states such as Michigan are famous for their fruit. Orchards are crowded with apple and cherry trees. Fields of berries are everywhere. In the summer and fall, these fruits, along with peaches and grapes, fill local farmers' markets.

Dairy farms are also common in the Midwest. Dairy farmers raise cows for their milk. Dairy is especially important in northern states, such as Wisconsin. This state is famous for its milk, cheese, butter, and other dairy products.

Raising animals for meat is also a huge part of Midwestern agriculture. Much of the country's pork comes from states such as Minnesota and Iowa. A lot of corn is grown in these states, and hogs feed on the corn. This makes the area a natural fit for raising hogs. For the same reason, a lot of beef is produced in the Midwest. Chickens are raised for meat and eggs in the Midwest. Iowa is the nation's top egg-producing state.

4. **Circle** the names of states that produce dairy products. Then **mark** the states that grow wheat.

Dairy products like milk are important to the region's economy.

231

Other Resources

Agricultural goods are not the Midwest's only products. Many nonagricultural resources contribute to the region's economy, as well.

Mining is important in the region. Mining for coal has provided jobs for people in Illinois for many years. Today, the state still has a quarter of the nation's supply of coal. Illinois coal provides power for millions of homes.

Minnesota's Mesabi Range is rich in iron. Between 1900 and 1980, the mines there produced more than half of the nation's supply of iron. Michigan is also a source of iron.

In Indiana, limestone is an important natural resource. The stone is dug out of huge deposits in the ground. These deposits form an underground layer of rock in the earth.

Manufacturing

The many natural resources of the Midwest help make the region a leader in manufacturing. For example, iron from Minnesota is manufactured into steel. The steel is used in construction and making machines. Indiana limestone is cut into blocks and used to build houses, bridges, and skyscrapers. The Empire State Building in New York City was constructed partly with Indiana limestone.

The Midwest is a key center for manufacturing. The region produces goods that are sold all over the world. Midwestern manufacturers make cars, appliances, and many other products.

5. ⊚ **Categorize Write** the following products and resources as agricultural or nonagricultural: *berries, cattle, coal, corn, dairy, eggs, iron, limestone, soybeans, wheat*

Agricultural

....

....

....

Nonagricultural

....

....

....

Limestone mined in Indiana is cut into big blocks that are used to construct buildings.

Resources From Lakes and Rivers

The Midwest's lakes and rivers also contain important resources. Fishing has long played a role in the economies of the Great Lakes states. Native Americans fished the waters of Lake Huron and Lake Michigan. Commercial fishing was a major industry there for many years. But pollution led to a decline in fish populations in the region. This caused commercial fishing to collapse.

Today, recreational fishing, or fishing for fun, is popular on Midwestern rivers and lakes. Even in winter, fishermen cut holes in the ice, drop a line, and wait to catch trout or perch.

Ice fishing is a popular winter pastime in the Midwest.

Got it?

6. ◉ **Summarize** How does the Midwest's physical environment enable farmers to do their jobs? And how do farmers affect, or change, the physical environment as they farm?

....

....

....

7. On a trip to the Midwest, you plan to meet a farmer. What kind of farmer would you like to meet? **Write** a few questions you might ask him or her.

my Story Ideas

....

....

....

⬛ **Stop!** I need help with ....

⏸ **Wait!** I have a question about ....

▶ **Go!** Now I know ....

Settling in the Midwest

Envision It!

This painting shows Comanche riders hunting bison. Bison provided many of the things the Comanche needed.

Native Americans have lived in the Midwest for thousands of years. Because the Midwest has varied landscapes, these groups lived in different ways.

Native Americans of the Midwest

Native American groups lived in the forests, river valleys, and flat areas of the eastern Midwest. Groups like the Fox and the Shawnee farmed corn, beans, and squash.

Wisconsin, Michigan, and Minnesota were home to the Ojibwa, also known as the Chippewa. The Ojibwa did little farming. Instead, they adapted to the Midwest's geography. They hunted in the forests. They fished in the region's many lakes and rivers. They gathered berries, fruit, and wild rice.

Other groups lived on the Great Plains. Eastern Plains groups like the Omaha and the Iowa farmed in river valleys. Western Plains groups like the Lakota were nomads. A **nomad** is a person who moves from place to place. Western Plains groups followed the bison.

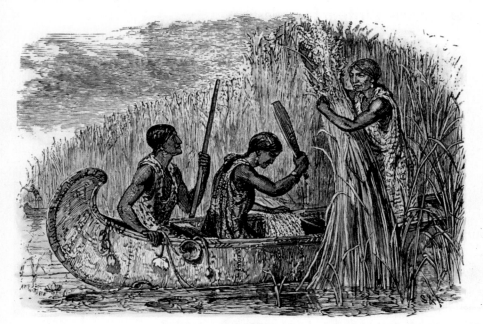

1. The Ojibwa used canoes to gather wild rice. **Underline** in the text another way they used natural resources.

I will understand that the Midwest's rich farmland and other resources attracted thousands of settlers.

Vocabulary

nomad
missionary
trading post

Northwest Ordinance
plow

Think about the ways that the Comanche would have used bison. Write your ideas in the space above.

The Fur Trade

Some of the first Europeans to arrive in the Midwest were missionaries. **Missionaries** are religious people who set up settlements to teach religion. Other settlers, many of them French, came because of the fur trade. Beaver, otter, and mink furs were valuable in Europe. They were used to make hats and coats.

French fur traders explored the Midwest from the north to the south. In 1673, explorers Jacques Marquette and Louis Jolliet traveled by canoe down some Midwestern waterways. They started on Lake Michigan. Then they explored parts of the Mississippi River.

Soon, the French were building forts and trading posts along waterways. A **trading post** is a small settlement where goods are traded. They traded European goods to Native Americans for furs. Often, the trading posts were built near Native Americans who would farm and trade their food with the Europeans. Some of these trading posts later grew into cities. Chicago is one of them. This major city began as a trading post.

2. **Circle** the trading post that was located close to the Native American group called the Fox.

Native Americans of the Midwest

KEY
▢ Midwest region
🏠 Trading post

Farmers Settle the Land

Farmers came to the Midwest as early as the 1770s. They were attracted to the region's rich farmland. They came from the East. The first to come settled in the Ohio River valley. Later, as farmland became harder to find there, settlers moved farther west. Many new settlers came west through the Great Lakes

At the time of the Revolutionary War, the Midwest was part of the frontier. Then, in the 1780s, the new United States government began organizing the region. Much of the Midwest became part of the Northwest Territory. In 1787, Congress passed the **Northwest Ordinance.** This law said the Northwest Territory must be divided into "not less than three nor more than five states." It also said these new states could not allow slavery. Five states came from this territory: Ohio, Illinois, Indiana, Wisconsin, and Michigan.

In the early 1800s, pioneers began coming to the Midwest by the thousands. Most wanted land to farm. The government was offering cheap land. There was a conflict, however. Native Americans were already living on much of this land. So the government forced the Native Americans to sell their land and move to reservations. By 1890, all of the Midwest had been organized into states.

3. ◎ **Compare and Contrast** When families moved to the Midwest, their lives changed. For example, living in log cabins (left) or sod houses (right) may have been unfamiliar. **Write** about other possible changes for families.

....

....

....

....

Immigrants Come to the Midwest

In the mid-1800s, immigrants from Europe started coming to the Midwest. These settlers looked for land in the Northeast first. Soon however, the Midwest became the first choice for new immigrants. Many of these immigrants came from northern and central Europe. They came from countries such as Germany, Ireland, Sweden, Norway, and Hungary. Some of these new immigrants started farms. Others moved to growing Midwestern cities, port towns, and trading posts.

Farming Changes

Although Midwestern land was great for farming, it was hard work to clear it. Farmers had to remove trees. They had to clear prairie grass from the plains. Then they had to turn over the soil to get it ready for planting. The tool they used for this was a **plow.** But plows had a hard time digging through the thick prairie grass roots.

Then, in 1837, a man named John Deere invented a new steel plow. This plow made farming easier. It could break through the toughest prairie grass roots. Soon, oxen or horses were pulling bigger plows. Years later, plows were pulled by tractors. This made it possible to farm huge areas of the Midwest's prairies. More and more pioneers began settling the Great Plains. They hoped to start big, successful farms.

4. ◎ **Categorize** Write what kinds of plows allowed more people to settle the Great Plains.

....

....

....

....

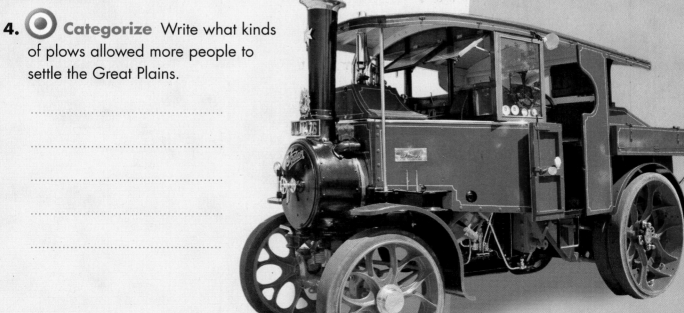

This early tractor is powered by a steam engine. Tractors prepare fields for planting faster than a horse pulling a small plow.

Midwestern Cities

As more people settled the Midwest, some trading posts grew into towns and cities. These communities were often on waterways used for transportation. As trade grew, so did the communities.

In 1784, African American pioneer Jean Baptiste Point Du Sable established a trading post. It was at the mouth of the Chicago River, near Lake Michigan's southern tip.

Soon Du Sable's trading post was the largest in the Midwest. It had a bakery, a mill, and a poultry house. In the early 1830s, Chicago had a few hundred people. By 1890, it had more than a million. Today, it is the largest city in the Midwest and the third-largest city in the country.

Other Midwestern cities began as trading posts. In 1701, a French trader founded Detroit on a river that connected Lake Huron to Lake Erie. Cleveland was founded in 1796 on the Cuyahoga River. In 1764, another French trader settled St. Louis on the Mississippi River. St. Louis soon became a center of shipping and transportation. This was true for other Midwestern cities. Slowly, the Midwest was becoming more urban.

5. ◎ **Summarize** This painting shows Chicago, Illinois, in 1820. Chicago started as a trading post. **Write** a sentence summarizing why so many Midwestern cities grew near waterways.

....

....

From Trade to Factories

As the United States became more industrial in the late 1800s, so did the Midwest. Many Midwestern cities were good sites for factories because they were on the water. The raw materials used to manufacture goods could be shipped to these cities easily. Finished products could also be shipped easily.

In the early 1900s, Detroit became the center of the car industry. Companies like the Ford Motor Company were located there. Soon almost every car in the United States was made in Detroit. The city was nicknamed "the Motor City."

Of course, all these new industries brought people in search of jobs and better lives. Some of these new settlers were immigrants from other countries. Others were African Americans from the Southeast. They came to escape segregation and to find jobs.

Henry Ford was an entrepreneur who owned his own business, the Ford Motor Company. It was based in Detroit, Michigan.

Got it?

6. ◉ **Summarize** How did the Midwest's geography affect the way it was settled?

....

....

....

....

7. ❓ During a trip to the Midwest, you want to visit a city. Which city would you choose, and why?   **my Story Ideas**

....

....

▢ **Stop!** I need help with ....

❚❚ **Wait!** I have a question about ....

▶ **Go!** Now I know ....

The Midwest on the Move

Envision It!

The Midwest is a center for many kinds of transportation. People and goods move by truck, train, and boat.

The Midwest grew as more and more people settled there. These new Midwesterners farmed, ran stores, and worked in factories. All had one thing in common: they used and needed transportation.

Native American Trade in the 1200s

Long before Europeans arrived, Native Americans moved goods and people all over the region. The Midwest's many lakes and rivers made transportation by water easy. Trading centers like Cahokia developed. Located in Illinois, Cahokia was the site of the largest Native American city in North America.

Cahokia was close to the **junction,** or meeting point, of three rivers: the Illinois, the Missouri, and the Mississippi. These waterways connected Cahokia to the north, south, west, and northeast. Traders from the Great Lakes area shipped copper to Cahokia. Southern traders in the Mississippi valley shipped shells, jewelry, and pottery. Cahokia was a meeting place of many cultures.

1. **Summarize** This is an illustration of Cahokia. How did the physical environment of the Midwest affect Cahokia's success as a trading center?

....

....

....

....

UNLOCK THE BIG ?

I will understand how a central location made the Midwest important in the nation's transportation and trade.

Vocabulary

junction   interstate
hub   highway

Which kind of transportation would be most likely to deliver goods to your neighborhood?

Changes in Transportation

In the early 1800s, few roads existed west of the Appalachian Mountains. The best way to travel was on the water. This was especially true in the Midwest, with its many rivers and lakes. Most transportation in the region was by boat.

Until the early 1800s, boats needed wind or human power to move them. Sailing ships could travel down the St. Lawrence River and around the Great Lakes. On the shallower rivers, such as the Mississippi, people had to use canoes or flatboats. Flatboats could float downstream, but they had to be paddled upstream. The upstream journeys were long and difficult.

The invention of the steamboat changed everything. These new boats were bigger and faster than human-powered boats. By the 1830s, steamboats carrying tons of cargo and hundreds of passengers sailed up Midwestern rivers daily. Such steamboats turned the great rivers of the Midwest into major water highways.

2. ◎ **Cause and Effect** **Underline** what effect steamboats had on river transportation.

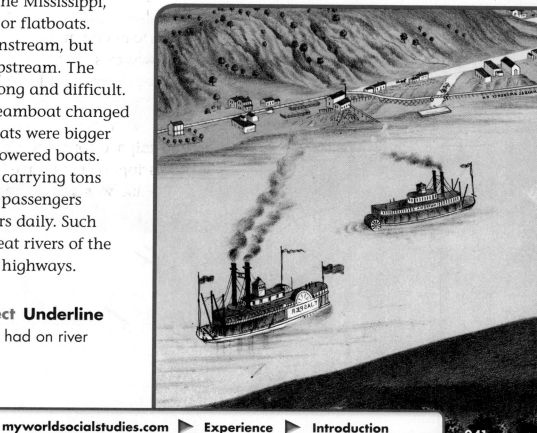

Steamboats could go both downstream and upstream easily.

Railroads and Shipping

By the mid-1800s the steamboat was no longer the most modern form of transportation. Trains had taken over. In 1869, the transcontinental railroad was completed. Now goods could travel from the Midwest to either coast. The Midwest became the **hub,** or center, of the country's rail transportation network. It was now even easier for Midwesterners to trade goods.

Shipping continued to be very important to the Midwest. Large ships are able to carry people and goods more cheaply than trains. And, because of the St. Lawrence Seaway, ships can travel from the Atlantic Ocean all the way to the Great Lakes. The St. Lawrence Seaway is a system of canals and waterways that connects the Midwest to the Atlantic Ocean. Because of the importance of shipping, many important ports developed in the Midwest. Like Chicago, Detroit, and Cleveland, cities such as Milwaukee, Wisconsin, and Duluth, Minnesota, became major shipping centers.

Today, these port cities remain important shipping centers. More than 200 million tons of cargo crosses the Great Lakes and their waterways each year. As in the 1850s, this cargo includes iron ore, coal, limestone, grain, and other farm products.

The Aerial Lift Bridge in Duluth, Minnesota, goes across a canal that connects to the city's harbor. Duluth is one of the most important port cities in the United States.

3. You need to send iron ore from Duluth to Cleveland. **Look** at the chart. Would you ship by land or by water? Why?

....

....

Shipping From Duluth, MN, to Cleveland, OH

	Land	Water
Cargo	iron ore	iron ore
Travel Time	2.2 days	1.7 days
Distance	813 miles	549 miles
Cost	$2,811	$1,725

Highways

In the early 1900s, cars became very popular in the United States. At first, there were few good roads. Then the United States government began building better ones. In 1956, the government began building an **interstate highway** system. This system of wide, fast roads connected all the states.

Trucks used the new highways, too. Soon, trucks became a popular way of transporting goods. Today, most of the goods we buy are shipped by truck. Because of the Midwest's central location, its highways are important truck routes.

New Industries

Though farming and manufacturing are still important in the Midwest, its economy has changed. Today, many Midwesterners have jobs in the technology and service industries. There are many new companies in the Midwest. Companies go where the workers are. A quarter of the nation's workforce is in the Midwest.

Today, instead of working in a car factory, Midwesterners might work at a factory that manufactures solar panels. Instead of farming, they might work in the health care field.

As the Midwest's economy has changed, so has life for Midwesterners. For example, people might live in apartment buildings that were once factories. They might also live along cleaned-up rivers that were once polluted by those factories.

4. ◎ **Categorize** The economy of the Midwest is changing. **Underline** examples of new industries in the text.

This is the Minneapolis skyline. Minneapolis and St. Paul are Minnesota's "Twin Cities." Both have growing new industries.

Tourism in the Midwest

Another important industry in the Midwest is tourism. Many Midwesterners work in this field. They might be tour guides in Chicago or lead canoe trips across lakes in Michigan.

There is plenty for tourists to see and do in this region. Tourists depend on the Midwest's many forms of transporation to plan their visits. Visitors might drive on highways to visit Mount Rushmore in the Black Hills of South Dakota. Or they might fly into Chicago's busy O'Hare International Airport. Then they could take a bus into the city and spend the afternoon in Millennium Park.

Arts and Culture

Arts and culture are thriving in the Midwest. The Chicago Symphony Orchestra is one of the world's best. And the Guthrie Theater in Minneapolis is second only to New York's Broadway. Music lovers visit the Rock and Roll Hall of Fame on the shores of Lake Erie in Cleveland. More than 8 million visitors have visited this museum since it opened in 1995.

5. ◉ **Summarize Write** why tourism is an important industry in the Midwest.

....

....

The Gateway Arch in St. Louis sits on the western bank of the Mississippi River. It is the tallest national monument in the United States.

Many tourists enjoy visiting the magnificent Milwaukee Art Museum. The building itself is as big an attraction as the art inside.

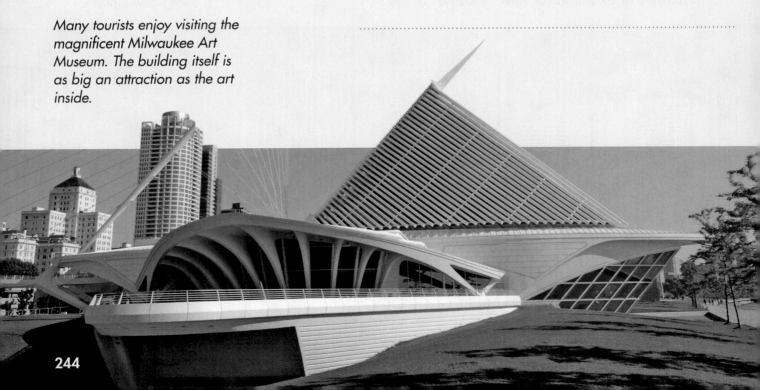

It took hundreds of workers more than six years to shape the figures on Mount Rushmore in the Black Hills of South Dakota.

6. ⦿ **Compare and Contrast Describe** how the economy of the Midwest has changed since the mid-1800s. Then tell how it has stayed the same.

....

....

....

....

7. ❓ What form or forms of transportation would you like to use on your trip to the Midwest? Why?

my Story Ideas

....

....

....

....

⬛ **Stop!** I need help with ....

⏸ **Wait!** I have a question about ....

▶ **Go!** Now I know ....

Lesson 1

In the Heart of the Nation

- The Midwest is on the broad plains in the center of the United States.
- The largest lakes and rivers in the United States are in the Midwest.
- The Midwest generally has cold winters and hot summers.
- Midwestern wildlife includes bison and many kinds of birds and fish.

Lesson 2

Resources and Farming

- The Midwest's agricultural resources make it one of the world's leading producers of farm products.
- The Midwest has other natural resources, such as iron, coal, and limestone that give the region a balanced economy.

Lesson 3

Settling in the Midwest

- Many Native American groups were the first to live in the Midwest.
- French missionaries and fur traders were the first Europeans to settle in the Midwest, followed by other pioneers.
- Settlers turned the Midwest into a productive region of farms and cities.

Lesson 4

The Midwest on the Move

- Waterways, railroads, and highways are all used for transportation.
- The Midwest's railroads, ports, and highways make it a shipping hub.
- New industries and dynamic cities show that the Midwest's culture and economy are thriving.

Review and Assessment

Lesson 1

In the Heart of the Nation

1. In the list below, **circle** the features and landforms found in the Midwest.

   A. Lake Huron

   B. Coastal Plain

   C. Ohio River

   D. prairie

   E. Lake Ontario

   F. rain forest

2. **Write** the names of four Great Lakes and two major rivers found in the Midwest.

   ....

   ....

   ....

   ....

   ....

3. Which of these best describes the climate of the Midwest?

   A. hot and dry

   B. wet and humid

   C. mild winters and cool summers

   D. cold winters and hot summers

Lesson 2

Resources and Farming

4. **Write** the correct answers in the blanks.

   The .... Plains are great for growing corn. The drier .... Plains are better for growing wheat.

5. ◉ **Categorize** **Write** *A* for agricultural and *N* for nonagricultural for each resource.

   _____ limestone

   _____ sunshine

   _____ iron

   _____ coal

   _____ rich soil

   _____ level land

6. The Midwest is sometimes called "the nation's breadbasket." **Write** why you think it was given this nickname.

   ....

   ....

   ....

   ....

   ....

Lesson 3

Settling in the Midwest

7. **Write** the correct answers in the blanks.

.... and ....
were the first Europeans to settle in the
Midwest.

8. Which of the following Midwestern cities
began as a trading post?

A. Detroit

B. Chicago

C. Cleveland

D. all of the above

Lesson 4

The Midwest on the Move

9. What makes the Midwest so important to
the nation's transportation and trade?

....

....

....

....

10. **Write** *F* if a statement is a fact. **Write** *O*
if a statement is an opinion.

The steamboat changed river transportation
in the Midwest. _____

Chicago is the nicest city in the United
States. _____

11. How does where we live
affect who we are?

Use the photograph and question
below to think more about this
chapter's Big Question.

Describe who might live in the place
shown above and what kind of work
they might do. Would that work be
different if they lived somewhere else?

....

....

....

....

....

....

....

Go online to write and illustrate your own **myStory Book** using the **myStory Ideas** from this chapter.

 # How does where we live affect who we are?

People live where they do for many reasons. They may enjoy a region's geography or climate. The culture and history of a place might be attractive, as well. Another reason to live in a region may be its strong economy and many different kinds of jobs.

Think about why you like living in your region or community. **Write** some reasons in the space below.

....

....

....

....

Now **draw** a picture of the best part about living in your region or community.

While you're online, check out the **myStory Current Events** area where you can create your own book on a topic that's in the news.

Regions: The Southwest

How does where we live affect who we are?

Native Americans have lived in the Southwest for thousands of years. In the 1500s, Spanish settlers arrived. Today, people from many different cultures live in the Southwest. **Think** about the different cultures of people in your community. **Write** about how different cultures affect your life.

....

....

....

....

The desert Southwest

Arizona
A Sunny Wonderland

my Story Video

Just like other states in the Southwest region, Arizona is a place of remarkable geography, history, and culture. For Daniel, Arizona is home. "I've lived here my whole life," he says. "I can't imagine living anywhere else."

Today, Daniel is going to take us to some of his favorite places in his home state. "Can you think of a more perfect place to play?" he asks as he practices his golf swing. Golfing is a favorite sport in Arizona. People come from all over the world to try the state's famous courses. It's the mild winter days that are most popular for golfers, but some also brave the hot summer to play here. "Playing in the summer can be hot, but the shade of large trees helps keep you cool," Daniel says.

Mountains and rocks line some golf courses in the Southwest.

251

More than 1 million people live in Phoenix, Arizona.

Daniel tours what was once a mound built by Native Americans.

Phoenix is Arizona's largest city. Over the past 20 years, Phoenix and the surrounding areas have grown quickly. In fact, the city's population has grown so much, it is now one of the largest cities in the nation. But, Daniel assures us, "there is still plenty of natural beauty." The amazing red rocks found at Phoenix's Papago Park offer some of the most unusual and beautiful scenery in the area. Daniel loves to hike these hills. "See the cactus?" he says, being careful not to get too close. "These are really neat, but they sure can hurt!" Cactus plants grow in many parts of Arizona. "Have you ever touched a cactus?" Daniel asks.

Daniel's next stop is a Native American museum and archeological park. He has some research to do for a school essay.

"Hi, Daniel. Welcome!" says Stacey. "These are sites of what is left of mounds built by the Hohokam group. They lived in this area since the year 450." she explains. "Wow, that was a long, long time ago!" replies Daniel. Stacey is happy to give Daniel a tour and answer his questions. Outside the museum, Daniel listens closely as she shows him the ruins.

At a museum in Arizona, people have built structures to show what an ancient pit house looked like.

In Arizona, you can find both hot and cold temperatures.

Many people think of deserts as places where few plants grow. However, flowers and cactus bloom in the dry land.

He is amazed that more than 1,000 years later, he can see traces of a structure that was as long as a football field and three stories high! These sites are carefully preserved.

Arizona is still home to many Native American groups. Hopi, Mojave, Pima, Navajo, and many other Native Americans live throughout the state and region.

While the Southwest is home to most of the United States desert land, this region also has stretches of lush plains and snow-covered mountains. Pine, fir, and aspen forests are found in the mountains near Flagstaff, Arizona. Arizona's highest peak is often covered with snow during winter months. "That's San Francisco Peaks over there," Daniel says as he points to the tall mountain range. "My family likes to play in the snow during winter!" Flagstaff is only about 150 miles north of Phoenix, but it has a very different look and feel. "It's kind of hard to believe that you'll find snow in the Southwest, isn't it?" Daniel says. "Brrr!"

The sun is setting now after Daniel's long day, and it's time for him to go home. "Thanks for checking out part of the Southwest region with me," he says. "Now you know a little more about me, and I hope you learned a lot about Arizona."

The Hohokam made pottery such as this clay container.

Think About It Daniel's family likes to play in the snow found on some of Arizona's high mountains. Where is the closest place your family could go to find snow? As you read this chapter, think about ways that people can enjoy the land where they live.

Southwestern Land and Water

Envision It!

Water wears away the soil and rock in a canyon.

Flying over the Southwest, you cross four states: Texas, Oklahoma, New Mexico, and Arizona. On your flight you will see some of the landforms of the region. In Texas and Oklahoma, farms and cities stretch across the plains. Farther west, the land rises. On the high plateaus, you see herds of cattle. Forests cover some mountains.

The Land

Much of Texas and Oklahoma is flat. The Coastal Plain extends inland from the Gulf of Mexico. It covers almost half of Texas. The Great Plains sweep south through the Midwest into Oklahoma, Texas, and New Mexico.

Much of New Mexico and Arizona is plateaus and mountains. In fact, most of New Mexico lies more than 4,000 feet above sea level. Arizona, too, is a mix of high plateaus and mountains. In southern New Mexico and Arizona, many mountain ranges rise up from the land. The ranges are separated by basins. Basins are low, slightly hollowed areas of land.

At the southern border of the region, the Rio Grande winds through Big Bend National Park.

1. **Draw Conclusions** **Write** why parts of New Mexico and Arizona are called the basin and range region.

....

....

....

I will know about the landforms and natural resources in the Southwest.

Vocabulary

erosion
natural gas
refinery

What do you think will happen in this canyon over a long period of time? Draw a picture to show it.

Rivers and the Gulf

The states of the Southwest form part of the southern border of the United States. In Texas, the Gulf of Mexico and the Rio Grande form part of the border. The Rio Grande separates Texas and Mexico.

The Rio Grande is one of the great rivers of the nation. In fact, its name means "great river" in Spanish. The Rio Grande begins in the Rocky Mountains in the state of Colorado. It is one of the longest rivers in North America. It flows 1,900 miles south and east to the Gulf of Mexico.

The Colorado River is another major river. It begins in the Rocky Mountains and empties in the Gulf of California. The Colorado River drains a large part of North America. That means that the rivers in the area flow into the Colorado. This river also forms most of the western border of Arizona.

2. **Underline** the names of states that border Mexico.

The Southwest, Political

Colorado River
Flagstaff
Arizona
★ Phoenix
Yuma
Tucson
El Paso
★ Santa Fe
Albuquerque
New Mexico
Amarillo
Oklahoma City ★
Tulsa
Oklahoma
Red River
Fort Worth ● ● Dallas
Texas
Austin ★
San Antonio
Houston
Beaumont
Rio Grande
MEXICO
Gulf of Mexico

KEY
Southwest region
★ Capital city

N W E S

0 — 200 mi
0 — 200 km

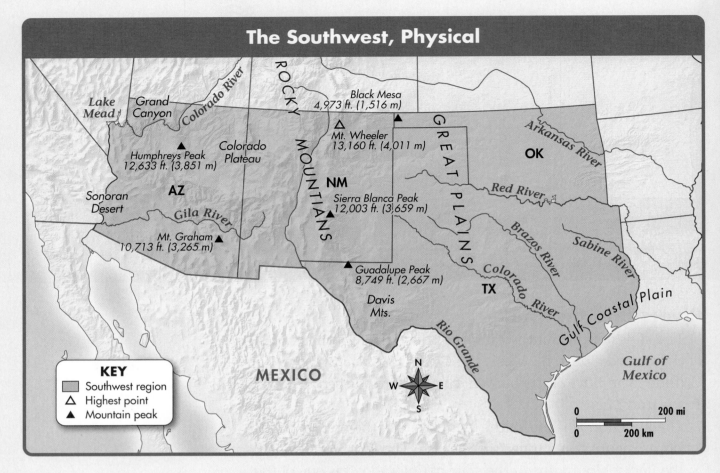

The Southwest, Physical

Lake Mead
Grand Canyon
Colorado River
ROCKY MOUNTAINS
Black Mesa 4,973 ft. (1,516 m)
GREAT PLAINS
Arkansas River
OK
Humphreys Peak 12,633 ft. (3,851 m)
Colorado Plateau
Mt. Wheeler 13,160 ft. (4,011 m)
Red River
AZ
NM
Sierra Blanca Peak 12,003 ft. (3,659 m)
Brazos River
Sonoran Desert
Gila River
Sabine River
Mt. Graham 10,713 ft. (3,265 m)
Colorado River
Gulf Coastal Plain
Guadalupe Peak 8,749 ft. (2,667 m)
TX
Davis Mts.
Rio Grande
MEXICO
Gulf of Mexico

KEY
Southwest region
△ Highest point
▲ Mountain peak

N W E S

0   200 mi
0   200 km

The Remarkable Grand Canyon

Suppose that you are in northwest Arizona, about to begin a hike down into the Grand Canyon. Looking out, you understand why 5 million people visit each year. The canyon seems to go on forever. In places, the Grand Canyon is more than 18 miles wide. It is 6,000 feet deep at its deepest point. That is more than one mile!

Birds fly thousands of feet below you in the canyon, including the rare California condor. At the bottom is the Colorado River. The land near the river is desert-like. There, rattlesnakes hunt their prey. At the top of the canyon are forests. The different types of vegetation make a journey down into the canyon like a trip from Canada to Mexico.

The Grand Canyon is a World Heritage Site. This means it is one of 911 places on Earth that are prized for their unique cultural or natural environment. It is one of the world's wonders.

Visitors can ride mules into the canyon.

The Work of Erosion

No one knows exactly how the Grand Canyon was formed. Scientists do know that erosion played a big part in it. **Erosion** is a gradual process of wearing away soil and rock. Scientists say that the rushing water of the Colorado River helped wear away the rock to form the Grand Canyon. This process may have taken millions of years. The water itself gradually wears away the rock. Sand, gravel, and boulders in the river also cut the canyon walls.

Erosion is not only caused by rivers. It can also be caused by rainwater, by melting and moving glaciers, and even by the wind. Rainwater causes erosion when it washes away dirt and soil. It also dissolves certain kinds of rock, such as limestone.

Wind plays a role in erosion when it picks up sand and blows it against rocks or mountains. Even though sand seems harmless, its small, sharp edges wear away the surface of the rocks and mountains.

Every minute of every day, erosion is taking place in the canyons and in other places. The changes happen very slowly over many years.

3. ◎ **Cause and Effect**
Fill in the effect in the chart.

Erosion

> **Cause**
> River water flows over rock.

⬇

> **Effect**

Window Rock, in Arizona, was formed through the process of erosion.

257

Natural Resources

Rich mineral resources are found underground in the Southwest region. Minerals play a key role in the economy in all four states of the region.

In the high lands of New Mexico and Arizona, mining is important to the economy. Some miners in the region say, "If it can't be grown, it must be mined." Arizona is the leading producer of copper in the United States. Today, Arizona copper is mined in two ways. Some mines are underground. Others are what are called open-pit mines. In these, miners blast copper out the ground at the surface. Copper from Arizona is used in everything from coins to computers. Arizona and New Mexico also have gold, silver, and coal mines.

Just as oil is found underground, so is natural gas. **Natural gas** is a fossil fuel like oil. Texas produces more oil and natural gas than any other state. There is oil under more than two thirds of the state, and there are more than 350,000 oil wells there. Oil is processed, or made into chemicals, at a **refinery.**

4. **Study** the map. **Circle** the symbols for oil and natural gas. Where is most of the oil in the Southwest found?

....

....

....

....

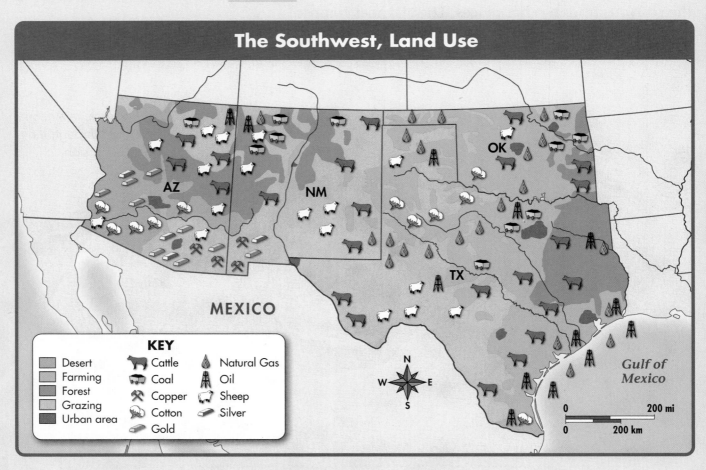

The Southwest, Land Use

KEY

Desert	Cattle
Farming	Coal
Forest	Copper
Grazing	Cotton
Urban area	Gold

Natural Gas
Oil
Sheep
Silver

AZ

NM

OK

TX

MEXICO

Gulf of Mexico

N W E S

0   200 mi
0   200 km

People in the Southwest also farm. Even though there are many mountains and deserts, the Southwest also has productive farmland. Arizona is one of the nation's largest producers of cotton, and Texas has more farms than any other state. In Oklahoma, farmers raise large crops of wheat.

The grasslands of the region are used to raise livestock. People in Texas and Oklahoma raise cattle, goats, and sheep. The Navajo people have been raising sheep in the region since the 1500s.

5. ◉ **Draw Conclusions** What conclusions can you make about the products made in the Southwest?

....

....

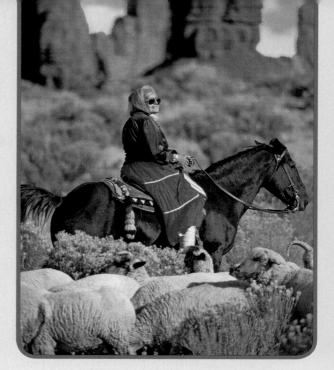

A woman herds sheep.

Got it?

6. ◉ **Fact and Opinion** **Write** one fact and one opinion about the Grand Canyon.

....

....

....

7. ❓ Suppose you were moving to the Southwest from another country. Where would you want to live? How would the landforms affect your decision?

my Story Ideas

....

....

....

⬛ **Stop!** I need help with ....

⏸ **Wait!** I have a question about ....

▶ **Go!** Now I know ....

Search for Information on the Internet

You have just learned about the land and water of the Southwest. Your textbook cannot cover everything about the region, however. Where can you find more information?

To learn more, you can use the Internet. The Internet is a huge network of computers from all around the world. Each site, or place, on the Internet has its own address. The collection of sites on the Internet is called the World Wide Web. Individual sites are called Web sites.

There are millions of Web sites on the Internet. How can you find ones that will help the most? One of the best ways is to use a search engine. A search engine, or browser, is a place on the Internet that provides information about Web sites. Follow the steps to complete a search on the Internet.

Step 1 Type in keywords for your search.

Step 2 Click on the word "Search."

Step 3 Click on the title of the Web site you think will be best. Web sites that end in .edu and .gov are usually reliable Web sites.

Big Bend National Park

Search   Advanced search

About 6,540,000 results (0.21 seconds)

Big Bend National Park
Big Bend National Park, TX 79834. Phone. Visitor Information (432) 477-2251. Weather Information Hotline (432) 477-1183. Fax. (432) 477-1175. Climate ...
Lodging - Campgrounds - Daily Report - Weather www.nps.gov;

Come to Big Bend
Research the history while visiting the National Park
www.come2bigbend.com

Big Bend Park
Big Bend National Park is home to mountains and plateaus. There are many places to find lodging nearby.
www.learnabbigbend.com

Suppose a student wanted to find out about Big Bend National Park in Texas. The student did an Internet search. The first part is on the screen on the opposite page. Use it to answer the questions below.

1. What keywords did the student use?

....

2. What is another term the student could have used to search?

....

....

3. Why is it important to use keywords in a search of the Internet?

....

....

4. Which Web sites in the search seem most reliable? **Circle** one reliable Web site. **Explain**.

....

....

5. Suppose you want to learn the history of the Grand Canyon. Write keywords you would search for. Then list possible sources.

....

....

....

....

Climate of the Southwest

Look at the contrast in the photograph. The brown areas are very dry. Circle the green areas.

In eastern Texas, Caddo Lake is a wet and humid area.

Just as the landforms of the Southwest vary, so does the climate. In Arizona, the summers are hot and dry. More than 1,000 miles away, however, on the coast of Texas, it will still be hot, but there is much more precipitation.

A Range of Climates

Some parts of the region, such as southern Arizona and New Mexico, have an **arid**, or very dry, climate. They may receive some rain, but often go for a long time with little or no rain. Other parts of Arizona and New Mexico receive more rain, but they are still dry, or **semiarid.**

Texas has contrasting climates. The western half of the state is semiarid. As you travel east, however, the climate becomes wetter and more humid. In fact, a storm in Texas holds the record for the most rain in one day. It rained 43 inches! Like Texas, Oklahoma is dry in the western part of the state and receives more rain in the eastern part. In one year, western Oklahoma received less than 15 inches of rain. However, in the east it had about 57 inches of rain.

1. ⊙ **Draw Conclusions Write** a conclusion about how the climate in the Southwest might affect people.

....

....

....

Write why some areas are green and others are brown.

UNLOCK THE BIG ?

I will know that the climate of the Southwest ranges from dry deserts in the west to damper lands in the east.

Vocabulary

arid

semiarid

air mass

savanna

Tornado Alley

The weather in the Southwest can change quickly. Large storms can develop. Then you might see a tornado come out of the sky. The powerful winds are twisting and tearing at nearby trees, cars, and buildings.

More tornadoes occur in Texas than in any other state in the nation. Oklahoma has the second-highest number of tornadoes each year. Both states are part of Tornado Alley. On the map, you see how different air masses meet in the Southwest. An **air mass** is a body of air with the same temperature and humidity. Tornadoes can form when the contrasting air masses clash.

These tornadoes can be deadly. The strong winds can rip roofs off houses and overturn cars. In one year, Oklahoma suffered more than $1 billion in property damage as a result of tornadoes.

2. **Circle** the air masses that can cause tornadoes. Then **write** the names of the states in the Southwest that are part of Tornado Alley.

....

....

....

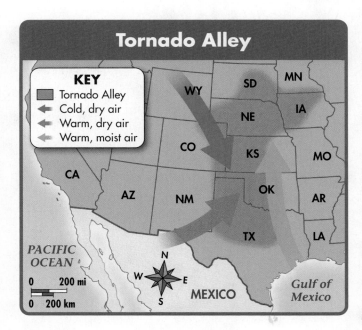

Tornado Alley

KEY
Tornado Alley
◄ Cold, dry air
◄ Warm, dry air
◄ Warm, moist air

WY SD MN
NE IA
CO KS MO
CA AZ NM OK AR
TX LA
PACIFIC OCEAN
N W E S
0 200 mi
0 200 km
MEXICO
Gulf of Mexico

Climate and Vegetation

Since the climate changes from the western part of the region to the eastern part, the types of vegetation change, too. In western Arizona is the Sonoran Desert. Here cactus such as the barrel cactus and the prickly pear are found. There are also large saguaro cactus. Like other plants in the region, this cactus grows long, shallow roots to get water from underground. Its trunk and branches also expand to store the water so that it will survive during the long, dry periods.

As you move to the east, there is enough precipitation to keep the soil moister. The land changes to prairie and grassland. In fact, the Cibola (SEE boh lah) National Forests and National Grasslands cover more than 263,000 acres of land in northern New Mexico, western Oklahoma, and northern Texas.

Farther east, in parts of Texas and Oklahoma, there is an area called Cross Timbers. This area includes a **savanna**, or a grassland with few, scattered trees. It also has thick forests. The forests of the Cross Timbers were often viewed as a starting point for settlers traveling to the West.

Along the eastern edge of the Southwest, in Texas, are swamps and wetlands. In this watery, humid area, reeds and other marsh plants grow. Some areas of land are covered with water most of the year.

A desert owl

In between the eastern and western parts of the region, there are open plains and partly wooded areas like the Cross Timbers in Texas.

Animals of the Southwest

Suppose you could visit one of the Southwest's deserts, such as the Sonoran Desert in Arizona. You might think there were no animals there. You could easily see a golden eagle in the sky, but where are the animals on the ground? They are hiding from the sun. Some, like elf owls and lizards, find protection in the saguaro cactus. Rattlesnakes take shelter under rocks. Gila monsters are poisonous lizards. Like snakes, they find protection under rocks and in holes in the ground.

The prairies and grasslands of the region are home to many different animals. Deer, armadillos, and even bald eagles are found here. American bison graze on the grasslands of Oklahoma. Other animals, such as coyotes, can be found across the grasslands, too. Bighorn sheep live high up in the mountains and forests of New Mexico.

Farther east, in Texas, there are more than 300 miles of coast on the Gulf of Mexico. At Padre Island National Seashore, nearly 400 different kinds of birds live in or pass through the parkland each year. You can find seagulls, egrets, and pelicans here. There are also sea turtles that lay their eggs on the beaches.

3. **Write** where each animal can be found.

American bison ....

egret ....

Gila monster ....

An egret in wetlands

265

The Higher You Go . . .

Not only does the climate change as you travel from west to east, but also it changes from lower to higher. One hot afternoon in Phoenix, Arizona, you decide to go someplace cooler. A drive to Flagstaff changes everything. If Phoenix is more than 100°F, Flagstaff, might be 30 degrees cooler. The two cities are just 150 miles apart, but the difference in elevation is huge. Phoenix is a little more than 1,000 feet above sea level. Located in the mountains, Flagstaff is almost 6,000 feet higher. They are both in one state, but their climates are very different.

In Phoenix, the land is drier as well as lower. When you move to higher elevations, there is more precipitation. In the Sonoran Desert, for example, the lowest areas are at sea level, and the temperatures are high most of the time. But in parts of the Sonoran Desert there are mountain peaks. The highest is 9,000 feet above sea level. In the low areas, you will see cactus plants. In the mountains, there is enough precipitation so that you will see ponderosa pine trees and aspen trees. These trees grow well in the damper high elevations.

4. ◉ **Compare and Contrast Write** C on the area that appears to be the coldest.

Taos Mountain

People's activities vary according to elevation, too. In the low areas of Arizona and New Mexico, people bike and hike on nature trails. People also go on guided horseback tours through places such as the Sonoran Desert. In the mountains, people also hike, but they can ski, sled, and snowboard in addition. Another popular sport in the mountains is mountain biking. Wherever you are in the Southwest, elevation matters.

People climb the large rocks and boulders in the region.

Got it?

5. ◉ **Summarize Write** a summary of how the climate of the Southwest changes as you travel from the west to the east.

....

....

....

....

6. ❓ Sometimes an animal represents a culture. A bald eagle is the national bird of the United States. **Think** about an eagle flying in the sky over the Southwest. **Write** about how an eagle might represent American culture.

my Story Ideas

....

....

....

⬛ **Stop!** I need help with ....

⏸ **Wait!** I have a question about ....

▶ **Go!** Now I know ....

The Southwest's Past

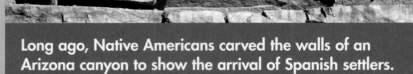

Long ago, Native Americans carved the walls of an Arizona canyon to show the arrival of Spanish settlers.

An Ancient Puebloan cliff dwelling

In 1908, George McJunkin, an African American cowhand, made an amazing discovery. He found bones from long ago near Folsom, New Mexico. At the site was a spear point made by humans more than 10,000 years ago. Twenty-one years later, near Clovis, New Mexico, bones and a spear point were discovered that were even older. Archeologists learned that humans lived in what is now the Southwest far earlier than anyone had thought.

Ancient Cultures of the Region

Archeologists still don't know much about the people who made the Folsom and Clovis spear points. However, they have learned a lot about people who came after them. More than 3,000 years ago, many different groups lived in what is now the Southwest. One of the earliest of these groups was the Ancient Puebloans, or Anasazi (ah nuh SAH zee). The Ancient Puebloans built **cliff dwellings,** or homes in the cliffs, in present-day New Mexico and Arizona. The Hohokam lived in what is now central Arizona. They built a system of canals. These canals brought water from the Salt River and the Gila River to their farms. The Mogollon people lived along rivers in Arizona and New Mexico. There, they farmed and hunted.

Think about an important event that took place in your school. Draw a picture to show a detail of this event.

UNLOCK THE BIG ?

I will know that Native Americans and Spanish settlers have shaped the history and culture of the Southwest.

Vocabulary

cliff dwelling
pueblo
mission

Native Americans in the 1500s

The Ancient Puebloans, Hohokam, and Mogollon groups are the ancestors to some of today's Native Americans. Like the Ancient Puebloans, the Hopi and Zuni built large villages. When the Spanish came, they called these villages **pueblos.** That is the Spanish word for "village." The Hopi and Zuni farmed crops such as corn, beans, and cotton.

The Pima people were farmers, too. They used the canal systems that the Hohokam built to irrigate their crops. The Mojave and Yuma farmed in the river valleys.

Some Native Americans came to the Southwest from other places. The Apache and Comanche people came from the north. Both the Apache and the Comanche were nomads. Nomads are people who move from place to place. The Navajo people came from the north, too. Like other groups, they were farmers. In time, they began to raise sheep.

1. **Underline** on the map each of the tribes named in the text.

Native Americans of the Southwest

Colorado River
Hopi
ROCKY MOUNTAINS
Pueblo
Navajo
Mojave
Zuni
Red River
Papago
Comanche
Wichita
Pima
Apache
N
W E
S
Rio Grande
Apache
Gulf of Mexico

KEY
Southwest region
Map shows present-day borders.

0   200 mi
0   200 km

Coronado explored much of the Southwest. He searched for, but never found, cities of gold.

The Spanish Arrive

In the 1500s, Spain sent explorers to the Americas. Álvar Núñez Cabeza de Vaca was part of an early expedition. In 1528, the expedition landed on the coast of what is now Texas. Soon, however, Cabeza de Vaca was one of only four survivors. Another was an African, Estevan. Cabeza de Vaca and Estevan set out to reach Mexico City. It was the capital of New Spain located in what is now Mexico. When they arrived in the city, they said that they heard about rich "cities of gold" while they were traveling. These cities could be found in what is now the Southwest region.

In 1539, Estevan and Father Marcos de Niza set out to find the cities. Father Marcos de Niza was a Spanish missionary. When they reached southeastern Arizona, Father Marcos de Niza saw what he thought were cities of gold shining in the sun.

When the governor of New Spain heard of cities with "walls of gold blocks . . . and streets paved with silver," he wanted to find them. In 1540, he sent Francisco Vásquez de Coronado to find the golden cities, called Cíbola. Near the present-day border of New Mexico and Arizona, Coronado reached the Zuni pueblo. He found that it was not made of gold after all.

2. ◉ **Cause and Effect** **Underline** the effects of the arrival of Cabeza de Vaca and Estevan in Mexico City.

The Colonial Period

Some Spanish explorers would not give up the dream of finding gold in the Southwest. One was Juan de Oñate. In 1598, he led 400 settlers north to build a colony and to find riches. The settlers found no riches, and many were afraid of the Native Americans that lived nearby. As a result, most of them returned to Mexico. However, the Spanish soon built other colonies in the Southwest.

At the heart of the Spanish colonies were missions. A **mission** is the headquarters of missionaries. The goal of the missions was to claim land and teach Christian beliefs to the Native Americans. The Spanish set up missions across the Southwest. Near many, they built settlements called presidios. Soldiers lived at the presidios so that they could protect the missions.

At the missions, Native Americans were given food and protected from enemies. They were put to work farming or making goods. Sometimes, they were forced to live and work at the missions. At times they were treated poorly. At other times, however, the Spanish treated them with kindness.

In 1687, Father Eusebio Kino (eh oh SEH bee oh KEE noh) started three missions in what is now Arizona. Here he taught the Pima and Yuma groups for 25 years.

3. ◎ **Draw Conclusions**
Look at the mission.
Write clues that show that the people on missions grew or made most of what they needed.

....

....

....

....

San José Mission in Texas

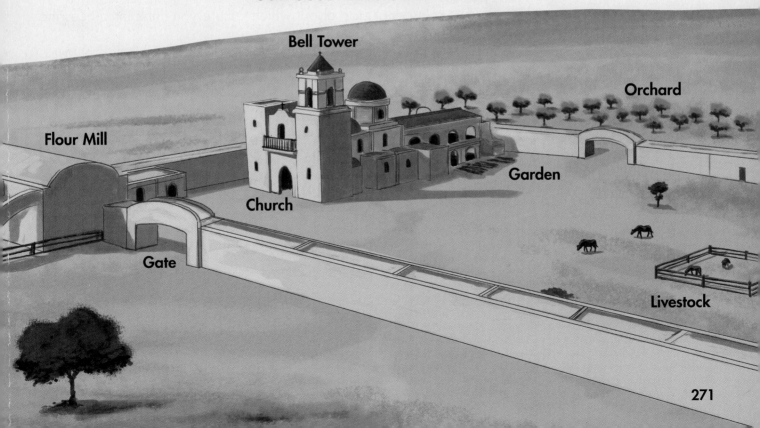

Bell Tower

Orchard

Flour Mill

Garden

Church

Gate

Livestock

271

Influences Past and Present

Like much of the nation, the Southwest has great diversity, or mixture of cultures. People from all over the world have come to live in the region. However, the Spanish, Mexican, and Native American cultures have been especially influential in the Southwest.

In Arizona, New Mexico, and Texas, many people have Spanish or Mexican roots. Many people speak both English and Spanish. You see Spanish-style buildings, and you can eat Mexican and Spanish foods. People in the Southwest also celebrate two important holidays from Mexico. One is Cinco de Mayo on May 5, which celebrates a Mexican military victory. The other is on September 16, which is Mexican Independence Day.

The Southwest region is also still home to Native Americans. Many Navajo, Hopi, and Mojave live on reservations. The Navajo Reservation covers about 26,000 square miles. There are other Native American reservations in the Southwest, too. These include the Gila River Reservation and the Colorado River Indian Tribes Reservation in Arizona.

4. ◉ **Draw Conclusions** **Underline** three of the different cultures in the Southwest. Then **write** a conclusion about which culture you think influences the region the most.

....
....
....
....
....
....

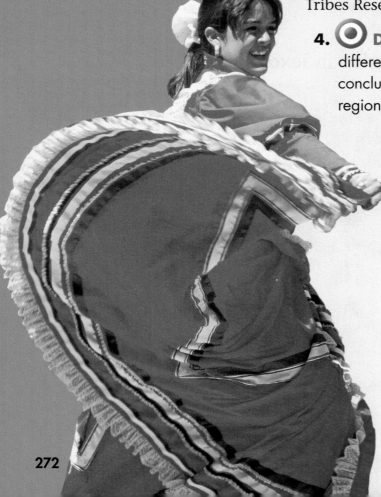

People in the Southwest perform traditional dances from Mexico.

Visiting the Southwest

Every year, millions of people visit the Southwest. Many of these people come to experience the mix of cultures. They come to see the cultural life in places from San Antonio, Texas, to Santa Fe, New Mexico. They attend festivals, eat Mexican food, hear music, and see settlements that were once missions.

Tourists come, too, to visit Native American sites. At places like Canyon de Chelly, they see the carvings and cliff dwellings of ancient Native Americans. They also visit pueblos. They learn more about the Navajo, Hopi, and Zuni people. They learn that, like Mexican and Spanish culture, Native Americans and their culture are a key part of the Southwest.

Weavings, pottery, and jewelry made by Navajo artists are popular with collectors.

Got it?

5. **⊙ Draw Conclusions** How did the arrival of Spanish settlers change the lives of Native Americans?

....

....

....

6. **?** Which Native American groups live or lived in your area? What would you like to learn about them? **Write** one question you would ask if you could visit the group.

my **Story Ideas**

....

....

....

◻ Stop! I need help with ....

⏸ Wait! I have a question about ....

▶ Go! Now I know ....

Growth of the Southwest

Envision It!

People today continue to practice the skills that some of the first cowboys used.

Stephen F. Austin

Inside the Alamo were more than 200 Texas soldiers and colonists. The Alamo was a Spanish mission in present-day San Antonio, Texas. During a war in 1836, several thousand Mexican soldiers attacked the Alamo. More than 180 Texas soldiers died. Who were these men? Why were they willing to die for Texas?

New Arrivals

In 1821, an American named Stephen F. Austin led a group of American settlers into Texas. At this time, Texas was part of Mexico. Over the next 15 years, more settlers from the United States moved to Texas. With each married man promised more than 4,000 acres, many Americans saw opportunity in this land.

By the 1830s, many Texans wanted to break away from Mexico. Mexico did not want to let Texas go, and soon a war started. Although the Mexicans won at the Alamo, they lost the war. People in Texas declared Texas a new country, the Republic of Texas. Sam Houston, a settler and soldier, became its president.

In 1845, Texas was annexed to the United States. To **annex** means to add to. The battles with Mexico were not over, though. The annexation of Texas led the United States into the Mexican-American War. At the end of the war, the United States won even more land. This land included what is now New Mexico and California, and most of Arizona.

What do you think these people are doing? Write your answer above.

UNLOCK THE BIG ?

I will know that the Southwest continued to grow as settlers from the United States moved into the region.

Vocabulary

annex

meat-packing

ranch

homestead

gusher

metropolitan area

Changing Life for Native Americans

Settlers from other states poured into Texas, Arizona, and New Mexico. So did immigrants from Europe. Many of these settlers moved to the river valleys, including the Pecos and Rio Grande valleys. Here there was both water and good soil for farming. Some of this land was used by Native Americans. Since the 1830s, the United States had forced many Native Americans to move to reservations. The largest was the Indian Territory, in present-day Oklahoma.

In 1863 and 1864, the Navajo were driven from their land. The United States government wanted to stop the fighting between the Navajo and settlers in New Mexico. Led by an officer named Kit Carson, United States soldiers forced the Navajo to move to a reservation. The Navajo had to walk about 300 miles during the winter months. During the walk, many Navajo died. This difficult journey is called "The Long Walk."

In 1868, the government returned some of the land in present-day Arizona, New Mexico, and Utah, to the Navajo. This land is still the home of the Navajo Nation today.

Members of the Navajo Nation today

1. ◎ **Draw Conclusions** How did the desire for land in the Southwest lead to fighting?

....

....

Cattle Country

Settlers in Texas raised cattle to sell. In 1867, a man named Philip Armour started the largest meat-packing plant in Chicago, Illinois. A **meat-packing** plant processes the meat from animals for food. In time, this plant and others began to process beef.

People in Texas could raise cattle on their ranches to supply the beef. A **ranch** is a large farm where livestock is raised. The challenge was getting the cattle to the meat-packing plants. How did the cattle get there? Cattle drives and the railroad were the answer. Cowhands "drove" the cattle north along cattle trails. These trails met the railroads at places such as Kansas and Missouri. Cattle were loaded onto freight cars. The cars carried the cattle to meat-packing plants in Chicago and Kansas City.

2. On the map, **mark** a route for a cattle drive. Go from southern Texas to a railroad stop.

Nat Love was a well-known African American cowhand on the cattle trails of the Southwest.

Cattle Trails Meet the Railroads

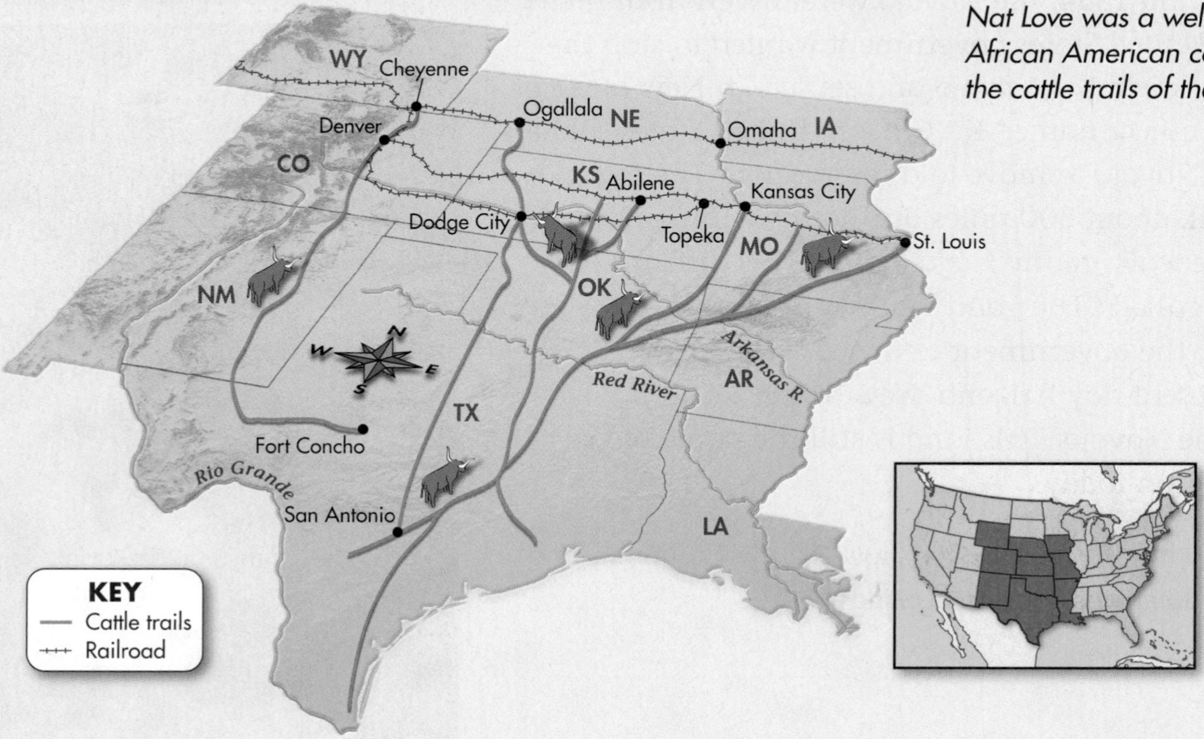

WY
Cheyenne
Denver
CO
Ogallala NE
Omaha IA
KS Abilene
Dodge City
Topeka
Kansas City
St. Louis
MO
NM
OK
Arkansas R.
Red River
AR
TX
Fort Concho
Rio Grande
San Antonio
LA

KEY
— Cattle trails
+++ Railroad

Cattle ranching quickly became a big business. As the demand for beef grew, so did ranching. Ranches were started across the Southwest, as well as in the states of the northern plains. These lands where bison once grazed were now filling with cattle.

Over time, however, ranching changed. Railroad lines were laid in the Southwest. Also, more settlers were moving to the region. The government gave them land to start farms called **homesteads.** To protect their crops, homesteaders, as the farmers were called, put up fences. Cattle could no longer freely roam the grasslands, and the routes the cattle drives followed were often blocked by fences. The days of the long cattle drives came to an end.

Birth of the Oil Industry

More changes came to the Southwest in the 1900s. On January 10, 1901, workers were drilling an oil well at Spindletop, near Beaumont, Texas. At 10:30 that morning, the well exploded. Six tons of pipe shot out of the ground. Out came mud and gas, and then oil shot up more than 100 feet in the air. It took workers nine days to stop the flow of oil called a **gusher.**

The discovery of oil at Spindletop amazed people. Few people had ever seen this much oil before. Soon, land around Spindletop went from $150 to $50,000 for one lot. Oil derricks, or the frames that hold the drills, became a common site. Workers and oil companies rushed to the area. Oil companies spent billions of dollars looking for oil and natural gas in the Southwest. Today, the oil industry is still important to the region.

Oil derricks covered the land over oil fields in Texas.

3. ⊙ **Draw Conclusions Write** a conclusion about how land might be used near an oil field.

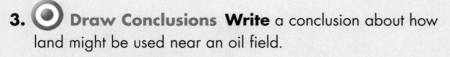

Still Growing

The Southwest is still a region of wide-open spaces. However, it is also a region of large cities and growth. In fact, Houston, Texas; San Antonio, Texas; Dallas, Texas; and Phoenix, Arizona, are four of the nation's fastest growing metropolitan areas. A **metropolitan area** is a large city and its surrounding area. Texas has more farms than any other state. However, most of the population lives in cities. So do most of the people in Arizona. In New Mexico and Oklahoma, too, most people live in cities.

Why are people moving to cities in the Southwest? High-tech industries and medical centers draw people to cities like Dallas and Houston. Many people come to Phoenix to work in the service industry. Across the region, "snowbirds," or people from states with cold climates, come to enjoy the warm weather of the Southwest and its beauty. People retire to the region for the same reasons. Immigrants come, too, largely from Mexico and Central America.

Not all of the people in cities in the Southwest have come to live there. Tourists come to experience the beauty of the region. In fact, tourism is New Mexico's largest industry.

As more people move to the Southwest, there are new job opportunities in industries such as construction.

The area around Phoenix is called the Valley of the Sun.

4. ◎ **Compare and Contrast Compare** the reasons these people settled in the Southwest.

Reasons for Settlement	
Group	**Reasons**
Early American settlers	land
Homesteaders	to start farms
Oil workers	
Retired people	

Got it?

5. ◎ **Draw Conclusions Write** a conclusion about how railroads changed cattle ranching.

....

....

....

....

6. ❓ What cultures influenced the history of the area where you live? **Write** a description of a talk you could give to tourists.

my Story Ideas

....

....

....

▪ **Stop!** I need help with ....

❚❚ **Wait!** I have a question about ....

▶ **Go!** Now I know ....

Life in a Dry Land

Envision It!

Average Water Use

Use	Gallons per day
Bathing	80
Bathroom	108
Cooking/drinking	12
Dishwashing	15
Laundry	35

A family of four can use about 250 gallons of water each day. That is enough water to fill a bathtub almost 8 times!

You look at your new front yard. Once it was covered with bright green grass and flower gardens. In the hot New Mexico sun, however, the yard had to be watered every day. Your family used hundreds of gallons of water every time you turned on the sprinklers! Your parents explained that there are water shortages in the Southwest. You're all finding ways to conserve water. One way is to get rid of all that grass. Now your yard has a cactus garden. It has native flowers that grow without a lot of moisture. It's a beautiful yard, and you are proud of it.

Where Does the Water Come From?

People cannot live without water. Neither can plants or animals. Yet water has always been a scarce resource in the Southwest. Even though some places in the Southwest get plenty of rainfall, remember that much of the region has a climate that is either arid or semiarid.

Cactus grow in the desert because they can survive with very little water.

Vocabulary

reservoir
aqueduct
drought
gray water

Circle one use of water on the chart that you think you could cut down on. How would you do it?

Anywhere in the world, there are two main sources of water. These are ground water and surface water. Ground water is water that is underground. Ground water resources are called aquifers. Rainwater and melted snow soak into the ground and become part of an aquifer. When people dig wells, they are tapping into aquifers.

Surface water is water in lakes, streams, and rivers. Of course, the oceans are also surface water, but salt water is not useful for most human needs. In the Southwest, there are two main sources of surface water: the Colorado River and the Rio Grande.

The Colorado River is especially important. It is the main supply of water for almost 30 million people. High in the mountains, the source of the river is rain and melting snow. States in the Southwest and the West agree on how to share the Colorado's water. In the 1930s, the United States built Hoover Dam on the river. The dam created a reservoir. A **reservoir** is a lake where water is stored. The Lake Mead reservoir was created by Hoover Dam. It extends more than 100 miles behind the dam. It is a key part of the Southwest's water supply.

Lake Mead, created by Hoover Dam, is one of the world's largest human-made lakes.

1. **Underline** the source of the Colorado River. **Write** how the weather could affect the amount of water in the river.

....

....

Who Uses the Water and How?

In both Arizona and New Mexico, most of the water is used for agriculture. Through irrigation, farmers turn dry soil into rich farmland. That takes a lot of water, though. Experts say that it takes over 1,000 gallons of water to grow the food needed for a typical family dinner.

Who uses the rest of the water? Cities supply water to their residents, or the people who live there. Many businesses use water, too. Other water is used by power plants. These plants use flowing water to turn machines to produce electricity. Dams are one of the places that create electricity. In fact, Hoover Dam makes electricity for more than 1 million people.

Experts study the water supply and the amount of water that people use. They try to predict future needs. Many expect that more water will be used in residences, or homes, in the future. Why? The answer is "more people." The population in the dry areas of the Southwest continues to grow.

2. 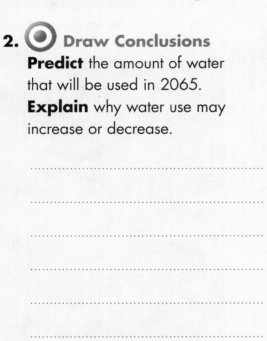 **Draw Conclusions**
Predict the amount of water that will be used in 2065.
Explain why water use may increase or decrease.

....

....

....

....

....

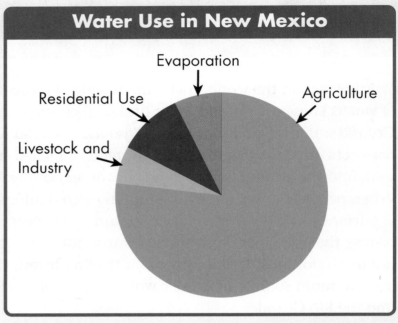

Water Use in New Mexico

Source: NM Office of the State Engineer

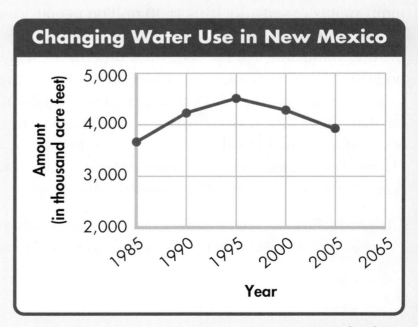

Changing Water Use in New Mexico

Source: U.S. Geological Survey

Life in a Hot, Dry Land

The warm climate has drawn people to the Southwest for many years. People have adapted to both the heat and the limited amount of water.

If it is 104° in New Mexico, you may not want to stand outside in the sun. Most likely, you would rather be in your cool home or even a movie theater. Today, most public places are air conditioned. Air conditioning was invented more than 100 years ago. The first large air-conditioned office building opened in San Antonio, Texas, in 1928. Air conditioning made life in the Southwest more comfortable. People could go inside to escape the heat. Since life in the region became less harsh, the population grew.

Evidence of how people have adapted to the Southwest can be found at people's homes. This home has a yard that uses less water than a yard filled with grass.

As more people moved to the Southwest, cities grew in areas without much water. Phoenix, Arizona, is one of these cities. How does Phoenix supply enough water for people to live? It uses aqueducts. **Aqueducts** are systems with pipes that carry water long distances. Aqueducts bring water from the Colorado River to Phoenix. Farmers also use aqueducts to bring water to their farms.

3.  **Cause and Effect Fill in** the effects.

Ways People Adapt

Causes		Effects
People use air conditioning to cool homes and businesses.	→	
Aqueducts bring water to cities.	→	

Water Shortages

The Southwest is one of the fastest-growing regions in the country. Arizona is a good example. Its population is nearly four times larger now than it was just 40 years ago. This means there is a need for more water.

However, recently there has been a water shortage. Parts of Arizona and New Mexico have experienced a drought. A **drought** is a period of time when there is little or no rain. When there is a drought, less water is available for use. In times of severe drought, there may not be enough water for farmers to raise crops. Animals in the wild may also have less water as rivers and streams dry up.

The people in the Southwest are meeting the challenge of the water shortage. Scientists, experts, and ordinary citizens are working to use water more wisely. Farmers have developed ways to use less water for irrigation. Many now use drip irrigation. In drip irrigation, less water is lost through evaporation since the water drips directly onto the base of the plants.

Cities and industries are helping, too. Some use new sources of water. They use "gray water" to water public lands or in factories. **Gray water** is recycled water. It is not safe for drinking by people or washing the fruit and vegetables that people eat, but it is useful in other ways.

In the 1930s, a severe drought in the Great Plains lasted many years. The drought left farmers in Oklahoma, Texas, and New Mexico with dry, dusty soil.

Families are also working to save water. In twenty years, for example, people in Phoenix, Arizona, have cut their water use by about 20 percent. Many new showers, toilets, and washing machines are designed to use less water. Families also try to use less water outdoors. They follow city guidelines that recommend that they water their yard less often and water only at night or early morning. This way, less water is lost through evaporation. Many people also have stopped washing their cars to save water. Across the Southwest, people know that their lives and their region depend on water.

Signs remind people to fix leaking faucets so that water is not wasted.

We need to save every drop!

4. How can you and your family save water? **Write** two tips.

....

....

....

Got it?

5. ⊙ **Summarize** **Write** a summary of how technology helps people adapt to the Southwest.

....

....

....

....

6. ❓ "The bigger, the better" is a saying in American culture. But growth my Story Ideas
brings challenges. **Write** a new saying that takes a shortage of resources into account.

....

....

■ **Stop!** I need help with ....

❚❚ **Wait!** I have a question about ....

▶ **Go!** Now I know ....

Study Guide

Southwestern Land and Water

- Landforms of the Southwest include plains, mountains, and canyons.
- Along with the Gulf of Mexico, the Colorado River and the Rio Grande shape the region.
- The Southwest is a rich source of minerals.

Lesson 2

Climate of the Southwest

- The range of Southwest climates, from humid to arid, affects the vegetation that grows in the region.
- Tornadoes are common in Tornado Alley.
- The climate in the Southwest changes as the elevation changes.

Lesson 3

The Southwest's Past

- Native Americans have lived in the Southwest for thousands of years.
- Spanish explorers and missionaries changed the region beginning in the 1500s.
- Visitors come to enjoy the mix of cultures in the Southwest.

Lesson 4

Growth of the Southwest

- Availability of land and rich resources, such as oil, have drawn people to the Southwest for hundreds of years.
- Many Native Americans of the Southwest were uprooted in the past.
- The Southwest today is one of the fastest-growing parts of the country.

Lesson 5

Life in a Dry Land

- Water is a scarce resource in much of the Southwest.
- Ground water from aquifers and surface water from the Colorado River and the Rio Grande are the region's main water sources.
- Southwestern residents are learning to save water in new ways.

Lesson 1

Southwestern Land and Water

1. **Match** the words and phrases.

_____ plains   a. high, flat land

_____ basin and range   b. flat land, good for farming

_____ mountains   c. low areas and mountain ranges

_____ plateaus   d. high peaks

Lesson 2

Climate of the Southwest

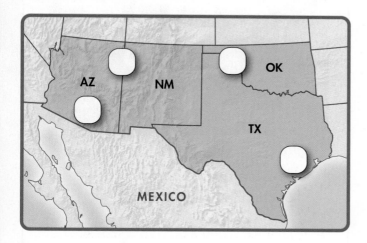

2. **Label** one location for each item below.

A   Arid land

G   Gulf Coastal Plains

T   Tornado Alley

P   Plateaus

Lesson 3

The Southwest's Past

3. Place these events in chronological order. Number them 1 for the earliest through 4 for the latest event.

_____ The Hohokam farmed in Arizona.

_____ Coronado saw the Zuni pueblos.

_____ Folsom people carved spear points.

_____ Father Kino started missions.

4. **List** two reasons why Spanish settlers came to the Southwest.

....

....

....

....

5. ◉ **Draw Conclusions** **Write** a conclusion about what makes the cultural diversity in the Southwest special.

....

....

....

....

....

....

....

Review and Assessment

Lesson 4

Growth of the Southwest

6. ◎ **Cause and Effect Fill in** the cause-and-effect chart.

Cause	Effect
....	Many Americans move to Texas after 1821.

7. What was the goal of a cattle drive?

....

....

....

8. Why was Spindletop important?

....

....

....

Lesson 5

Life in a Dry Land

9. Why is there a water shortage in the Southwest?

....

....

....

10. ❓ **How does where we live affect who we are?**

Use the photograph and question below to think more about this chapter's Big Question.

How are people adapting to the dry land in the Southwest?

....

....

....

....

....

....

Go online to write and illustrate your own **myStory Book** using the **myStory Ideas** from this chapter.

How does where we live affect who we are?

By now you have learned a lot about the geography of the Southwest region. You have also learned ways that geography affects how people live. Remember that *culture* means the way of life of a group of people. The Navajo had one culture. The Spanish had another. Both were affected by the physical geography of the Southwest.

Think about your way of life. How do landforms and climate affect it?
Write about one way in which geography affects your culture.

....

....

....

....

Now, **draw** a picture to illustrate your writing.

While you're online, check out the **myStory Current** Events area where you can create your own book on a topic that's in the news.

Regions: The West

How does where we live affect who we are?

Many people first settled in the West because of the region's rich resources and the chance to make a better life for themselves. **Think** about your community. **List** some reasons why people might have settled there.

....

....

....

....

San Diego's Balboa Park has gardens, museums, theaters, and a zoo.

San Diego
The City by the Sea

my Story Video

Catalina has lived in the West her whole life. "We have it all here in California," she says. Today, Catalina, or Cat as she is usually called, is going to show us some of her favorite places in her hometown of San Diego.

The city of San Diego has a climate and environment that many people say is nearly perfect. "It's almost always sunny and warm. But there's enough rain to keep it green," says Cat. Lush greenery, enormous parks, and beautiful beaches make San Diego a very popular city. "We have lots to see," she says. "Let's get going!"

As Cat arrives at Mission Basilica San Diego de Alcala, a tour guide greets her. "Welcome, I'm Janet. What's your name?" Janet asks. "I'm Catalina, but my friends call me Cat. Who built this gorgeous place and when?" Cat asks.

The Mission Basilica San Diego de Alcala

Janet, the tour guide, gives Cat a tour of the Mission Basilica San Diego de Alcala.

The USS *Midway*, which is now a museum, is docked in San Diego Bay.

"This mission was founded by Spain in 1769 and was California's first mission," answers Janet. Cat has seen other California missions. She never realized that the one in her hometown was California's first! California's culture reflects the state's Spanish history in lots of places. Many missions, built during the Spanish colonial period, still exist in California.

Cat's next stop is San Diego Bay. She loves to watch the activity in this busy waterway. "Those cruise ships are returning from vacationing in the Pacific Ocean!" she shouts over the noise. The bay is filled with cargo ships loaded with exports.

Shipping is a major industry in the West. Ships carry lumber, agricultural products, and other goods from United States ports to countries along the Pacific Rim. These are the nations that border the Pacific Ocean. "I love the sound of seagulls," Cat says. As a navy ship floats by, Cat remembers our next stop. "Come on," she says, "we're just getting started."

Cat stands alongside San Diego Bay and enjoys the scene.

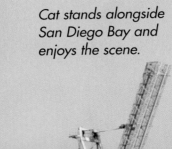

Cat takes a ride on a ferry boat. Behind her is the city of San Diego.

A perfect shell found at a San Diego beach

Just up the shore, we arrive at Tuna Harbor Park. Towering over the park is the USS *Midway,* which floats in the bay. This ship is the longest-serving Navy aircraft carrier of the twentieth century. "Whoa!" Cat exclaims, "It's so amazing and huge!"

From the end of World War II to the first Gulf War, this carrier has housed more than 225,000 service men and women. "A 47-year tour of duty," Cat says. "Now that's a long time." Today the USS *Midway* stays at its home on the bay. Visitors can get a tour of the grand ship.

Close to Tuna Harbor Park is the Broadway Pier ferry landing. "Ready for a ferry ride?" Cat asks as she gets on the boat. This ferry crosses San Diego Bay and takes passengers to nearby Coronado Island. From the ferry you get a great view of San Diego. "That is my city," Cat says proudly.

When the boat reaches the Coronado ferry landing, Cat rushes off the boat toward a beautiful beach nearby. She is ready to explore her favorite destination on today's journey. "I love the beach. I could stay here all day!" she says as she hurries to change into her swimming suit.

Sunny beaches are one of the West's most popular attractions. Cat does look quite at home building her sandcastle near the water's edge. "Adios! Thanks for coming!" she says as she skips down the beach. "Come see me again!" It's just another fantastic ending to a perfect day in the West.

Think About It The West's Spanish history is seen in its missions and elsewhere. What buildings or locations near you show history in the same way? As you read this chapter, look for other ways the West's history is seen today.

A Varied Land

Envision It!

THIS WAY TO THE PACIFIC

THIS WAY TO THE ATLANTIC

The Continental Divide is a line of high land that runs north and south along the Rocky Mountains.

Mount Rainier is part of the Cascade Range.

The West is a region with many different landforms. A person could hike a mountain trail in the morning and then splash in the Pacific Ocean in the evening. The West has been shaped by volcanoes and earthquakes and mighty rivers that wind like ribbons through the region. The West includes the states of California, Oregon, Montana, Wyoming, Colorado, Utah, Nevada, Idaho, Washington, Alaska, and Hawaii.

Mountains of the West

From Alaska, through Canada, and on south through New Mexico, the Rocky Mountains form the largest mountain range in North America. They stretch more than 3,000 miles in length and more than 300 miles in width in some places.

The Rockies, as they are often called, rise up in steep peaks and form the western border of the Great Plains. Coming west from the east, they tower over the plain's flat lands.

West of the Rocky Mountains is another mountain range located in eastern California and western Nevada called the Sierra Nevada. Some of these mountains are more than 14,000 feet above sea level. Sea level is the height of the surface of the ocean.

1. **Identify** the largest mountain range in North America.

....

Write what you think happens when rain falls to the east and west of the Continental Divide.

UNLOCK THE BIG ?

I will know that the land of the West is varied and sometimes reshaped by earthquakes and volcanoes.

Vocabulary

volcano

geyser

magma

tsunami

Another mountain range, called the Cascades, extends from northern California up through Oregon and Washington. Mount Rainier, the tallest mountain in this range is more than 14,400 feet above sea level.

To see the highest mountain peak in North America, visitors head north to Alaska. Rising to a height of more than 20,000 feet above sea level is Mount McKinley. This mountain is also known as Denali.

The Long Coast

The Pacific Coast is the land along the western border of the United States. This is where the land meets the Pacific Ocean. California, Oregon, Washington, and Alaska are the states that share this coastline.

Sea arches and sea stacks are unusual landforms that visitors can spot along the coast. A sea arch is formed by waves wearing away large rocks along a coast. Over time, the waves erode the middle of a rock to form an arch. As erosion continues, part of the arch may break. The pile of rocks that is left behind is called a sea stack.

The West, Political

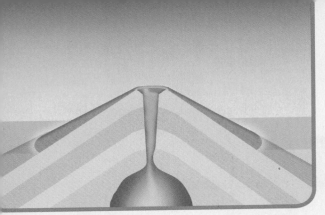

This diagram shows magma rising under an active volcano in Hawaii.

Volcanoes

Some of the high peaks that make up the mountain ranges of the West are actually volcanoes. A **volcano** is an opening in the surface of the earth through which gas, ash, and lava are forced out. As hot lava flows from the volcano, it begins to cool and harden. More lava flows on top and begins to build up, creating land. In some cases, underwater volcanoes in the ocean erupt. The hot lava soon cools and hardens. Eventually, after enough undersea eruptions, the cooled lava will rise above sea level and form an island.

The Cascade Range, which spreads from northern California up through Oregon and Washington, has many volcanoes. Most of them are not erupting. However, Washington's Mount Saint Helens is an active volcano that erupted violently in 1980.

Hawaii is our only state made up of islands. Some of these islands began forming from undersea eruptions about 70 million years ago. Eventually, the islands rose above the Pacific Ocean.

2. Circle the region's highest and lowest points.

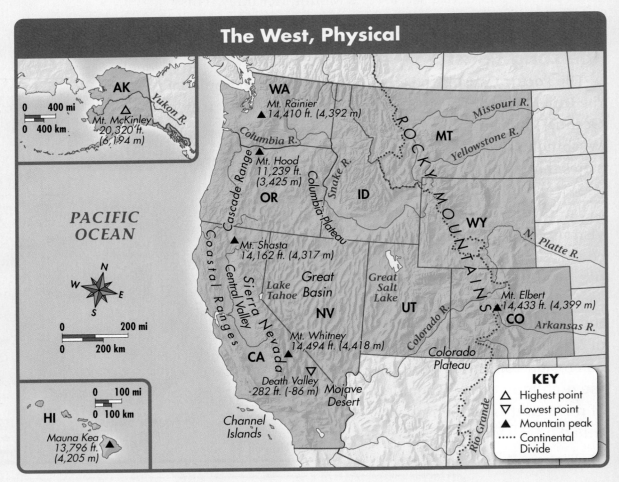

The West, Physical

AK
0 400 mi
0 400 km
Mt. McKinley 20,320 ft. (6,194 m)
Yukon R.

PACIFIC OCEAN

0 200 mi
0 200 km

HI
0 100 mi
0 100 km
Mauna Kea 13,796 ft. (4,205 m)

WA
Mt. Rainier ▲14,410 ft. (4,392 m)
Columbia R.
Mt. Hood 11,239 ft. (3,425 m)
Cascade Range
OR
Coastal Ranges
Central Valley
Mt. Shasta 14,162 ft. (4,317 m)
Sierra Nevada
Lake Tahoe
Great Basin
CA
Mt. Whitney 14,494 ft. (4,418 m)
Death Valley -282 ft. (-86 m)
Mojave Desert
Channel Islands

Columbia Plateau
Snake R.
ID
MT
Yellowstone R.
Missouri R.
ROCKY MOUNTAINS
WY
N. Platte R.
Great Salt Lake
UT
Colorado R.
NV
Mt. Elbert ▲14,433 ft. (4,399 m)
CO
Arkansas R.
Colorado Plateau
Rio Grande

KEY
△ Highest point
▽ Lowest point
▲ Mountain peak
····· Continental Divide

Geysers and Hot Springs

In Wyoming's Yellowstone National Park, more than 10,000 hot springs and hundreds of geysers attract tourists from around the globe. A **geyser** is a hot, underground spring that shoots steam and boiling water high into the air. The park's most famous geyser is Old Faithful, which erupts about every 60 to 110 minutes.

The geysers and hot springs of Yellowstone occur because groundwater there is heated by **magma**, or melted rock that is underneath Earth's surface. Pools of heated water that form are known as hot springs. Only when these pools of hot water erupt, such as Old Faithful does, are they called geysers.

Earthquakes

A fault is a break in Earth's crust that is created by the movement of giant blocks of Earth. These massive blocks sometimes overlap or slip past each other. When the blocks finally break free of each other, the energy that is released is an earthquake. There are a great number of faults in the West, especially along the coastline.

Earthquakes can cause terrible damage. Landslides of rocks, mud, snow, and ice can slide down mountains, knocking down forests and burying buildings. When huge blocks of Earth shift along the fault lines, roads, highways, and railroads can split apart. Buildings and bridges can collapse from the shaking.

In March 1964, an earthquake hit Prince William Sound in Alaska. In some places the earthquake pushed the land up by 82 feet. This same earthquake created a number of tsunamis. A **tsunami** is a wall of water that can be 100 feet higher than an average wave. These enormous waves are dangerous when they crash along the shore. In March 2011, an earthquake in Japan created tsunamis that killed many thousands of people.

3. **⊙ Cause and Effect Underline** why the West is more likely to suffer an earthquake than other regions.

During an eruption, Old Faithful can spray more than 8,000 gallons of water into the air in about five minutes.

Rivers and Lakes of the West

When people first settled in the West, they often made their homes near rivers, streams, and lakes. The main reason is that people and their animals needed water to survive. Another reason is that long ago, it was easier for people to travel and transport goods by water than by land.

One important western river is the Columbia, which begins its journey of more than 1,200 miles in the Rocky Mountains of Canada. It then winds south and west through Washington and Oregon before spilling into the Pacific Ocean. Over time, the river cut through rock to form the beautiful Columbia River Gorge, a deep valley that is set between mountains.

The many dams on the Columbia River and its tributaries, or the smaller rivers that flow into the Columbia, provide electricity for homes and businesses. The energy created by this blocked water is a valuable resource in the region. However, the dams have not been good for the river's fish. The salmon population has decreased sharply since the dams were built. Scientists and other experts are studying the problem and looking for ways to solve it.

The Willamette River is an important river in Oregon that feeds into the Columbia. As the Willamette drains, the rich soil stays behind in the Willamette Valley. The soil provides ideal conditions to grow a variety of fruits and vegetables.

The Columbia River Gorge forms part of the boundary between Washington and Oregon.

Many lakes in the West are freshwater lakes. Alaska has more than 3 million lakes. Lake Iliamna, about 200 miles southwest of Anchorage, is Alaska's largest lake.

Utah's Great Salt Lake is a saltwater lake. This lake is also known as a sump lake because it does not flow into another body of water. The Great Salt lake has an even higher salt content than the oceans. Rivers that feed into the lake carry small amounts of salt in their water. As the water evaporates, the salt is left behind and the lake becomes saltier.

Salt crystals form at the edges of the Great Salt Lake.

4. ⊙ **Compare and Contrast Write** how a sump lake is different from other lakes.

....

....

Got it?

5. ⊙ **Summarize Write** how the islands of Hawaii were formed.

....

....

....

6. ? On your vacation to the West, you saw a sea arch, a landform created by wind and water. **Write** a postcard to a friend to describe the sea arch and how it was formed.

my Story Ideas

....

....

....

⬜ **Stop!** I need help with ....

⏸ **Wait!** I have a question about ....

▶ **Go!** Now I know ....

Climate of the West

Bettles, AK, -19°F

Death Valley, CA, 115°F

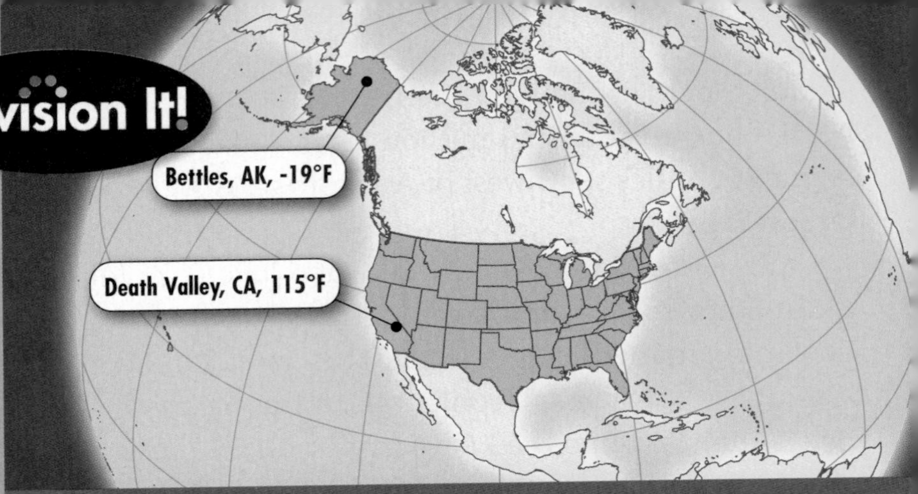

This map shows a January temperature in part of Alaska and a July temperature in part of California.

From the baking heat of a summer day in the desert to a snowy, frozen plain in winter, the West region has a range of climates. Climate is the average weather patterns in an area throughout a year.

Extreme Heat and Cold

Many areas in the West have hot summers. Death Valley, a desert in southern California, has the most extreme heat. In the summer, the temperature often rises to 120°F. In 1913, a North American record was set when the temperature there reached 134°F.

Death Valley is located in the Great Basin, a desert region in the West. This area is called a basin because it is like a sink that holds water. Nearby rivers and streams drain into the area. They do not flow away to the ocean. Utah's Great Salt Lake is one area that collects this water. The desert areas in the Great Basin have hot, dry summers.

People who live in Idaho, Montana, Wyoming, Colorado, and parts of Washington are used to heavy snows and freezing winter temperatures. However, the most extreme winter temperatures occur in Alaska, our northernmost state.

Death Valley, California, gets an average of less than 2 inches of rain each year.

UNLOCK
THE BIG
?

I will know how weather and climate vary in different parts of the West.

_____

Write how living in these two places would compare.

Tundra is a level, frozen area in the far north where the temperatures are so cold that trees cannot grow. In winter, the Alaskan tundra often has extremely cold temperatures. On January 23, 1971, the temperature in Prospect Creek, Alaska, dropped to −80° F.

Moderate Climates

Many areas in the West have climates that are more moderate. This means that the temperatures are warm, not hot, in the summer. Winters are cool, not cold. In some areas of California, such as San Diego, people enjoy mild temperatures throughout the year.

Hawaii has a tropical climate, which means that it is warm all year. The average high temperature for Hawaii is about 85° F. The average low temperature is about 70° F. Tropical rain forests filled with plants and flowers grow on some of Hawaii's islands.

1. **Write** how a moderate climate is different than the climate of the Alaskan tundra.

....

....

....

....

This photo shows part of Alaska north of the Arctic Circle. About a third of Alaska is above this imaginary line.

Precipitation

Just as temperatures vary in the West, so does rainfall. Extreme examples of rainfall include Death Valley, California, and Mount Waialeale, Hawaii. In one part of Death Valley, between October 3, 1912, and November 8, 1914, no precipitation fell. Two years with no rain! At the other extreme is Hawaii's Mount Waialeale. It receives about 450 inches of rain in an average year.

The Rain Shadow Effect

The tall mountains that make up the Cascade Range affect the amount of precipitation that falls nearby. In parts of Washington's Olympic Peninsula, which lies to the west of the Cascades, the yearly precipitation averages about 140 inches. However, Yakima, Washington, which is east of the Cascades, receives less than 8 inches of precipitation each year.

How do mountains affect the amount of rain or snow that falls on an area? Warm, moist air is carried in from the Pacific Ocean. As the warm air blows to the east, it forms clouds. As the clouds rise up over the mountains, they become cooler and can no longer hold as much moisture. The water inside the cooled clouds falls as rain or snow. When the clouds begin to pass over the eastern side of the mountains, they have little moisture left inside. Because the eastern side of the Cascades lies in the **rain shadow**, it receives less rain than the western side.

2. Identify on which side of the Cascade Range you would find a rain forest.

....

....

....

The Rain Shadow Effect

Warm, moist air from the Pacific Ocean rises and moves up the mountains.

Moisture falls from the cooled clouds as rain or snow.

As the clouds reach the eastern side, they have lost most of their moisture.

The area in the rain shadow receives little moisture.

Trees such as firs and spruce grow in Washington's Hoh Rain Forest. The forest floor is covered with moisture-loving mosses and ferns.

Wildlife of the Western Plains and Deserts

The Great Plains is a large area of land that lies in the rain shadow created by the Rocky Mountains. Most of the Great Plains is a prairie, a place where grass grows well but trees are scarce. The Great Plains often experiences hot summers and cold winters. This area is also known for sudden storms that seem to form without warning. Animals that make their home in the Great Plains must adapt to this grassland area where the weather can change quickly.

Pronghorns are found mostly in the high plains area of Wyoming and Montana. The light brown coat of the pronghorn helps it to blend in with the dry, brown grasses of the high plains. But the pronghorn also relies on its speed and keen eyesight. These are important since this animal needs to see and outrun wolves and coyotes.

Desert animals have found interesting ways to survive the hot and sandy environment of Death Valley. Some animals spend the hottest part of the day asleep in a hole in the ground. The Mojave rattlesnake is **nocturnal**, meaning that it is only active at night. The desert jackrabbit survives by feeding on small desert plants. The jackrabbit's long ears move heat away from its body, helping it to stay cool. The fringe-toed lizard has scales on its feet that help it run quickly across the sand to escape predators.

The Mojave rattlesnake has sharp fangs that deliver a deadly bite.

Wildlife of Hawaii

The ocean surrounding the Hawaiian Islands is home to dolphins, sharks, whales, and the monk seal, which is one of Hawaii's native mammals.

The nene, or Hawaiian goose, is the state bird. The nene is often spotted in the Hawaii Volcanoes National Park showing off its tan and black feathers. Male and female nenes look alike, although the male nene is slightly larger in size.

Hawaiian honeycreepers are colorful birds found in the tropical rain forests. They feed on insects, snails, fruit, seeds, and the nectar from flowers.

The curved bill of the Hawaiian honeycreeper helps it to gather nectar.

Wildlife of Alaska

Many people think of Alaska as a land of ice and snow. But Alaska has many climates. Areas in its southern climate zone have average winter temperatures of about 20 to 40° F. Average summer temperatures are about 40 to 60° F.

Alaska is home to a variety of wildlife, including birds such as snowy owls and tundra swans, as well as black and white puffins that live near the arctic waters.

Down in the cold sea, walruses keep warm with a thick layer of blubber, or fat. Other sea creatures, such as dolphins, sharks, and whales, live in the waters off Alaska's coast.

Alaskan mammals include the arctic fox, which has a white coat in the winter. In the summer, its coat turns reddish brown to help it blend in with the native grasses. This helps the fox sneak up on its prey without being seen.

The arctic fox has the warmest fur of any mammal.

3. **Compare and Contrast Use** the Venn diagram to list two animals that have adapted to Alaska and two that have adapted to Hawaii. In the shared section, list two animals that have adapted to both places.

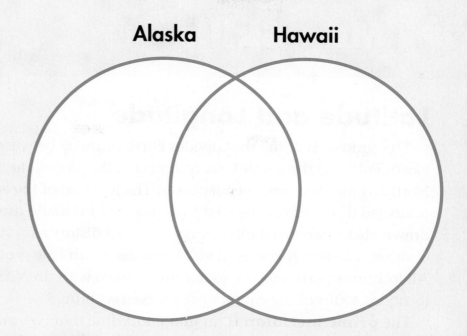

Alaska   Hawaii

Got it?

4. **Cause and Effect** What effect does the Cascade Range have on the climate east of the mountains?

....

....

....

5. You are packing for a vacation to see the Great Salt Lake in Utah. Because the West has so many different climates, what do you need to know about Utah to help you pack?

my Story Ideas

....

....

....

....

Stop! I need help with ....

Wait! I have a question about ....

Go! Now I know ....

Latitude and Longitude

The equator is a line that divides Earth halfway between the North Pole and the South Pole. It separates the globe into the Northern and Southern hemispheres. The location of the equator is labeled 0°, or zero degrees latitude. Lines of **latitude** are drawn east to west and are always an equal distance from one another. The North Pole is at 90°N and the South Pole is at 90°S. All locations north of the equator are marked with an *N*, and all locations south of the equator are marked with an *S*.

The **prime meridian** is an imaginary line that is drawn from the North Pole to the South Pole on a globe. The prime meridian passes through Europe and Africa. It divides Earth into the Eastern Hemisphere, or all those locations east of the prime meridian, and the Western Hemisphere, or all locations west of the prime meridian. Just as the equator is the starting point for latitude, the prime meridian is the starting point for lines of **longitude.** The prime meridian is labeled 0°, or zero degrees longitude. Lines of longitude are labeled from 0° to 180°. All locations east of the prime meridian are marked with an *E,* and all locations west of the prime meridian are marked with a *W*.

This map of Montana shows lines of latitude and longitude.

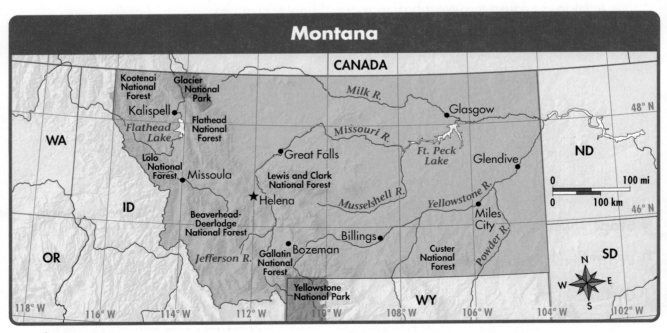

I will know how to use latitude and longitude to find locations on a map.

Lines of latitude and longitude on a map form a grid. Draw a circle around the city of Glasgow, Montana, on the map. Trace the line of latitude that is near Glasgow. Then trace the line of longitude that is near Glasgow. Notice that the two lines intersect, or come together, near 48°N and 106°W. This is one way that an **absolute location** on Earth can be identified.

A GPS is a machine that shows latitude and longitude. It is useful when traveling someplace new.

Try it!

Landmarks such as large rocks and unusual trees are often used to give people directions. But we can find the location of places on Earth easier when we know their latitude and longitude.

1. **Find** Kalispell on the map. What is the nearest latitude? ....

   Now find Billings. What is the nearest latitude? ....

2. Which location is nearer to the equator? ....

   Which location is nearer to the North Pole? ....

3. Use latitude, longitude, and the compass rose to give someone directions to Miles City, Montana.

   ....

   ....

   ....

4. Which city is at 112°W? ....

5. **Apply** Locate a place on this map of Montana that you might like to visit. Place an **X** next to it. What is the nearest latitude and longitude?

   ....

   ....

Western Resources

Envision It!

The West's many natural resources include forests. Wood from trees is used for making paper and books.

The West is a region rich in natural resources. People in the western states use their land, forests, and waters to produce goods that are shipped from the West to other regions and overseas.

The Great West

Although the West contains many mountain ranges, farmers use valleys and broad, level plateaus to grow vegetables, fruits, and grains. These same plateaus are just right for cattle and sheep ranching. In fact, animals that are raised on farms and ranches are the main source of farming income in some western states. This includes beef from western ranches, as well as milk from dairy cows. Sheep and sheep products, such as wool, are also important.

Western forests provide trees to make many different products. Trees are cut down and then sawed into lumber. The lumber is used to build homes and furniture. Other wood products include paper to make paper towels and books. To keep forests productive, timber companies usually **reforest.** This means they plant new trees to replace the ones that have been cut.

Fishing is important to the western coastal economy. In Alaska, the harvesting and processing of fish brings in about $3.3 billion a year to the state's economy. Government groups and others help protect fish in the West. They alert the public about fish that are in danger because too many are being caught.

1. **Write** how ranching in the West creates income.

....

....

....

....

Draw a picture of yourself in which you are using a product made from wood.

Vocabulary

reforest
Central Valley
canal
vineyard

Mountains and Minerals

In some areas of the West, what is hidden in the ground is a prized resource, too. Certain areas are rich in minerals, such as silver, copper, gold, and lead. Other areas are rich in fuels, such as coal and oil.

Colorado has a large supply of coal, gold, and lead. Coal is burned to make electricity in power plants. It is also used to make steel. Much of Colorado's coal is used in other states.

Silver, which is mined in Nevada and Utah, is used to make jewelry and coins. Silver is also used for photography, electronics, and materials for dentists.

Utah is rich in copper. The Bingham Canyon Mine in Utah is a leading copper producer. Because copper has an excellent ability to carry electricity and heat, it is often used in electrical wiring and pots and pans.

Gold is used to make jewelry and computer parts. California's Kennedy Gold Mine is one of the world's deepest gold mines. A tunnel that was first dug in 1898 eventually reached almost 6,000 feet.

Another early gold mine was the Crow Creek Mine in Alaska. This mine was started in 1896. Today, the area attracts tourists. They come to try their luck searching for gold nuggets, or small lumps of gold.

Open pit mines are dug to remove minerals that are near Earth's surface.

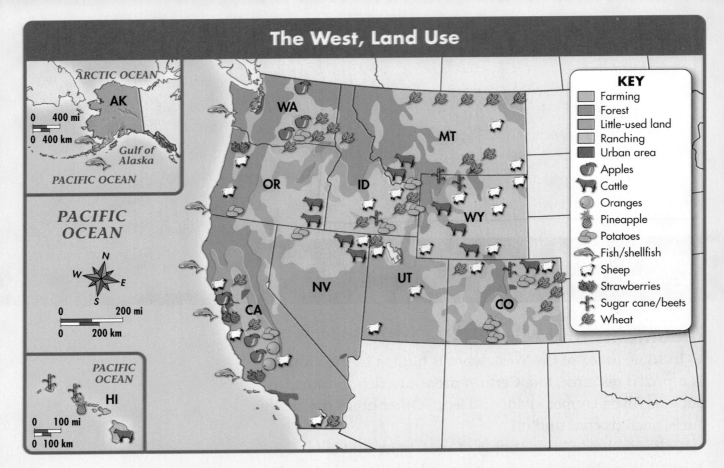

KEY
- Farming
- Forest
- Little-used land
- Ranching
- Urban area
- Apples
- Cattle
- Oranges
- Pineapple
- Potatoes
- Fish/shellfish
- Sheep
- Strawberries
- Sugar cane/beets
- Wheat

Western Agriculture

The West, with its variety of climates, produces many different agricultural products. The large plateau of the Great Plains is an ideal location to grow wheat and to raise cattle and sheep. Livestock has been an important product of these grasslands since the cattle drives of the 1870s. Back then, cowboys would round up the cattle and move them to another grazing area or to a market to be sold.

In parts of Washington, where the climate is perfect for growing apples, orchards dot the land. Apples and apple products, such as juice, jellies, jams, and applesauce, are shipped to countries all over the world. Washington is also known for its cherries, pears, and potatoes. Farms in Oregon's rich Willamette Valley produce strawberries, nuts, berries, and a variety of vegetables.

The tropical climate of Hawaii makes it a good place to grow sugar cane and pineapples, the state's most important crops. Sugar cane is a type of grass that produces long stalks or canes. The canes are boiled and processed to make sugar. Macadamia nuts and coffee are also well-suited to Hawaii's year-round warmth.

2. **Circle** the state or states that provide apples. **Draw** an X on states that produce cattle.

California Agriculture

California is the top-producing farm state in the nation. Of all the states in the West, California produces the widest variety of agricultural goods. Many crops are grown in California's **Central Valley**, the long valley set between the Sierra Nevada mountain range to the east and the Coastal Range to the west. Rich soil and a long growing season make this area ideal for farming. Although the Central Valley doesn't receive a lot of rainfall, farmers irrigate their crops with water from rivers that flow down from the mountains. The water is transported in Canals. **Canals** are waterways that are dug to hold water.

Almonds are an important crop in California's Central Valley. This area produces almost 100 percent of the nation's almonds. California is also a key producer of garlic. This member of the onion family is a central ingredient in many dishes all around the world.

California farmers grow strawberries, oranges, tomatoes, and broccoli. **Vineyards,** or places that grow grapes, are an important part of California's agriculture, too. Climate, precipitation, and the amount of sunlight all contribute to making this an ideal spot for growing red and white grapes. Grapes are also used to make dried grapes, or raisins, and jelly.

The Imperial Valley in southeastern California is known for its farmland even though it receives little rainfall. A canal from the Colorado River irrigates the land. Farmers in this valley grow citrus fruit, figs, and dates. Farmers here also grow vegetables, such as onions, peppers, carrots, spinach, and lettuce.

3. Underline how crops in the Imperial Valley receive water.

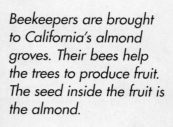

Beekeepers are brought to California's almond groves. Their bees help the trees to produce fruit. The seed inside the fruit is the almond.

Top Western Fishing Ports

Fishing Port	Pounds of Fish Landed (in millions)	Dollar Value of Fish Landed (in millions)
Dutch Harbor-Unalaska, AK	777	$174
Astoria, OR	153	$28
Los Angeles, CA	141	$19
Westport, WA	120	$32
Honolulu, HI	24	$64

Source: National Ocean Economics Program

Fishing in the West

The fishing industry is very important to Alaska. Salmon, cod, perch, and halibut are just a few of the fish pulled from the chilly Alaskan waters. The fisheries where the fish, crab, and shrimp are made ready for shipping provide thousands of jobs for workers.

Based on the amount of seafood that is caught there, Dutch Harbor in Unalaska, Alaska is one of the nation's largest fishing ports. One important resource in the area is the king crab. Fishing for king crabs takes place during the freezing winter months and is a dangerous job. Fishermen must protect themselves from the cold temperatures and the rough waters where the king crab is found.

Another busy fishing port in Alaska is Kodiak. Commercial fishing fleets catch enormous numbers of fish and several types of crab in that area.

Off the California and Oregon coast, sardines, crab, sole, shrimp, tuna, and swordfish are caught. In Hawaii, tuna and swordfish are major catches. Washington fishermen bring in salmon, tuna, halibut, and shrimp.

4. **Read** the table and then **list** the western state with the busiest fishing port.

....

The Alaskan king crab is one of the largest crabs. Some weigh more than 11 pounds.

Where Are the Salmon?

Salmon is a native fish that lives both in the ocean and in the fresh water of streams and rivers. A salmon begins its life in the fresh water of the Pacific Northwest. As they mature, the fish travel downstream to the Pacific Ocean, where they live as adults. When it is time to spawn, or lay their eggs, salmon swim back to the rivers and streams where they were born. The fish that survive the journey lay their eggs in the same stream where they were hatched.

About 50 years ago, many dams were built along the rivers where the salmon spawn. The salmon population began to decline. The dams blocked salmon that were heading upstream. Some fish that made it past the dams into the reservoir, or pooled water behind the dam, became confused. The fish couldn't find their way to the waters where they needed to lay their eggs. Today, dams are being changed to give the salmon a better chance to make the journey to their spawning ground.

Salmon are able to leap up steep rapids as they swim upstream to the place where they will lay eggs.

Got it?

5. ⊙ **Compare and Contrast** **List** some western resources that come from land and some resources that come from the ocean.

....

....

6. ❓ You are leading a group that is fishing for Alaskan king crab. **Write** a plan for your trip that details how to protect your crew.

my Story Ideas

....

....

....

⬜ **Stop!** I need help with ....

⏸ **Wait!** I have a question about ....

▶ **Go!** Now I know ....

Growth of the West

Walking: 20 miles per day

Stagecoach: 60 miles per day

Steam-Powered Train: 200 miles per day

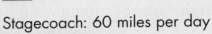

As transportation improved, people and goods could travel to and from the West in less time.

The Tlingit, a Native American group of the West, created this totem pole.

The West's rich lands and resources have long attracted people to the region. From the first people who came to the West thousands of years ago to those who live there today, all have contributed to the region's growth.

Native American Past

The forests and rivers of Alaska's southeastern coast offered plenty of fish and game for the Native Americans who settled there long ago. One such group, the Tlingit (TLING giht), built their homes from large planks cut from trees found in the forests. Some Tlingit families placed a totem pole outside their homes. A **totem pole** is a tall post carved with the images of people and animals. The Tlingit traded canoes, wool blankets, and seal oil with other Native Americans. Today, many Tlingit people still live in the region. They live on lands where their families have survived for hundreds of years.

The Inuit live in the arctic region of northern Alaska. They have survived on fish and game. But for a few months each year, the tundra thaws and the Inuit add berries to their meals. The Inuit passed their history and culture down to their children through stories and songs.

The Blackfeet people live in what is now Montana. The Blackfeet worked together to gather food and to protect their villages. Each group, or band, had a leader known as the chief. There was also a council of older people that met to make important decisions.

I will know how growth has affected the states in the West.

Vocabulary

totem pole
ranch
gold rush
boomtown

Describe how these transportation improvements might have affected the population of the West.

The Chumash lived along the California coast for thousands of years before explorers from Europe arrived. They fished in the ocean using canoes made from redwood trees. The Chumash were known for the tools they made from stone, wood, and the bones of whales.

Long ago, people from Polynesia migrated to the islands of Hawaii. Polynesia is a group of islands far to the west in the Pacific Ocean. These people told stories about Pele, the goddess of fire. They believed she was responsible for the volcanoes and lava flows on the islands.

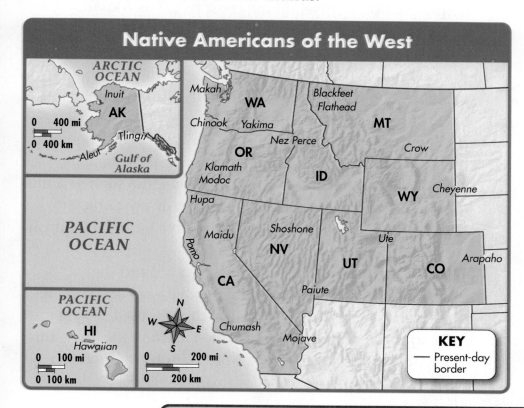

Native Americans of the West

KEY
— Present-day border

1. **Circle** a Native American group that lived in Wyoming.

This painting shows Spanish priests, soldiers, and Native Americans outside a mission. Presidios, or Spanish military posts, were built near missions to offer protection.

2. Identify some cities in California that began as missions.

....

....

....

....

Early Spanish Settlers

In 1542, the explorer Juan Rodriguez Cabrillo sailed from the west coast of what is now Mexico and headed north. Like Christopher Columbus, Cabrillo was exploring on behalf of Spain. His plan was to search the Pacific coast for riches and a possible route to connect the Pacific and Atlantic oceans. Cabrillo was probably the first European to land along the California coast. Eventually, Spanish explorers would travel up the coast as far as Alaska.

Spain later sent other explorers to California. The Spanish wanted to start colonies in this new land, even though native people had been there for thousands of years. Spanish explorers eventually started settlements as far up the coast as Alaska.

By 1769, a priest named Father Junipero Serra (hoo NEE peh roh SEHR rah) built the first mission in what is now San Diego, California. Other California cities such as Santa Barbara and San Francisco also began as missions. By 1823, 21 missions had been built to serve both the Spanish settlers and the Native Americans.

To encourage settlement of the area around the missions, the Spanish government gave land and supplies to settlers. These plots of land, which were used mostly for raising cattle and sheep, were called *ranchos.* It is from this Spanish word that we get the word **ranch.** A ranch is a large area of land set aside for raising livestock.

In Search of Opportunity

Jedediah Smith was a New Yorker who joined a group of fur traders who wanted to explore the West. In 1826, Smith crossed the Mojave Desert into what is now California. Smith may have been the first white man to enter the region from the East. Later, other American explorers and some settlers began to head west.

In 1848, a man named James Marshall was building a sawmill for a businessman named John Sutter. The mill was on the American River in the foothills of the Sierra Nevada. In the water, Marshall saw sparkling yellow flakes that he recognized as gold. News of his discovery spread quickly, and thousands of people came to California in what became known as the **gold rush.**

This sudden increase in people and business activity created towns called **boomtowns.** The prospectors, or people who search for gold or other minerals, were nicknamed "forty-niners." This was because it was in 1849 when the rush of gold miners first hit the area.

Life was hard for people in the crowded mining camps. The tunnels the miners dug to find the gold often collapsed. It took a long time to find small amounts of gold by chipping away at rocks deep underground or searching for it in streams.

Other groups that came to the West included Russian settlers who moved into northern California and the Alaskan territory for the fur-trading industry. Many Easterners moved west for opportunities in farming and logging. Some traveled hundreds of miles by wagon trains over the Oregon and California Trails.

Some settlers came west for religious freedom. The Mormons, a religious group, settled in the area that is now Salt Lake City, Utah.

Prospectors sifted sand and rocks through a cradle, hoping to find gold left behind.

After the gold miners left, many boomtowns were deserted. These empty towns became known as ghost towns.

Workers help dig out a Union Pacific train buried in the snow near Ogden, Utah, in the 1870s.

Growth Continues

As news of the 1849 gold rush spread, people from all across the globe came to the West. People in China saw flyers from mining companies advertising for workers. Some Chinese came for the work while others sought gold. Companies building railroads also hired foreign workers. The transcontinental railroad, or a railroad that crossed the entire continent, was one such project. The completed railroad made it possible for new businesses in the West to ship their products east. The railroad also sped up communication.

Almost one hundred years after the gold rush, in 1959, Hawaii became a state. How did this chain of islands in the Pacific Ocean become a state? As trade increased between the United States and Asia, the Hawaiian Islands were an important stop on the trading route. Passengers could get off the ship when it reached the Hawaiian Islands to refuel and take on supplies. Hawaii was also an important base in the Pacific for the United States Navy. In 1900, Hawaii became a U.S. territory.

Alaska was another territory that became a state in the 1950s. The United States bought it from Russia in 1867. Many thought this land of snow and ice a waste of money. When gold and oil were discovered there, the public changed its mind. Alaska became a state in 1959.

3. **Underline** how the United States acquired the Alaskan territory.

This is an early image of Sitka, Alaska, in 1869.

Cities in the West

As farmers, loggers, miners, ranchers, and railroad workers moved to the West, the number of people who lived in the region grew quickly. By 1900, the West had a population of about 4 million people. This number was still smaller than any other region in the United States. Many of these people lived in western cities.

By 1920, western cities had grown so much that four of them were among the 25 largest cities in the United States. These were Los Angeles and San Francisco in California; Seattle, Washington; and Denver, Colorado.

Today, western cities are just as varied as the region's land and climate. Although Anchorage, Alaska, does not have a very large population, at 1,697 square miles, it has the largest area of any city in the nation.

The Space Needle in Seattle, Washington

Got it?

4. ● **Compare and Contrast** **Write** how a boomtown is different from a ghost town.

....

....

....

5. ❓ You are living in the Hawaiian territory in the 1950s. People are talking about Hawaii becoming a state. **Write** a diary entry about how this may affect life in Hawaii.

my Story Ideas

....

....

....

▢ **Stop!** I need help with ....

❚❚ **Wait!** I have a question about ....

▶ **Go!** Now I know ....

The West Today

Envision It! Greetings from OREGON

States use colorful advertisements to show tourists what is special about their state.

A computer's circuit board has chips that run the computer.

1. List two industries in the West.

....

....

....

Over time, the West has changed. Communities have grown into cities, and many cities have grown into large urban areas. There are still wide-open spaces in the West, but not as many as before. People continue to move to the West for jobs. Many visitors also come to see the region's national parks and exciting cities.

Working in the West

In the early 1900s, southern California's sunny weather drew film and then television companies to the West. Entertainment has been important to the area's economy ever since. Another part of California is often called "Silicon Valley." **Silicon** is obtained from rocks. It is used to make key computer parts. Starting in the 1970s, computer companies began popping up in this area and started a high-tech industry. High-tech refers to computers and other goods that are made using advanced processes.

The economy of Seattle, Washington, grew quickly during World War II when large numbers of planes were needed. At the time, the Boeing Company of Seattle, a maker of military planes, became one of the city's largest employers.

Another boom began in the 1970s in northern Alaska. After large amounts of oil were discovered there, an 800 mile pipe was built to move the oil. This pipe system is still used to carry the oil from the arctic coast down to harbors on Alaska's southern coast. From there it is shipped around the world.

Create a postcard to encourage tourists to visit a part of the West that you yourself would like to visit.

UNLOCK THE BIG ?

I will know about work and recreation in the West today and the challenges in its future.

Vocabulary

silicon

Pacific Rim

international trade

Nevada has recently become a leader in producing energy that is clean and renewable. This includes geothermal energy, in which heat from deep in the Earth is used to make electricity. Solar energy is also produced in Nevada and other sunny western states.

Tourism in the West

Tourism is an important part of the West's economy. From outdoor thrills to indoor fun, each state has something to offer.

Wyoming's Yellowstone National Park and Montana's Glacier National Park let visitors enjoy beautiful views of mountains and forests. These parks offer many trails for hikers. These states also have many natural areas where people can hunt and fish.

The mountains of the West have many fine spots for winter skiing. During the spring and summer, the water flows so quickly on some western rivers that it looks white. Tourists can test their skills and enjoy the thrill of taking a raft down these fast-running rivers.

California and Hawaii have warm beaches and big waves that are popular with surfers. Other tourists may prefer to spread a towel on the sand and relax.

For indoor fun, tourists in Las Vegas, Nevada, can attend shows by entertainers from around the world. Many large cities in the West, including Los Angeles and San Francisco, California, are home to museums and theaters.

Utah's Bryce Canyon

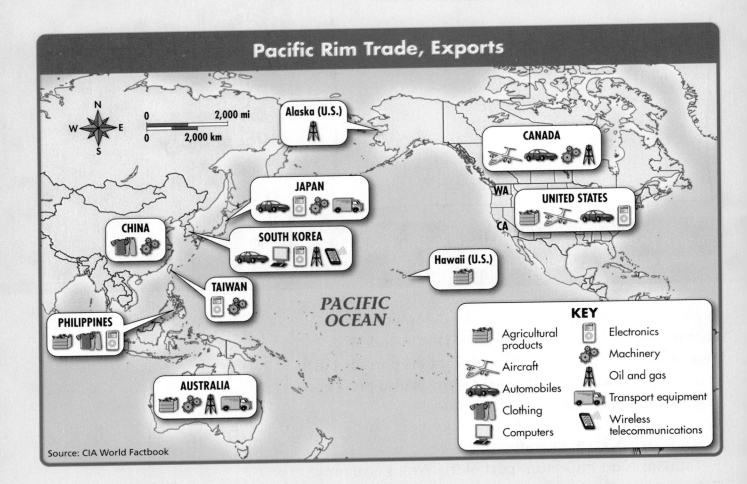

Pacific Rim Trade, Exports

Alaska (U.S.)

CANADA

JAPAN

WA

UNITED STATES

CHINA

CA

SOUTH KOREA

Hawaii (U.S.)

TAIWAN

PACIFIC
OCEAN

PHILIPPINES

KEY

Agricultural products

Electronics

Aircraft

Machinery

Automobiles

Oil and gas

AUSTRALIA

Clothing

Transport equipment

Computers

Wireless telecommunications

Source: CIA World Factbook

The Pacific Rim and International Trade

The **Pacific Rim** is a geographic area made up of countries that border the Pacific Ocean. Because Pacific Rim nations all face the Pacific, they trade many resources, goods, and services with each other. The map above shows goods that Pacific Rim nations export to other nations.

In the past, much of the United States' **international trade,** or the trade with other countries, was with European nations. Beginning in the 1960s, however, Japan and then other East Asian nations began exporting goods to the United States on a large scale. An export is an item that is sent from one country to be sold in another. When an item enters a country, it is called an import, or an item from abroad that is offered for sale.

It is not just the trading of goods and services that increase with international trade. Languages, ideas, and cultural traditions are shared, too.

2. **Circle** the names of Pacific Rim nations that export automobiles.

Imports and Exports

Most imports and exports that are traded between countries of the Pacific Rim are shipped from one nation's ports to another. In the West, three of the busiest ports are in Los Angeles and San Francisco in California, and Seattle, Washington.

Imports that come into western ports include electronic equipment and automobiles from Japan. From Australia, the United States receives meat and minerals. Cargo ships from China bring clothing, food, electronics, and toys.

The United States exports products to other Pacific Rim nations from the same ports that receive imports. Los Angeles, California, with its busy entertainment industry, exports movies. Computer software from Silicon Valley and Seattle are major United States exports, too. Alaska's busy ports export seafood and minerals. Hawaii ships out agricultural products, including pineapples, coffee, and sugar cane.

A cargo ship heading to port passes under San Francisco's Golden Gate Bridge.

Oregon lumber waiting to be exported

3. ⊙ **Compare and Contrast**
Write how imports are different from exports.

....

....

....

....

....

The Western Future

For more than 200 years, the West has continued to grow and change. Some changes result in challenges. As the West continues to grow, these challenges must be met to ensure a promising future for the region.

In many areas of the West, farmers and ranchers depend on rain and snow to provide water for their land. But what happens when there isn't enough rainfall, and water is in short supply, or scarce? Also, as the population increases in large urban areas such as Los Angeles, California, and Las Vegas, Nevada, the water needs of the population increase as well. Water scarcity is a major challenge in the West.

The problem of making sure there is enough water for everyone is difficult to solve. Learning to conserve water helps, but it also takes cooperation and enforcement. Some states, such as California, have rules that homes must have plumbing that uses water efficiently. Other states try to educate the public. Utah's Division of Water Resources reminds the state's residents that "We live in a desert."

Green roofs, like this one in San Francisco, California, keep buildings cooler and collect rainwater that would ordinarily go to waste.

4. **Write** how California's government is helping people to conserve water.

....

....

....

Portland, Oregon, the largest city in the state, is known for being a successful "green" city. This means that the city has rules that help keep the city and its resources clean and green. Bike lanes throughout the city allow people to safely ride bikes to work, school, and markets. The city offers free public transportation in the downtown area to encourage people to leave their cars at home. With fewer cars on the road there is less air pollution.

Portland's farmers' markets offer fruits, vegetables, meats, and other food that is raised locally. This means that the products do not have to be shipped in from long distances. The city also has a strong recycling program. The people of Portland found ways to balance the needs of a growing city with the needs of our planet.

A biker rides in a bike lane in Portland, Oregon. Cars and buses are not allowed in these lanes.

Got it?

5. ◉ **Summarize** **Write** how the West might change in the future.

....

....

....

....

6. ❓ You are making a Hollywood movie about sports in the West and must choose two locations for your film. **List** two locations and the scenes you would like to shoot.

my Story Ideas

....

....

⬜ **Stop!** I need help with ....

⏸ **Wait!** I have a question about ....

▶ **Go!** Now I know ....

Lesson 1

A Varied Land

- The West is a region with many different landforms.
- The region has many mountain ranges and a long coast.
- Volcanoes and earthquakes create or change landforms.
- Lakes, rivers, and other bodies of water are important in the West.

Lesson 2

Climate of the West

- There are a variety of climates in the West.
- Precipitation varies greatly in the region.
- Climate has an impact on wildlife and their habitats.

Lesson 3

Western Resources

- The West has many different resources.
- Mining for minerals has contributed to growth in the West.
- The West produces many agricultural products.
- The sea is an important resource in the West.

Lesson 4

Growth of the West

- Native Americans made their homes in the West before Europeans arrived.
- Settlers, including the Spanish, came to the West for new opportunities.
- In the 1900s, the population of cities in the West increased.

Lesson 5

The West Today

- The West offers a variety of industries and jobs for people.
- Tourism is an important industry in the West.
- The Pacific Rim nations trade with one another.
- Conserving resources is important to the future of the West.

Lesson 1

A Varied Land

1. **List** five landforms that can be found in the West.

   ....

   ....

2. **Write** a sentence using the words *weathering* and *landforms*.

   ....

   ....

   ....

   ....

   ....

   ....

3. **Explain** why many settlers made their homes near bodies of water.

   ....

   ....

   ....

   ....

Lesson 2

Climate of the West

4. Match each word with its meaning.

   _____ tundra   a. a very cold area where trees cannot grow

   _____ prairie   b. active at night

   _____ nocturnal   c. an area where grass grows well but trees are rare

5. **Write** a description of how the arctic fox has adapted to its climate.

   ....

   ....

   ....

   ....

   ....

   ....

6. **Circle** the letter below of an effect created by the Cascade rain shadow.

   A. The Cascades receive no rain.

   B. The western side of the mountains receives more rain than the eastern side does.

   C. The mountains have a desert climate.

   D. The north side of the Cascades receive more rain than the southern side.

Lesson 3

Western Resources

7. ⦿ **Compare and Contrast** How are the resources of Alaska and Hawaii alike? How are they different?

....

....

....

....

8. **Complete** the sentence. .... is the leading producer of agricultural products in the nation.

Lesson 4

Growth of the West

9. **Write** one way the Native Americans used natural resources.

....

....

....

10. **Circle** the nickname for the gold miners who came during the gold rush.

   A. the prospectors

   B. the trailblazers

   C. the mountain men

   D. the forty-niners

Lesson 5

The West Today

11. **Write** one reason that the West continues to grow.

....

....

12. **Write** one way that western cities and states try to improve the environment.

....

....

....

13. ❓ **How does where we live affect who we are?**

Based on what you've learned in Chapter 9, **write** how people in the West are affected by resources.

....

....

....

....

....

Go online to write and illustrate your own **myStory Book** using the **myStory Ideas** from this chapter.

How does where we live affect who we are?

Sometimes people live in an area because it is where they were born. Other people may move to a new area because of work. What if you were raised in a warm, mild climate, such as Hawaii, and then moved to a colder climate, such as Alaska?

Write how your home, clothing, and activities might change. Then **draw** a picture of yourself after you have adapted to this change in climate.

While you're online, check out the **myStory Current Events** area where you can create your own book on a topic that's in the news.

Atlas

The United States of America, Political

Washington
★ Olympia

★ Salem
Oregon

★ Boise
Idaho

Montana
★ Helena

Wyoming

North Dakota
★ Bismarck

South Dakota
Pierre ★

Carson City ★
★ Sacramento
Nevada
California

Salt Lake City ★
Utah

Cheyenne ★

Denver ★
Colorado

Nebraska
Lincoln ★

Topeka ★
Kansas

Arizona
★ Phoenix

Santa Fe ★
New Mexico

Oklahoma
Oklahoma City ★

Texas
★ Austin

Alaska
Juneau ★

Honolulu ★
Hawaii

Minnesota

St. Paul ★
Wisconsin
Madison ★

Iowa
Des Moines ★

Michigan
Lansing ★

Springfield ★
Illinois

Indiana
Indianapolis ★

★ Jefferson
City
Missouri

Arkansas

Little ★
Rock

Mississippi

Alabama

★ Jackson

Louisiana

Baton
Rouge ★

New Hampshire

Vermont

Montpelier ★

Albany
New York ★

Hartford

Ohio
Columbus ★

Harrisburg ★

Pennsylvania

West
Virginia

Charleston
★

★ Frankfort

Kentucky

Richmond ★

Annapolis

★ Trenton
Dover ★

Maine

★ Augusta
Concord ★

Massachusetts
★ Boston
★ Providence
Rhode Island
Connecticut
New Jersey

Delaware
Maryland
Washington, D.C.
Virginia

★ Nashville

Tennessee

Raleigh ★ North
Carolina

Columbia
★

South
Carolina

★ Atlanta

Montgomery
★

Georgia

★ Tallahassee

Florida

N
W   E
S

KEY

⬟ National capital

★ State capital

R1

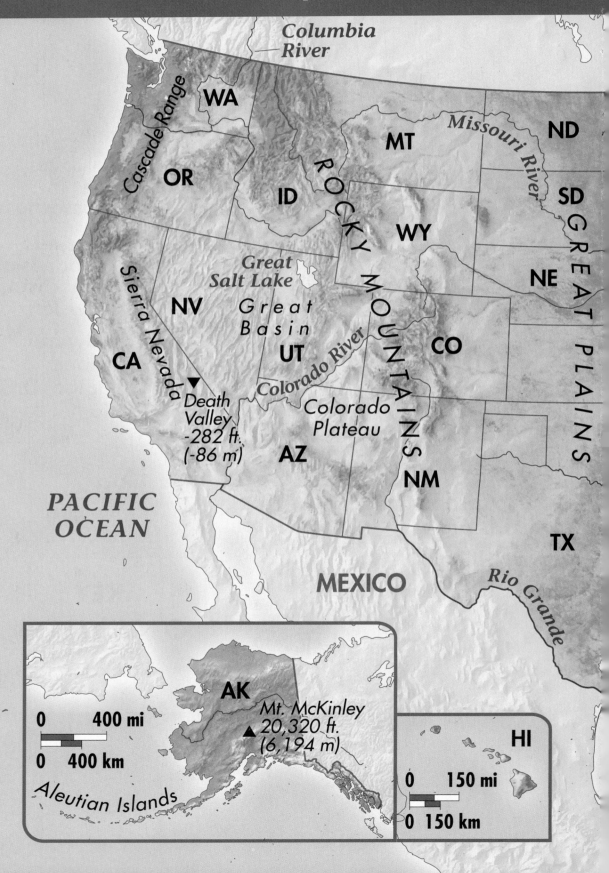

Columbia River

Cascade Range

WA

OR

MT

ROCKY MOUNTAINS

Missouri River

ND

SD

GREAT PLAINS

ID

WY

NE

Sierra Nevada

Great Salt Lake

NV

Great Basin

UT

Colorado River

CO

CA

▼ Death Valley -282 ft. (-86 m)

Colorado Plateau

AZ

NM

PACIFIC OCEAN

MEXICO

TX

Rio Grande

AK

Mt. McKinley 20,320 ft. (6,194 m) ▲

0   400 mi

0   400 km

Aleutian Islands

HI

0   150 mi

0   150 km

CANADA

Lake Superior

0   400 mi

0   400 km

St. Lawrence River

VT   ME

NH
MA

MN

WI

Lake
Huron

Lake
Ontario

MI

Lake
Michigan

NY

CT

RI

Lake Erie

APPALACHIAN MOUNTAINS

PA

IA

IL

IN

OH

NJ

N

E

W

DE
MD

S

KS

Central
Plains

Ohio River

WV

VA

Atlantic Coastal Plain

MO

KY

OK

AR

TN

NC

ATLANTIC
OCEAN

Mississippi River

SC

MS

AL

GA

LA

Gulf Coastal Plain

FL

BAHAMAS

Lake
Okeechobee

Gulf of
Mexico

CUBA

KEY

— National border
— State border
▲ Highest point
▼ Lowest point

The World

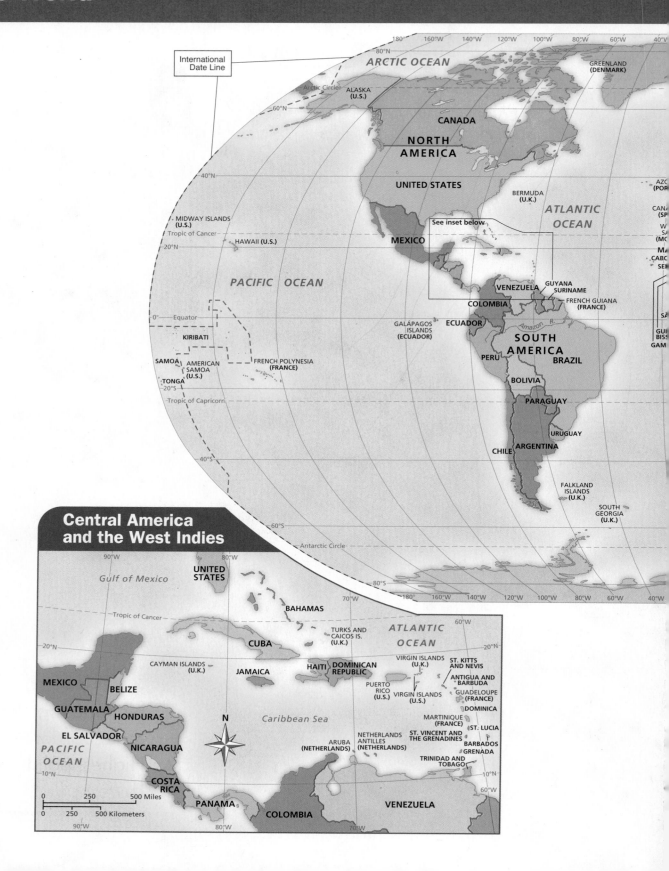

International Date Line

ARCTIC OCEAN

180° 160°W 140°W 120°W 100°W 80°W 60°W 40°W

80°N

Arctic Circle

GREENLAND (DENMARK)

ALASKA (U.S.)

60°N

CANADA

NORTH AMERICA

40°N

UNITED STATES

BERMUDA (U.K.)

ATLANTIC OCEAN

AZO (POR

CAN (SP

See inset below

MIDWAY ISLANDS (U.S.)

Tropic of Cancer

MEXICO

20°N

HAWAII (U.S.)

W SA (MC

Ma CABO SEN

PACIFIC OCEAN

VENEZUELA GUYANA SURINAME

FRENCH GUIANA (FRANCE)

COLOMBIA

SA

0° Equator

GALÁPAGOS ISLANDS (ECUADOR)

ECUADOR

Amazon R.

GUI BISS GAM

KIRIBATI

SOUTH AMERICA

SAMOA

AMERICAN SAMOA (U.S.)

FRENCH POLYNESIA (FRANCE)

PERU

BRAZIL

TONGA

20°S

BOLIVIA

Tropic of Capricorn

PARAGUAY

URUGUAY

40°S

CHILE ARGENTINA

FALKLAND ISLANDS (U.K.)

SOUTH GEORGIA (U.K.)

60°S

Antarctic Circle

80°S

180° 160°W 140°W 120°W 100°W 80°W 60°W 40°W

Central America and the West Indies

90°W 80°W

Gulf of Mexico

UNITED STATES

70°W 60°W

Tropic of Cancer

BAHAMAS

ATLANTIC OCEAN

20°N

CUBA

TURKS AND CAICOS IS. (U.K.)

20°N

MEXICO

CAYMAN ISLANDS (U.K.)

JAMAICA

HAITI

DOMINICAN REPUBLIC

VIRGIN ISLANDS (U.K.)

ST. KITTS AND NEVIS

ANTIGUA AND BARBUDA

BELIZE

PUERTO RICO (U.S.)

VIRGIN ISLANDS (U.S.)

GUADELOUPE (FRANCE)

GUATEMALA

HONDURAS

N

Caribbean Sea

DOMINICA

MARTINIQUE (FRANCE)

ST. LUCIA

EL SALVADOR

NICARAGUA

NETHERLANDS ANTILLES (NETHERLANDS)

ARUBA (NETHERLANDS)

ST. VINCENT AND THE GRENADINES

BARBADOS

GRENADA

PACIFIC OCEAN

TRINIDAD AND TOBAGO

10°N

COSTA RICA

10°N

0 250 500 Miles

0 250 500 Kilometers

PANAMA

COLOMBIA

VENEZUELA

90°W 80°W 70°W 60°W

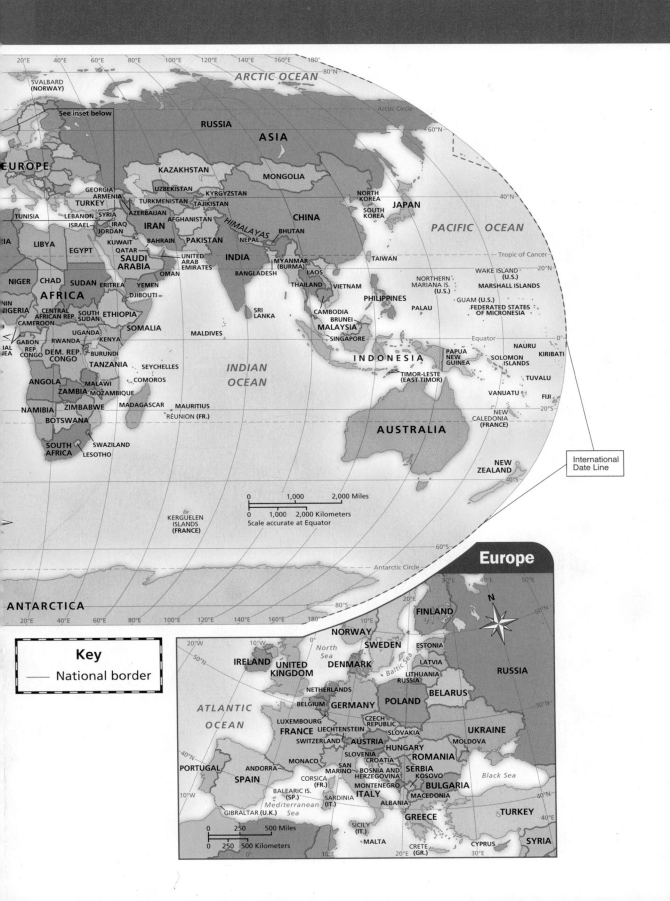

ARCTIC OCEAN

80°N

SVALBARD
(NORWAY)

Arctic Circle

See inset below

60°N

RUSSIA

ASIA

EUROPE

KAZAKHSTAN

MONGOLIA

40°N

GEORGIA
ARMENIA
TURKEY

UZBEKISTAN

KYRGYZSTAN

NORTH
KOREA

JAPAN

TURKMENISTAN

TAJIKISTAN

SOUTH
KOREA

PACIFIC OCEAN

TUNISIA

LEBANON SYRIA

AZERBAIJAN

AFGHANISTAN

CHINA

ISRAEL
JORDAN

IRAQ

IRAN

HIMALAYAS

TAIWAN

LIBYA

EGYPT

KUWAIT
QATAR

BAHRAIN

PAKISTAN

NEPAL

BHUTAN

Tropic of Cancer

20°N

SAUDI
ARABIA

UNITED
ARAB
EMIRATES

INDIA

MYANMAR
(BURMA)

LAOS

WAKE ISLAND
(U.S.)

NIGER

CHAD

SUDAN

OMAN

ERITREA

YEMEN

BANGLADESH

THAILAND

VIETNAM

NORTHERN
MARIANA IS.
(U.S.)

MARSHALL ISLANDS

AFRICA

DJIBOUTI

PHILIPPINES

GUAM (U.S.)

NIGERIA

CENTRAL
AFRICAN REP.

SOUTH
SUDAN

ETHIOPIA

SRI
LANKA

CAMBODIA

PALAU

FEDERATED STATES
OF MICRONESIA

CAMEROON

UGANDA

SOMALIA

BRUNEI

KENYA

MALDIVES

MALAYSIA

IAL
EA

GABON

RWANDA

SINGAPORE

Equator

0°

REP.
CONGO

DEM. REP.
CONGO

BURUNDI

NAURU

KIRIBATI

TANZANIA

SEYCHELLES

INDONESIA

PAPUA
NEW
GUINEA

SOLOMON
ISLANDS

ANGOLA

MALAWI

COMOROS

INDIAN
OCEAN

TUVALU

ZAMBIA

MOZAMBIQUE

TIMOR-LESTE
(EAST TIMOR)

VANUATU

20°S

NAMIBIA

ZIMBABWE

MADAGASCAR

MAURITIUS

NEW
CALEDONIA
(FRANCE)

FIJI

BOTSWANA

RÉUNION (FR.)

AUSTRALIA

SOUTH
AFRICA

SWAZILAND

LESOTHO

International
Date Line

0   1,000   2,000 Miles

0   1,000   2,000 Kilometers

NEW
ZEALAND

40°S

Scale accurate at Equator

KERGUELEN
ISLANDS
(FRANCE)

60°S

Antarctic Circle

ANTARCTICA

80°S

20°E   40°E   60°E   80°E   100°E   120°E   140°E   160°E   180°

Key

—— National border

Europe

N

ATLANTIC
OCEAN

FINLAND

NORWAY

SWEDEN

ESTONIA

North
Sea

IRELAND

UNITED
KINGDOM

DENMARK

LATVIA

RUSSIA

Baltic Sea

LITHUANIA

RUSSIA

NETHERLANDS

BELARUS

50°N

BELGIUM

GERMANY

POLAND

LUXEMBOURG

CZECH
REPUBLIC

UKRAINE

FRANCE

LIECHTENSTEIN

SLOVAKIA

40°N

SWITZERLAND

AUSTRIA

HUNGARY

MOLDOVA

SLOVENIA

ROMANIA

PORTUGAL

MONACO

CROATIA

ANDORRA

SAN
MARINO

BOSNIA AND
HERZEGOVINA

SERBIA

KOSOVO

Black Sea

SPAIN

CORSICA
(FR.)

MONTENEGRO

BULGARIA

BALEARIC IS.
(SP.)

SARDINIA
(IT.)

ITALY

MACEDONIA

ALBANIA

40°N

GIBRALTAR (U.K.)

Mediterranean
Sea

GREECE

TURKEY

SICILY
(IT.)

0   250   500 Miles

0   250   500 Kilometers

MALTA

CRETE
(GR.)

CYPRUS

SYRIA

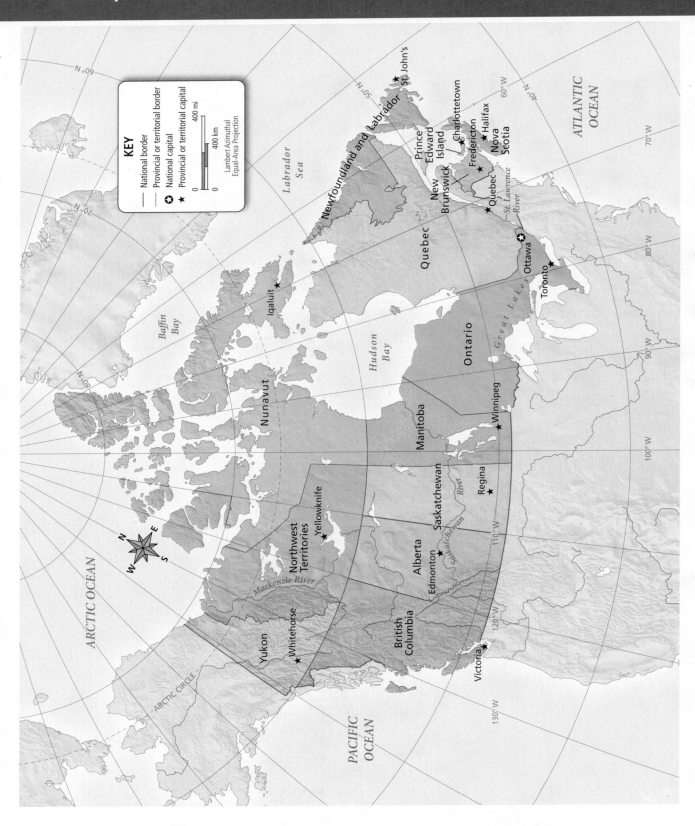

KEY
National border
Provincial or territorial border
National capital
Provincial or territorial capital
400 mi
400 km
Lambert Azimuthal
Equal-Area Projection

ARCTIC OCEAN

Baffin Bay

Labrador Sea

Newfoundland and Labrador

St. John's

Charlottetown
Prince Edward Island
New Brunswick
Fredericton
Halifax
Nova Scotia
Quebec
St. Lawrence River

ATLANTIC OCEAN

Quebec

Ottawa

Toronto

Great Lakes

Ontario

Hudson Bay

Iqaluit

Nunavut

Manitoba

Winnipeg

Saskatchewan

Regina

River

Saskatchewan River

Yellowknife

Northwest Territories

Alberta

Edmonton

Mackenzie River

Yukon

Whitehorse

British Columbia

Victoria

ARCTIC CIRCLE

PACIFIC OCEAN

N
W E
S

60°N

50°N

40°N

40°W

60°W

70°W

80°W

90°W

100°W

110°W

120°W

130°W

70°N

80°N

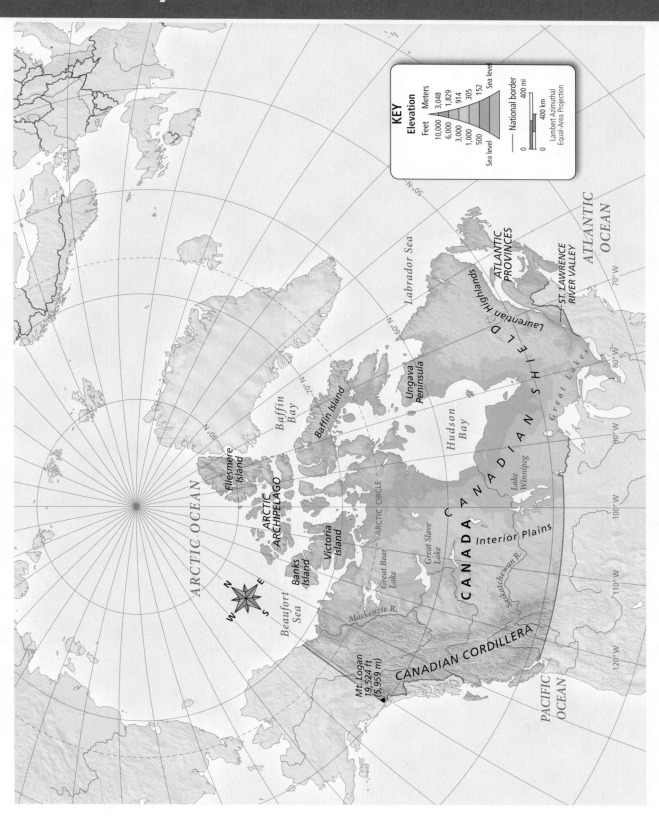

KEY

Elevation

Feet	Meters
10,000	3,048
6,000	1,829
3,000	914
1,000	305
500	152
Sea level	Sea level

— National border

400 mi

400 km

Lambert Azimuthal
Equal-Area Projection

ATLANTIC OCEAN

Labrador Sea

ATLANTIC PROVINCES

ST. LAWRENCE RIVER VALLEY

Laurentian Highlands

C A N A D I A N   S H I E L D

Great Lakes

Ungava Peninsula

Hudson Bay

Baffin Bay

Baffin Island

Lake Winnipeg

C A N A D A

Interior Plains

Ellesmere Island

ARCTIC ARCHIPELAGO

Victoria Island

ARCTIC CIRCLE

Great Slave Lake

Great Bear Lake

Saskatchewan R.

ARCTIC OCEAN

Banks Island

Beaufort Sea

Mackenzie R.

CANADIAN CORDILLERA

Mt. Logan
19,524 ft
(5,959 m)

PACIFIC OCEAN

70°W

80°W

90°W

100°W

110°W

120°W

60°N

50°N

70°N

80°N

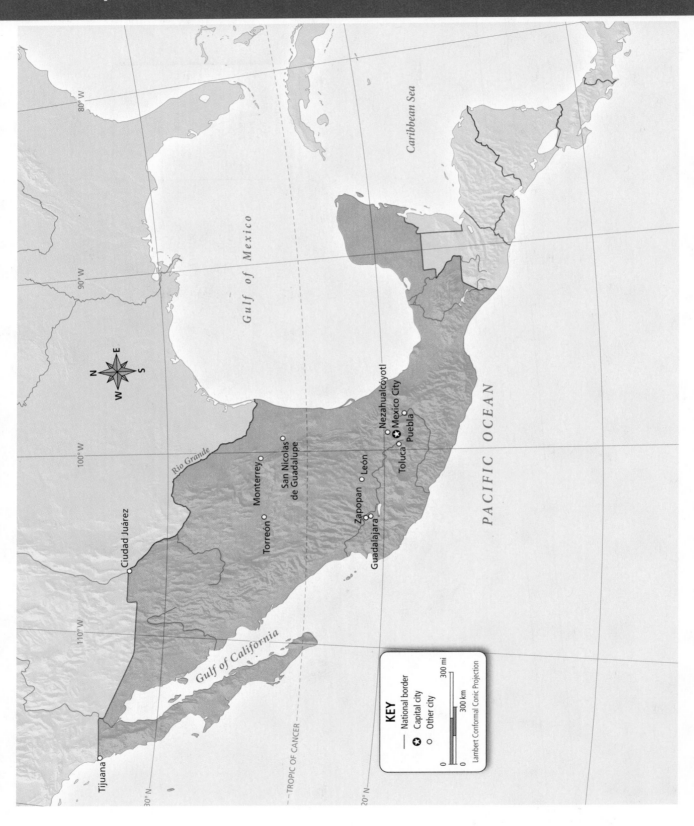

Caribbean Sea

Gulf of Mexico

80° W

90° W

100° W

110° W

N E W S

Rio Grande

Ciudad Juárez

Torreón

Monterrey

San Nicolas de Guadalupe

Zapopan

León

Guadalajara

Nezahualcoyotl

Mexico City

Puebla

Toluca

PACIFIC OCEAN

Gulf of California

Tijuana

TROPIC OF CANCER

30° N

20° N

KEY
National border
⊛ Capital city
○ Other city

300 mi
0

300 km
0

Lambert Conformal Conic Projection

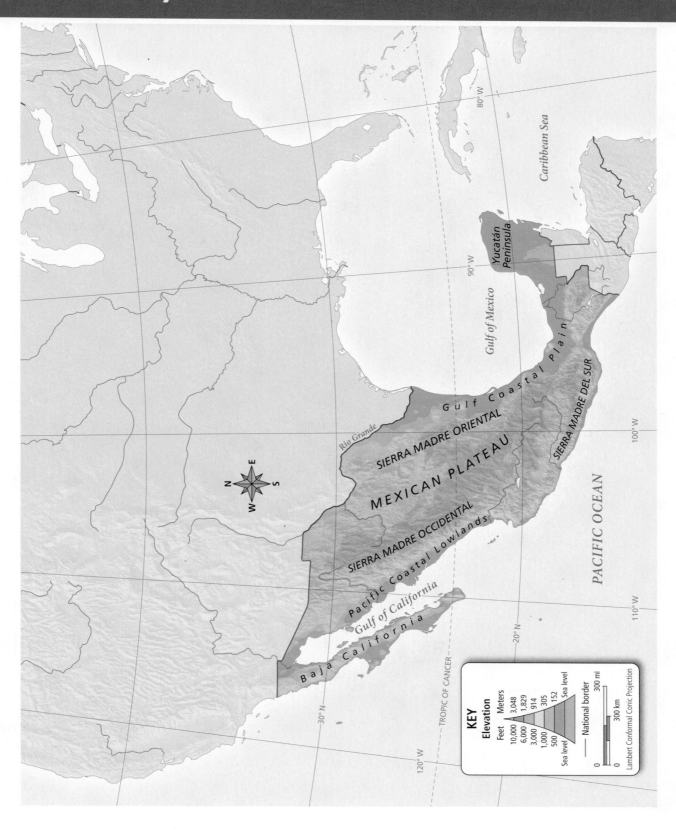

Caribbean Sea

80° W

90° W

Yucatán
Peninsula

Gulf Coastal Plain

Gulf of Mexico

SIERRA MADRE ORIENTAL

SIERRA MADRE DEL SUR

Rio Grande

MEXICAN PLATEAU

100° W

SIERRA MADRE OCCIDENTAL

Pacific Coastal Lowlands

PACIFIC OCEAN

Pacific Coastal Lowlands

Gulf of California

110° W

Baja California

20° N

30° N

TROPIC OF CANCER

120° W

KEY
Elevation

Feet	Meters
10,000	3,048
6,000	1,829
3,000	914
1,000	305
500	152
Sea level	Sea level

—— National border

0   300 mi

0   300 km

Lambert Conformal Conic Projection

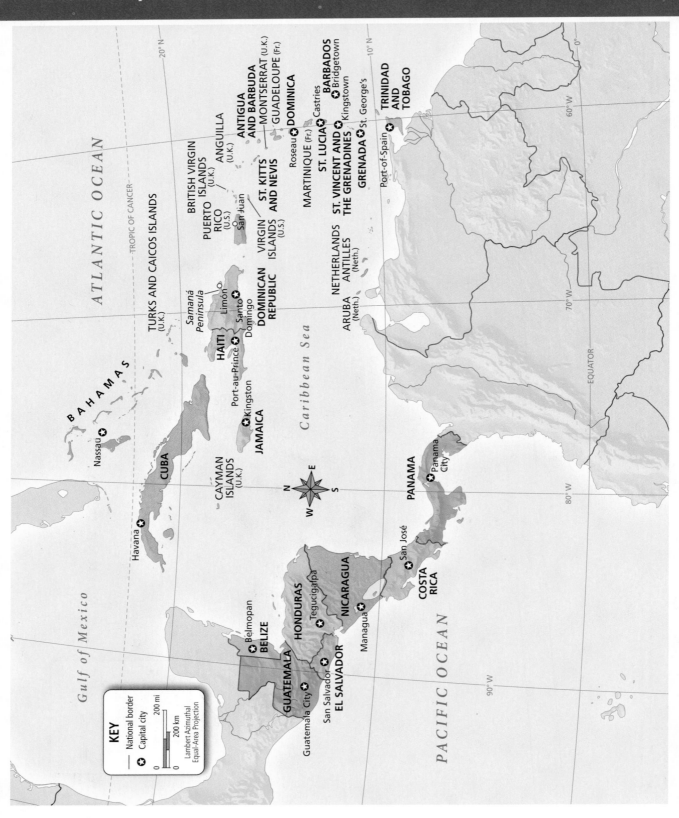

ATLANTIC OCEAN

20° N

TROPIC OF CANCER

TURKS AND CAICOS ISLANDS
(U.K.)

BRITISH VIRGIN
ISLANDS
(U.K.)

PUERTO
RICO
(U.S.)
San Juan

VIRGIN
ISLANDS
(U.S.)

ANGUILLA
(U.K.)

ST. KITTS
AND NEVIS

ANTIGUA
AND BARBUDA

MONTSERRAT (U.K.)

GUADELOUPE (Fr.)

Roseau ✪ DOMINICA

MARTINIQUE (Fr.)

ST. LUCIA ✪ Castries

ST. VINCENT AND
THE GRENADINES

GRENADA ✪ St. George's

BARBADOS
✪ Bridgetown

Kingstown

10° N

TRINIDAD
AND
TOBAGO

Port-of-Spain ✪

0°

60° W

70° W

Samaná
Peninsula

Limón

Santo
Domingo

DOMINICAN
REPUBLIC

HAITI

Port-au-Prince

NETHERLANDS
ANTILLES
(Neth.)

ARUBA
(Neth.)

Caribbean Sea

EQUATOR

B A H A M A S

Nassau ✪

CUBA

CAYMAN
ISLANDS
(U.K.)

Kingston
JAMAICA

Havana ✪

N
E
W S

PANAMA

Panama
City ✪

80° W

Gulf of Mexico

Belmopan ✪
BELIZE

HONDURAS

Tegucigalpa ✪

NICARAGUA

Managua ✪

San José ✪

COSTA
RICA

GUATEMALA

Guatemala City ✪

San Salvador ✪
EL SALVADOR

PACIFIC OCEAN

90° W

KEY

— National border

✪ Capital city

200 mi

200 km

0

Lambert Azimuthal
Equal-Area Projection

(ab′ə lish′ən ist) A person who ...o end or get rid of something, especially ...avery.

adapt (ə dapt′) To change to fit a new set of conditions.

advertising (ad′vər tīz′ing) The use of public notices to bring attention to a product or service.

agribusiness (ag′rə biz′nis) The farming industry.

agriculture (ag′ri kul′chər) The planting and growing of crops for food.

air mass (er mas) A body of air with the same temperature and humidity.

amendment (ə mend′mənt) A change to the Constitution of the United States.

annex (ə neks′) To take territory and join it to a state or country.

aqueduct (ak′wə dukt′) A channel used to carry water over a distance.

aquifer (ak′wə fər) An underground layer of porous rock that contains water.

arable (ar′ə bəl) Capable of growing crops.

archeologist (är′kē äl′ə jist) A scientist who studies the culture of people who lived long ago.

arid (ar′id) A very dry climate.

artifact (ärt′ə fakt) An object made by people, such as pottery.

atlas (at′ləs) A collection or book of maps.

B

Badlands (bad′landz′) A region of dry hills and sharp cliffs.

barrier island (bar′ē ər ī′lənd) An island along the coast that helps protect the mainland from pounding waves.

barter (bär′tər) To trade goods or services for other goods or services without using money.

blizzard (bliz′ərd) A severe storm with heavy snow and high winds.

bog (bäg) An area of soft, wet, spongy ground where moss grows.

boomtown (bōōm′toun) A fast-growing town often located near a place where gold or silver is discovered.

boundary (boun′drē) A line that divides one area or state from another.

boycott (boi′kät) A refusal to buy or use something.

C

canal (kə nal′) A waterway that has been dug across land to carry water for crops or for boats to travel through.

Pronunciation Key

a in hat	ō in open	'l in cattle
ā in age	ô in order	'n in sudden
ä in father	o͞o in tool	th in weather
e in let	u in cup	zh in measure
ē in equal	ʉ in reverse	
i in it	ə a in ago	
ī in ice	e in agent	
o in hot	o in collect	
	ʉ in focus	

candidate (kan′də dāt) A person who runs for a particular job or office.

canyon (kan′yən) A valley with steep rock sides.

capital resource (kap′ət ′l rē′sôrs) The human-made things such as a tractor that people use to grow or make other things.

cardinal direction (kard′n əl də rek′shən) One of the four main compass points north, south, east, and west.

Central Plains (sen′trəl plānz) Plains that include the eastern Midwest.

Central Valley (sen′trəl val′ē) A large valley in central California.

checks and balances (cheks and bal′əns es) The separation of powers in a democracy that gives each branch of government—the legislative, executive, and judicial—some form of authority over the others.

citizen (sit′ə zən) A member of a city, state, or town who has legal rights and responsibilities.

civil rights (siv′əl rīts) The rights that all people should have.

cliff dwelling (clif dwel′ing) Homes built into cliff sides, such as those built by the Ancient Puebloans of the Southwest.

climate (klī′mət) The pattern of weather an area has over a long period of time.

Cold War (kōld wôr) The conflict between the United States and the Soviet Union over economic and political ideas.

colony (käl′ə nē) A settlement ruled by another country.

command economy (kə mand′ i kän′ə mē) An economy in which the government decides what goods and services can be sold.

commerce (käm′ərs) The buying and selling of goods.

communism (käm′yoo niz′əm) An economic and political system in which the government owns all the land and most industries in the name of the people.

compass rose (kum′pəs rōz) A symbol on a map that shows directions.

confederation (kən fed′ər ā′shən) A union of states that agree to cooperate.

congress (kän′grəs) A group of people responsible for making a country's laws.

conserve (kən surv′) To limit the use of something.

constitution (kän′stə too′shən) A plan of government.

consumer (kən soom′ər) Someone who buys or uses goods and services.

craft (kraft) An object made by hand.

crop rotation (kräp rō tā′shən) The planting of different crops in different years.

culture (kul′chər) A way of life for a group of people.

currency (kur′ən sē) A country's money.

D

degree (di grē′) A unit of measure. There are 360 degrees of latitude and longitude used to locate places on Earth.

delegate (del′ə git) Someone who represents a group of people.

demand (di mand′) The amount of a particular good or service that consumers desire.

democracy (di mäk′rə sē) A government in which citizens have the power to make political decisions.

depression (dē presh′ən) A time when business activity is slow and many people are out of work.

desert (dez′ərt) An area that receives less than ten inches of rain in one year.

diverse (də vʉrs′) Showing much variety.

division of labor (də vizh′ən uv lā′bər) Dividing a job among skilled workers.

drought (drout) A long period with little or no rain.

E

economy (i kän′ə mē) The way a place uses its resources to produce goods and services.

elevation (el′ə vā′shən) The distance above or below sea level.

emancipation (ē man′sə pā′shən) The act of setting someone or something free.

endangered species (en dān′jərd spē′shēz) A kind of animal or plant that is in danger of becoming extinct.

enslaved (en slāvd′) To work without pay or freedom.

entrepreneur (än′trə prə noor′) A person who risks money and time to start a new business.

equator (ē kwāt′ər) An imaginary line that circles the globe halfway between the North and South Poles.

erosion (ē rō′zhən) The process of wearing away soil and rock.

evacuation (ē vak′yoo ā′shən) The action of moving a person to safety.

executive branch (eg zek′ yoo tiv branch) The branch of government that carries out the laws; the U.S. president and his or her administration.

export (ek sport′) To sell or trade something to another country.

extinct (ek stinkt′) No longer existing.

F

fall line (fôl līn) A line of waterfalls such as where a piedmont meets a coastal plain.

fascism (fash′iz′əm) A form of government that gives all power to the state, does away with individual freedoms, and uses the military to enforce the law.

flood plain (flud plān) A plain that is formed by flooding along a river.

fossil fuel (fäs′əl fyoo′əl) A fuel formed in the earth from the remains of plants and animals.

free enterprise system (frē ent′ər prīz sis′təm) An economy in which people are free to start their own businesses or to produce whatever good or service they want.

G

geyser (gī′zər) A hot spring that erupts and sends hot water from underground into the air.

glacier (glā′shər) A huge sheet of ice that covers land.

globe (glōb) A model of Earth.

gold rush (gōld rush) The quick movement of people to a place where gold has been discovered.

gray water (grā wat′ər) Water that is recycled.

Great Plains (grāt plānz) A vast area of plains east of the Rocky Mountains.

grid (grid) A system of lines that cross each other to form a pattern of squares. On a map, grids are used to locate places.

growing season (grō′ing sē′zən) A period of time when the temperature is high enough for plants to grow.

Gullah (gul′ə) A group of people in the Southeast who have kept much of their African heritage.

gusher (gush′ər) An oil well that produces a large amount of oil without being pumped.

hemisphere (hem′i sfir′) Half of a sphere. Earth's hemispheres are formed by the equator and the prime meridian.

heritage (her′ə tij) The customs and traditions of a cultural group that have been passed down from parents to children.

high-tech (hī tek) Using the newest or latest technology.

homestead (hōm′sted) Land given to settlers by the United States government if they lived and raised crops on it.

hub (hub) A center of activity.

human resource (hyōō′mən rē′sôrs) The people who work at a business.

humidity (hyōō mid′ə tē) The amount of moisture in the air.

hunter-gatherer (hunt′ər gath′ər ər) Someone who hunts animals and collects wild plants for food.

hurricane (hur′i kān) A strong, swirling storm with rain and winds blowing more than 74 miles per hour.

hydroelectric power (hī′drə ē lek′trik pou′ər) Power produced by capturing the energy of flowing water.

I

immigrant (im′ə grənt) A person who moves to one country from another.

import (im pôrt′) To bring something in from another country for sale or trade.

incentive (in sent′iv) Something that encourages one to take an action or do something.

income (in′kum′) The money a person or business earns for doing a job or providing a good or service.

indentured servant (in den′chərd sur′vənt) A person who agrees to work for a set period of time without pay, in exchange for necessities.

independence (in′dē pen′dəns) Freedom from rule by others.

industry (in′dəs trē) The part of the economy in which machines are used to do the work.

inflation (in flā′shən) A rise in the usual price of many goods and services.

innovation (in′ə vā′shən) New inventions or ideas.

interdependent (in′tər dē pen′dənt) When nations rely on one another for goods, services, or resources.

interest (in′trist) A small fee paid to bank customers in exchange for allowing the bank to use their money; a fee charged by banks for borrowing money.

intermediate direction (in′tər mē′dē it də rek′shən) A direction, such as northwest, that is between two cardinal directions.

international trade (in′tər nash′ə nəl trād) Trade between different countries.

interstate highway (in′tər stāt′ hī′wā′) Highways that connect states.

irrigation (ir ə gā′shən) The practice of bringing water to fields, usually by means of ditches and channels.

J

jazz (jaz) A type of music of African American origin.

judicial branch (jōō dish′əl branch) The part of government that decides what laws mean and makes sure that laws are applied fairly.

junction (junk′shən) A point where things, such as rivers, meet.

jury (jōōr′ē) A panel of ordinary citizens who make decisions in a court of law.

K

key (kē) A low island.

L

labor union (lā′bər yōōn′yən) A group of workers, usually in the same type of job, who have joined together to demand better wages and working conditions.

landform (land′fôrm) A natural feature of Earth's surface.

latitude (lat′ə tōōd) Lines that measure the distance north and south of the equator.

legislative branch (lej′is lā′tiv branch) The part of government that makes laws.

levee (lev′ē) A barrier of earth built to prevent flooding.

liberty (lib′ər tē) freedom to govern oneself.

lighthouse (līt′hous′) A tall tower with a very strong light used to guide ships at night.

livestock (līv′stäk′) Animals raised on farms and ranches for human use.

longitude (län′jə tōōd) Lines that measure the distances east and west of the prime meridian.

M

magma (mag′mə) Molten rock beneath Earth's surface.

manufacturing (man′yōō fak′chər ing) Making goods by machines, usually in factories.

map key (map kē) A map legend; the boxed list showing what the symbols on a map represent.

map scale (map skāl) A line drawn on a map that shows the relationship between a unit of measurement on the map and the real distance on Earth.

market economy (mär′kit i kän′ə mē) A free enterprise system in which supply and demand determines goods and services.

meat-packing (mēt′pak′ing) An industry that processes animals for food.

mesa (mā′sə) A flat-topped landform with slopes on all sides.

metropolitan area (me′trō päl′i tən er′ē ə) A large city and its surrounding area.

mineral (min′ər əl) Nonliving material that is found in the earth.

mission (mish′ən) A church and settlement where religion is taught.

missionary (mish′ən er′ē) A person sent to a new land to spread his or her religion.

natural gas (nach′ər əl gas) A fossil fuel.

natural resource (nach′ər əl rē′sôrs) Something in the environment that people use.

nocturnal (näk tur′nəl) Active at night.

nomad (nō′mad) A person who travels from place to place in order to survive.

nonrenewable (nän ri nōō′ə bəl) Something that cannot be replaced or would take a long time to form again.

Northwest Ordinance (nôrth′west ôrd′′n əns) A law that determined how the Northwest Territory would become states.

nutrients (nōō′trē əntz) Substances that help plants grow.

opportunity cost (äp′ər tōō′nə tē kôst) The value of something that must be given up to get the thing you want.

outsourcing (out′sôrs ing) When companies employ people to work outside of the company.

overfishing (ō′vər fish′ing) When people catch fish faster than natural processes can replace them.

Pacific Rim (pə sif′ik rim) A geographic area made up of countries that border the Pacific Ocean.

patent (pat′′nt) A government document that protects the ownership of a new idea or invention.

patriotism (pā′trē ət izm) The pride and support a people feel for their country.

peninsula (pə nin′sə lə) Land surrounded by water on three sides.

physical map (fiz′i kəl map) A map that shows geographic features of a place, such as mountains, valleys, and bodies of water.

piedmont (pēd′mänt) Foothills near mountains.

pioneer (pī′ə nir′) A person from a group that is the first to settle in an area.

plantation (plan tā′shən) A large farm with many workers.

plateau (pla tō′) A large, flat, raised area of land.

plow (plou) A farm tool, pulled by a tractor or animal, used to turn the soil.

political map (pə lit′i kəl map) A map that shows information such as borders, capitals, and important cities.

population density (päp′yə lā′shən den′sə tē) A measure of how many people, on average, live on each square mile of land in a certain area.

port (pôrt) A place where people or goods can enter or leave a country.

prairie (prer′ē) An area in which grass grows well but trees are rare.

precipitation (prē sip′ə tā′shən) The amount of moisture that falls as rain or snow.

prime meridian (prīm mə rid′ē ən) The starting point for measuring longitude.

private property (prī′vət präp′ər tē) The land or goods that people or companies own.

producer (prə dōōs′ər) A person who makes goods or services to sell.

product (präd′əkt) Something that people make or grow.

productivity (prō′dək tiv′ə tē) The amount of goods or services company workers can make or provide.

profit (präf′it) The money a business earns after all its expenses are paid.

pueblo (pweb′lō) A Spanish word meaning "village" that refers to some Native American groups in the Southwest.

pulp (pulp) A mix of wood chips, water, and chemicals used to make paper.

Q

quarry (kwôr′ē) A place where stone or marble is dug, cut, or blasted out of the ground.

R

rain shadow (rān shad′ō) An area such as the side of a mountain chain that receives less precipitation than the other side.

ranch (ranch) A large farm where cattle or other animals are raised.

ratify (rat′ə fī) To approve officially.

Reconstruction (rē′kən struk′shən) The period of rebuilding after the Civil War during which Southern states rejoined the Union.

refinery (ri fīn′ər ē) A factory that separates crude oil into different groups of chemicals.

reforest (rē fôr′ist) To plant young trees to replace ones that have been cut down.

region (rē′jən) An area defined by its common features.

renewable (ri nōō′ə bəl) Something that can be replaced.

republic (ri pub′lik) A type of government in which people elect leaders to represent them.

reservation (rez′ər vā′shən) An area of land set aside for Native Americans to live on.

reservoir (rez′ər vwär) A lake where water is stored for use.

rural (roor′əl) A country area.

sachem (sā′chəm) A ruler or leader among some Native American groups.

savanna (sə van′ə) A grassy plain with scattered trees.

scarcity (sker′sə tē) A shortage.

secede (si sēd′) To officially separate from an organization.

segregation (seg′rə gā′shən) A system under which people of different races are kept separate.

self-evident (self ev′i dənt) Something that does not need explaining or proof, such as basic rights.

semi-arid (sem′ē ar′id) A dry climate that receives some rain.

silicon (sil′i kän) A material from rocks and sand used to manufacture computers.

sound (sound) A large area of seawater that separates a mainland and an island.

sovereignty (säv′rən tē) The right to rule.

specialization (spesh′əl i zā′shən) A process in which each worker performs a single step in production.

states' rights (stāts rīts) The idea that the power of the state must be protected from the power of the federal government and that each state should solve its own problems.

steamboat (stēm′bōt) A boat powered by a steam engine.

storm surge (stôrm sʉrj) A rising of the sea caused by a storm.

suffrage (suf′rij) The right to vote.

supply (sə plī′) The amount of goods or services available for a consumer to buy.

sweatshop (swet′shäp) A factory with bad working conditions.

symbol (sim′bəl) A thing that stands for or represents something else.

technology (tek näl′ə jē) The use of scientific knowledge or tools to do work.

temperature (tem′pər ə chər) A measurement telling how hot or cold something is.

territory (ter′ə tôr′ē) A large area of land that is under the control of an outside government. In the United States, a territory does not have the same rights that a state does.

terrorist (ter′ər ist) A person who uses great fear or terror for political reasons.

timber (tim′bər) Trees that are cut or grown for wood.

tornado (tôr nā′dō) A storm with very fast winds that can form a funnel-shaped cloud.

totem pole (tōt′əm pōl) A tall post carved with images of people and animals to represent family history.

tourist (toor′ist) Someone who travels for pleasure.

trading post (trād′ing pōst) A store set up in a distant place to allow trade to take place.

tradition (trə dish′ən) A custom or belief that is passed on from one generation to the next.

transcontinental (trans′kän tə nent′′l) Across the continent.

tsunami (sōō nä′mē) A giant wave that can reach 50 feet high and cause great damage when it reaches land.

tundra (tun′drə) A cold area where trees cannot grow.

unalienable (un āl′yən ə bəl) Unable to be taken away, such as unalienable rights.

urban (ɥr′bən) A city area.

V

vineyard (vin′yərd) A farm where grapes are grown.

volcano (väl kā′nō) A vent in Earth's crust caused by molten rock forcing its way to the surface.

W

watershed (wôt′ər shed) An area drained by a river or group of rivers.

weather (we<u>th</u>′ər) The condition of the air at a certain place and time.

wetland (wet′land′) An area where water lies on or near the surface of the ground, as a swamp or marsh.

wetu (we′tōō) A structure made of wooden poles and covered in bark by some groups of Native Americans.

Index

In this index the letter *c* indicates a chart or table, *d* indicates a diagram, *g* indicates a graph, *m* indicates a map, and *p* indicates a photo or drawing. Bold page numbers indicate vocabulary definitions. The terms *See* and *See also* direct the reader to alternate entries.

F

G

Credits

Text Acknowledgments

Grateful acknowledgment is made to the following for copyrighted material:

Page 1 *The Everglades: River of Grass* by Marjory Stoneman Douglas. Copyright © Pineapple Press, Inc.

Note: Every effort has been made to locate the copyright owners of the material produced in this component. Omissions brought to our attention will be corrected in subsequent editions.

Illustrations

CVR2, 87, 88, 93, 98 Mattia Cerato; **viii, 114, 115, 122** Victor Rivas; **xiv, SSH1, SSH2, SSH3, SSH4, SSH5, SSH6, SSH7** Bill McGuire; **1, 2, 3** Kim Herbst; **4, 184, 302** Lyn Boyer; **12, 14, 31, 180, 296** Joe LeMonnier; **15** Frank Ippolito; **35, 36, 37** Raul Allen; **39, 42, 240, 271** James Palmer; **46** Tin Salamunic; **55** Scott Dawson; **75, 76, 77** John Royle; **103, 104, 105** Shingo Shimizu; **120, 125, 220, 240, 254, 294, 314** Dave Cockburn; **146** Ian Phillips; **152, 156, 192** Rick Whipple; **260** Robin Storesund.

Maps

XNR Productions, Inc.

Photographs

Every effort has been made to secure permission and provide appropriate credit for photographic material. The publisher deeply regrets any omission and pledges to correct errors called to its attention in subsequent editions.

Unless otherwise acknowledged, all photographs are the property of Pearson Education, Inc.

Photo locators denoted as follows: Top (T), Center (C), Bottom (B), Left (L), Right (R), Background (Bkgd)

Cover

CVR1 (T) ©Rick Dalton - Ag/Alamy Images, (BL) ©Ron Crabtree/Getty Images, (TL) Gleb Tarro/Shutterstock, (CL) Photos to Go/Photolibrary; **CVR2** (TCR) Cardaf/Shutterstock, (CR) Janeanne Gilchrist/©DK Images, (CL) Jon Spaull/©DK Images, (BC) Morgan Lane Photography/Shutterstock, (T) upthebanner/Shutterstock, (BL) National Archives

Front Matter

iv (BR) Stockbyte/Thinkstock; **v** (B) Design Pics/SuperStock; **vi** (L) Oleksiy Maksymenko/Alamy; **vii** (BR) Susan Law Cain/Shutterstock; **ix** (BR) Feng YuC/Shutterstock; **x** (BL) NewsCom; **xi** (BR) Transport Lesley/Alamy Images; **xii** (BL) Chuck Place/Alamy Images; **xiii** (BR) Mark Herreid/Shutterstock

Text

SSH10 (BL) Peter Arnold/PhotoLibrary Group, Inc.; **SSH11** (BR) Henryk Sadura/Shutterstock, (TL) RWP/Alamy Images, (CL) Walter Bibikow/mauritius images GmbH/Alamy Images; **SSH12** (B) Morgan Lane Photograph/Shutterstock, (T) Stockbyte/Thinkstock; **4** (TC) Kent Frost/Shutterstock; **9** (TR) Thinkstock; **12** (B) Design Pics/SuperStock, (CL) Janeanne Gilchrist/©DK Images; **17** (TR) SuperStock; **18** (TC) basel101658/Shutterstock, (B) Cultura Limited/SuperStock, (TR) Edgaras Kurauskas/Shutterstock; **19** (BR) ©Olly/Shutterstock, (TL) oncharuk/Shutterstock; **20** (BR) Christian Lagerek/Shutterstock, (BL) Lasse Kristensen/Shutterstock; **21** (BR) Big Cheese Photo/SuperStock, (BL) Henryk Sadura/Shutterstock; **22** (Bkgrd) StudioNewmarket/Shutterstock, (BR) SuperStock; **24** (CL) SuperStock, (TR) weberfoto/Alamy; **25** (B) Linda Whitwam/©DK Images; **26** (T) SuperStock; **27** (B) REDAV/Shutterstock; **28** (B) Terrance Emerson/Shutterstock; **30** (CL) Cultura Limited/SuperStock, (TL) Janeanne Gilchrist/©DK Images, (TL) Kent Frost/Shutterstock, (BL) weberfoto/Alamy; **32** (CR) Linda Whitwam/©DK Images; **34** (C) H. Mark Weidman Photography/Alamy Images; **38** (TR) Jeff Greenberg/PhotoEdit, Inc., (L) Oleksiy Maksymenko/Alamy; **41** (TR) North Wind Picture Archives/Alamy Images; **43** (TR) Ivy Close Images/Alamy; **44** (C) The Granger Collection; **47** (BR) Victorian Traditions/Shutterstock; **48** (TL) North Wind Picture Archives/Alamy Images; **49** (TR) GL Archive/Alamy Images; **51** (TR) ©The Granger Collection, NY; **52** (TR) North Wind Picture Archives/Alamy Images; **53** (BR) North Wind Picture Archives; **54** (TL, BL) North Wind Picture Archives/Alamy Images; **55** (TR) Prints & Photographs Division, LC-USZ62-11896/Library of Congress; **56** (TR) Prints & Photographs Division, LC-USZC4-2781/Library of Congress; **57** (TR) Curtis (Edward S.) Collection, Prints & Photographs Division, LC-USZ61-2088/Library of Congress; **58** (TR) AlexGul/Shutterstock, (L) Detroit Publishing Company, Prints & Photographs Division, LC-D4-11590/Library of Congress; **59** (BR) Pictorial Press Ltd/Alamy Images; **60** (TR) Pictorial Press Ltd/Alamy Images; **61** (BR) FSA/OWI Black-and-White Negatives, Prints & Photographs Division, LC-USE6-D-006594/Library of Congress; **62** (BL) FSA/OWI Black-and-White Negatives, Prints & Photographs Division, LC-USF34-072483-D/Library of Congress, (BR) H. ARMSTRONG ROBERTS/Alamy Images, (TR, CR) National Archives, (CL) Toni Frissell Collection, Prints & Photographs Division, LC-DIG-ppmsca-11759/Library of Congress; **63** (TR) Bettmann/Corbis; **64** (BR) JIM PRINGLE/©Associated Press, (TR) Marc Dietrich/Shutterstock; **65** (BR) NASA; **66** (T) Flip Schulke/Corbis; **67** (BR) ©Associated Press, (BL) CSU Archives/Alamy Images, (BC) Michael Germana/Newscom; **68** (B) Mark Pearson/Alamy Images; **70** (BL) NASA, (TL, CL) North Wind Picture Archives/Alamy Images, (CL) Pictorial Press Ltd/Alamy Images, (CL) Victorian Traditions/Shutterstock; **72** (CR) Visions of America, LLC/Alamy Images; **74** (C) fstockfoto/Shutterstock; **78** (B) Digital Vision/Thinkstock, (TR) Roy Morsch/PhotoLibrary

Group, Inc.; **79** (BR) Darren Green Photography/Alamy; **80** (B) Archive Images/Alamy Images; **81** (BR) Susan Law Cain/Shutterstock; **82** (B) Alamy Images; **83** (TR) dbimages/Alamy Images; **84** (CL) Susan Law Cain/Shutterstock; **86** (BL) KEVIN DIETSCH/NewsCom; **89** (T) Olivier Douliery/NewsCom; **90** (L) Alamy Images; **91** (TR) Henryk Sadura/Shutterstock; **92** (TR) Atlaspix/Shutterstock, (CL) Prints & Photographs Division, LC-USZC4-2542/Library of Congress; **95** (BL) Blend Images/SuperStock, (TR) Catchlight Visual Services/Alamy Images; **96** (BR) pandapaw/Shutterstock; **97** (TR) Russ Bishop/Alamy Images; **98** (TL) Alamy Images, (CL) Catchlight Visual Services/Alamy Images; **100** (CR) Susan Law Cain/Shutterstock; **102** (C) Spencer Grant/PhotoEdit, Inc.; **106** (TR) Alex Kosev/Shutterstock; **107** (BC) Lawrence Manning/Corbis RF/Alamy, (BL) Steve Hix/Somos Images/Corbis; **108** (T) Jack Kurtz/The Image Works, Inc.; **110** (BL) James Nesterwitz/Alamy Images, (BR) Tom Brakefield/SuperStock; **111** (TR) Purestock/Alamy; **114** (TR) Alistair Michael Thomas/Shutterstock; **116** (BR) David Johnson/©DK Images; **117** (BL) n08/NewsCom; **118** (BR) David Goldman/©Associated Press, (BL) dbimages/Alamy; **119** (TR) gr4/ZUMA Press/NewsCom; **120** (L) Creatas/Thinkstock; **121** (BR) Thinkstock; **123** (BR) Garth Blore/©DK Images, (BL) Magicinfoto/Shutterstock; **124** (TL) Robert Kneschke/Shutterstock, (BL) Tom Prettyman/PhotoEdit, Inc.; **126** (CL) North Wind Picture Archives, (B) Sascha Burkard/Shutterstock, (TR) Susan Van Etten/PhotoEdit, Inc.; **129** (B) Robert Landau/Alamy Images; **132** (TL) Steve Hix/Somos Images/Corbis, (CL) n08/NewsCom, (BL) Sascha Burkard/Shutterstock, (CL) Tom Prettyman/PhotoEdit, Inc.; **134** (BR) Susan Van Etten/PhotoEdit, Inc.; **136** (C) Ball Miwako/Alamy Images; **137** (Bkgd) Russell Kord/Alamy; **138** (TR) Iain Masterton/Alamy Images; **139** (B) Aeypix/Shutterstock, (TR) emin kuliyev/Shutterstock; **140** (TR) Galyna Andrushko/Shutterstock, (B) Michael G. Mill/Shutterstock; **142** (BL) Jaimie Duplass/Shutterstock; **144** (B) KennStilger47/Shutterstock, (TL) nialat/Shutterstock; **145** (TR) upthebanner/Shutterstock; **146** (BL) 7505811966/Shutterstock; **147** (B) Photos to Go/Photolibrary; **148** (R) Feng YuC/Shutterstock; **149** (TR) Lijuan Guo/Shutterstock; **150** (B) Michael Dwyer/Alamy Images; **151** (TR) RubberBall/SuperStock; **152** (L) Suchan/Shutterstock; **154** (BC) New York Public Library/Photo Researchers, Inc., (BR) North Wind Picture Archives/Alamy Images, (BL) Prints & Photographs Division, LC-USZ62-67573/Library of Congress; **155** (BR) Alamy Images, (BC) Prints & Photographs Division, LC-USZC4-7214/Library of Congress, (BL) SuperStock; **157** (TR) Thinkstock; **158** (TR) Alamy Images; **159** (BR) Philip Lange/Shutterstock; **160** (TL) Alamy Images, (BL) Brady-Handy Collection, Prints & Photographs Division, LC-DIG-cwpbh-04044/Library of Congress; **161** (TR) Mary Evans Picture Library/The Image Works, Inc.; **162** (BR) Bain Collection, Prints & Photographs Division, LC-USZ62-53176/Library of Congress, (TL) NewsCom; **163** (TR) Alamy Images; **164** (BL) StockbrokerC/SuperStock; **166** (TR) 1xpert/Shutterstock, (BL) Bill Cobb/SuperStock; **167** (B) Getty Images/Thinkstock; **168** (B) Visions of America, LLC/Alamy Images; **169** (BR) Jeffrey M. Frank/Shutterstock, (BL) Photos to Go/Photolibrary; **170** (L) Alamy Images, (B) Jeff Greenberg/Alamy Images; **172** (CL)

Alamy Images, (TL) Galyna Andrushko/Shutterstock, (BL) Jeff Greenberg/Alamy Images, (CL) Lijuan Guo/Shutterstock, (CL) Thinkstock; **176** (C) F1online digitale Bildagentur GmbH/Alamy Images; **180** (L) NASA Media Services Still Photo Lab/NASA; **183** (B) Daniel Dempster Photography/Alamy Images, (TR) Ed Metz/Shutterstock; **184** (TL) William Leaman/Alamy; **185** (TR) T. Kimmeskamp/Shutterstock; **188** (L) Morgan Lane Photography/Shutterstock; **189** (BR) Flirt/SuperStock; **190** (TL) Lionel Alvergnas/Shutterstock; **191** (BL) Jim West/Alamy Images; **193** (TR) Stacie Stauff Smith Photography/Shutterstock; **194** (L) Alamy Images, (TR) Sunsetman/Shutterstock; **195** (BR) Wayne Hughes/Alamy Images; **196** (BR) David Dobbs/Alamy Images; **197** (CR) Christina Handley/Masterfile Corporation; **198** (TL) Alamy; **199** (TR) Dean Pennala/Shutterstock; **200** (TR) Alamy Images, (L) David Lyons/Alamy Images; **202** (BL) Alamy Images; **203** (TR) INTERFOTO/Alamy Images, (B) NewsCom; **204** (CR) Andre Jenny/Alamy Images, (B) North Wind Picture Archives (Alamy); **205** (TR) ALEXIS C. GLENN/UPI/NewsCom; **206** (TR) Shutterstock, (BL) Stockbroker/Alamy; **207** (CR) CTK/Alamy Images; **208** (B) NewsCom; **209** (CR) AVAVA/Shutterstock, (TL) Patrick Lynch/Alamy Images; **210** (BL) Ariel Bravy/Shutterstock; **212** (BL) Ariel Bravy/Shutterstock, (CL) David Dobbs/Alamy Images, (CL) INTERFOTO/Alamy Images, (CL) Lionel Alvergnas/Shutterstock, (TL) NASA Media Services Still Photo Lab/NASA; **214** (CR) Daniel Korzeniewski/Shutterstock; **216** (C) Henryk Sadura/Shutterstock; **218** (TL) Esme/Shutterstock; **219** (BR) Andre Jenny/Alamy Images, (TL) Katherine Welles/Shutterstock, (TR) Photos to Go/Photolibrary; **220** (CL) Phil Schermeister/Corbis; **223** (CR) Flashon Studio/Shutterstock; **224** (TL) Sammy S. Lee/Shutterstock, (B) Tom Reichner/Shutterstock; **225** (TR) Tony Campbell/Shutterstock; **226** (BR) AVAVA/Shutterstock; **228** (CL) David R. Frazier Photolibrary, Inc/Alamy, (TR) Jim Wark/PhotoLibrary Group, Inc.; **230** (B) ©Rick Dalton - Ag/Alamy Images; **231** (BR) Medioimages/Thinkstock; **232** (B) Darron Cumming/©Associated Press; **233** (TR) Stephen Mcsweeny/Shutterstock; **234** (TR, BL) Alamy Images; **236** (TL) Nancy G Photography/Alamy Images, (TR) Prints & Photographs Division, LC-DIG-ppmsca-08379/Library of Congress; **237** (BR) Transport Lesley/Alamy Images; **238** (B) Niday Picture Library/Alamy Images; **239** (TR) Mondadori Portfolio/Newscom; **241** (BR) Prints & Photographs Division, Library of Congress; **242** (CL) Dennis MacDonald/Alamy Images; **243** (B) pakul54/Shutterstock; **244** (B) imac/Alamy, (TL) planet5D LLC/Shutterstock; **245** (TR) Jon Spaull/©DK Images; **246** (CL) David R. Frazier Photolibrary, Inc/Alamy, (CL) Dennis MacDonald/Alamy Images, (CL) Nancy G Photography/Alamy Images, (TL) Tom Reichner/Shutterstock; **248** (CR) David R. Frazier Photolibrary, Inc/Alamy; **250** (C) gary yim/Shutterstock; **252** (TL) Richard Levine/Alamy Images; **254** (B) Tom Baker/Shutterstock; **256** (BL) Charles T. Bennett/Shutterstock; **257** (B) Peter Horree/Alamy Images; **259** (TR) William Sutton/Alamy Images; **262** (L) Peter Wilson/©DK Images, (TR) Tim Roberts Photography/Shutterstock; **264** (L) Thinkstock, (B) William Manning/Alamy Images; **265** (R) Tony Campbell/Shutterstock; **266** (B) Jeff Banke/Shutterstock; **267** (TR) ©Masterfile Royalty-Free; **268** (BL) Cardaf/Shutterstock, (TR) Prisma Bildagentur AG/Alamy Images;

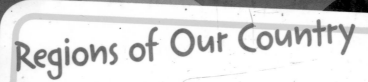

Regions of Our Country

PEARSON

myWorldSocialStudies.com

ISBN-13: 978-0-328-63918-2
ISBN-10:   0-328-63918-4